Quod scriptura, non iubet vetat

The Latin translates, "What is not commanded in scripture, is forbidden:'

On the Cover: Baptists rejoice to hold in common with other evangelicals the main principles of the orthodox Christian faith. However, there are points of difference and these differences are significant. In fact, because these differences arise out of God's revealed will, they are of vital importance. Hence, the barriers of separation between Baptists and others can hardly be considered a trifling matter. To suppose that Baptists are kept apart solely by their views on Baptism or the Lord's Supper is a regrettable misunderstanding. Baptists hold views which distinguish them from Catholics, Congregationalists, Episcopalians, Lutherans, Methodists, Pentecostals, and Presbyterians, and the differences are so great as not only to justify, but to demand, the separate denominational existence of Baptists. Some people think Baptists ought not teach and emphasize their differences but as E.J. Forrester stated in 1893, "Any denomination that has views which justify its separate existence, is bound to promulgate those views. If those views are of sufficient importance to justify a separate existence, they are important enough to create a duty for their promulgation ... the very same reasons which justify the separate existence of any denomination make it the duty of that denomination to teach the distinctive doctrines upon which its separate existence rests." If Baptists have a right to a separate denominational life, it is their duty to propagate their distinctive principles, without which their separate life cannot be justified or maintained.

Many among today's professing Baptists have an agenda to revise the Baptist distinctives and redefine what it means to be a Baptist. Others don't understand why it even matters. The books being reproduced in the *Baptist Distinctives Series* are republished in order that Baptists from the past may state, explain and defend the primary Baptist distinctives as they understood them. It is hoped that this Series will provide a more thorough historical perspective on what it means to be distinctively Baptist.

The Lord Jesus Christ asked, *"And why call ye me, Lord, Lord, and do not the things which I say?"* (Luke 6:46). The immediate context surrounding this question explains what it means to be a true disciple of Christ. Addressing the same issue, Christ's question is meant to show that a confession of discipleship to the Lord Jesus Christ is inconsistent and untrue if it is not accompanied with a corresponding submission to His authoritative commands. Christ's question teaches us that a true recognition of His authority as Lord inevitably includes a submission to the authority of His Word. Hence, with this question Christ has made it forever impossible to separate His authority as King from the authority of His Word. These two principles—the authority of Christ as King and the authority of His Word—are the two most fundamental Baptist distinctives. The first gives rise to the second and out of these two all the other Baptist distinctives emanate. As F.M. Iams wrote in 1894, "Loyalty to Christ as King, manifesting itself in a constant and unswerving obedience to His will as revealed in His written Word, is the real source of all the Baptist distinctives:' In the search for the *primary* Baptist distinctive many have settled on the Lordship of Christ as the most basic distinctive. Strangely, in doing this, some have attempted to separate Christ's Lordship from the authority of Scripture, as if you could embrace Christ's authority without submitting to what He commanded. However, while Christ's Lordship and Kingly authority can be isolated and considered essentially for discussion's sake, we see from Christ's own words in Luke 6:46 that His Lordship is really inseparable from His Word and, with regard to real Christian discipleship, there can be no practical submission to the one without a practical submission to the other.

In the symbol above the Kingly Crown and the Open Bible represent the inseparable truths of Christ's Kingly and Biblical authority. The Crown and Bible graphics are supplemented by three Bible verses (Ecclesiastes 8:4, Matthew 28:18-20, and Luke 6:46) that reiterate and reinforce the inextricable connection between the authority of Christ as King and the authority of His Word. The truths symbolized by these components are further emphasized by the Latin quotation - *quod scriptura, non iubet vetat*— i.e., "What is not commanded in scripture, is forbidden:' This Latin quote has been considered historically as a summary statement of the regulative principle of Scripture. Together these various symbolic components converge to exhibit the two most foundational Baptist Distinctives out of which all the other Baptist Distinctives arise. Consequently, we have chosen this composite symbol as a logo to represent the primary truths set forth in the *Baptist Distinctives Series*.

A Defense for The Baptists

ABRAHAM BOOTH
1734-1806

A DEFENSE FOR THE BAPTISTS

BEING A

DECLARATION AND A VINDICATION OF
THREE HISTORICALLY DISCINCTIVE BAPTIST PRINCIPLES
COMPILED AND SET FORTH
IN THE REPUBLISHING OF THE FOLLOWING THREE BOOKS:

AN APOLOGY FOR THE BAPTISTS, LONDON, 1778

AN ESSAY ON THE KINGDOM OF CHRIST, LONDON, 1788

PASTORAL CAUTIONS, LONDON, 1805

BY ABRAHAM BOOTH

WITH A BIOGRAPHICAL SKETCH OF THE AUTHOR BY
JOHN FRANKLIN JONES

The Baptist Standard Bearer, Inc.
NUMBER ONE IRON OAKS DRIVE • PARIS, ARKANSAS 72855

Thou hast given a *standard* to them that fear thee;
that it may be displayed because of the truth.
-- *Psalm 60:4*

Reprinted 2006

by

THE BAPTIST STANDARD BEARER, INC.
No. 1 Iron Oaks Drive
Paris, Arkansas 72855
(479) 963-3831

THE WALDENSIAN EMBLEM
lux lucet in tenebris
"The Light Shineth in the Darkness"

ISBN# 1579783678

TABLE OF CONTENTS

	PAGE
PUBLISHER'S FOREWORD	ix
MEMOIR OF THE LIFE AND WRITINGS OF ABRAHAM BOOTH	liii
BOOK I: AN APOLOGY FOR THE BAPTISTS	1
BOOK II: AN ESSAY ON THE KINGDOM OF CHRIST	145
BOOK III: PASTORAL CAUTIONS	215
A BIOGRAPHICAL SKETCH OF ABRAHAM BOOTH (1734-1806) BY JOHN FRANKLIN JONES	253

PUBLISHER'S FOREWORD[1]

The following book is a compilation of three books by Abraham Booth. Together they form a positive statement with regard to those views wherein Baptists differ from Protestant Pædobaptists, and we have several reasons for republishing them at this time. First, the reader should notice that the first book in this compilation of reprints addresses the age-old controversy of infant-baptism. The republication of this book does not mark a *public renewal* of that controversy, but, rather, a *public response* to the renewal of that controversy. While we recognize that a clear, definitive statement of Baptist beliefs regarding the nature of the New Testament Church, Baptism and the Lord's Supper has always sparked the charge of bigotry, sectarianism and narrow-mindedness, we also recognize that denunciation is oftentimes the last resort of a defeated opponent. We make no apology for publishing this work. We had rather bear the brunt of the unjustifiable charge of bigotry and enjoy the felicity of a cleared conscience, than bear the burden of the justifiable charge of apathy and suffer the misery of a seared conscience. Abraham Booth addresses himself in the first book to that unjustifiable charge of bigotry so often cast in our teeth. We exhort both friend and foe to prayerfully and seriously consider his answer.

Second, it should also be noted that, in all honesty, we would not make a brother "an offender for a word" (Isa. 29:21). We desire to "walk together" (Amos 3:3) "in truth" (III John 4)

---

[1] ©1985. "Publisher's Foreword" to Abraham Booth's – *A Defense for the Baptists*. (Paris, AR: The Baptist Standard Bearer, Inc., 1985).

with "all them that love our Lord Jesus Christ in sincerity" (Eph. 6:24), who "rejoiceth in the truth" (I Cor. 13:6), and who have determined in their hearts to "prove all things" and only "hold fast that which is good" (I Thess. 5:21). On the other hand, we can call no man master. We hold no man's "person in admiration because of advantage" (Jude 16). We seek not "honor from men" nor "one of another" (John 5:41, 44). If we know anything of ourselves, we desire "truth in the inward parts" (Ps. 51:6). Therefore, regarding this infant-baptism controversy (or any other controversy), God being our helper, we shall not purchase peace at the expense of the truth.

Third, the reader should also note that we realize there is probably no subject in Christianity about which such difference of opinion exists as baptism. The very word recalls to one's mind an endless list of strifes, disputes, divisions and controversies, regarding which J. C. Ryle said, "It is impossible to handle this question without coming into direct collision with the opinions of others. But I hope it is possible to handle it in a kindly and temperate spirit. At any rate it is no use to avoid discussion for fear of offending. Disputed points in theology are never likely to be settled unless men on both sides will say out plainly what they think, and give their reasons for their opinions. To avoid the subject, because it is a controversial one, is neither honest nor wise." *Knots Untied,* Chap. 5, p. 75. We are not vain enough to suppose that we can throw any NEW light on a controversy which so many able men have handled before. However, we do desire to uncover OLD light on this controversy about which most in this generation might not be aware. There is no need for us to spend ourselves producing NEW rebuttals to the errors of infant-baptism, when the Pædobaptists have never really answered our OLD rebuttals. Let the Pædobaptists first answer these, line for line, then we will consider what they have to say—not before. Where is their complete refutation to Abraham Booth's *Pædobaptism Examined,* Revised 3rd Edition with Replies to Dr. Williams and Peter Edwards, 3 vols. 1829? Where is their definitive answer to Alexander Carson's *Baptism in Its Mode and Subjects,* Edinburgh, 1831? Where is their complete answer to John Gale's *Reflections on Dr. Wall's*

PUBLISHER'S FOREWORD

History of Infant-Baptism, London, 1820? Where is their irrefutable reply to John Gill's *The Divine Right of Infant-Baptism Examined and Disproved,* Boston, 1746, or any of the other essays Dr. Gill wrote against infant-baptism? Until works like these be refuted, we see no benefit whatsoever in a ceaseless round of questions and of the vain and endless charges and counter-charges.

Fourth, in the republication of these books by Abraham Booth, we wish to strengthen the hands of those with whom we agree, to gather materials upon which future generations of younger Baptists can build, and to show them that we, as Baptists, have no reason to be ashamed of our opinions. Also, we desire to expose some of the Pædobaptists to some things they have, perhaps, never considered and to show the more credulous among the liberal Baptists and Pædobaptists of this generation that the Scriptural arguments in this matter are not, as they suppose, on their side. "To everything there is a season... a time to keep silence, and a time to speak." (Eccl. 3:1, 7). The time for silence has passed. The time to speak has come.

There are times when peculiar circumstances arise which draw special attention to specific doctrines of Christianity. The attacks by those who oppose the truth often make it necessary for Baptists to explain and emphasize some of their particular doctrinal views more than they normally would. The plausible assertion of some falsehood sometimes requires to be met by more than ordinary carefulness. Such are the times and circumstances in which we live with regard to the renewal of the infant-baptism controversy through the disproportionate publication of materials espousing Pædobaptist theology and vilifying and maligning Baptist theology and history. This recurring upsurge in publications emphasizing infant-baptism is neither surprising to us nor new for Protestants. After the Reformation (but prior to the founding of the American Republic, with full constitutional religious liberty), the Protestant Pædobaptists were usually in the majority and in control of the printing presses, through their connection with the political governments (except, of course, when everything was dominated by Roman Catholicism). Every time the

Pædobaptists felt their Baptist opponents were growing too much, or, when they sensed a doctrinal weakening of the Baptists, or, when they became over-confident in their own doctrinal position, or, when they became aware of any restless uncertainty among their own ranks, they repeatedly began to shore-up their Dagon by a renewed emphasis on infant-baptism and their aberrant views of the Abrahamic Covenant. What is surprising and new about the current situation of the infant-baptism controversy is some of the NEW arguments the Pædobaptists have adopted to attempt to defend their position. What we mean by NEW is, negatively, not just new in the sense of "what" they are saying, but new, positively, in "how" they are saying it. Regarding the mode of baptism, for example, there have always been Pædobaptists who espoused sprinkling and pouring as "acceptable" modes of baptism, but now some Pædobaptists are declaring them to be the ONLY acceptable modes; so what for 450 years they confessed were, at best, plausible, expedient, optional modes (sprinkling and pouring) have now become positively the ONLY Scriptural modes—at least this is what some of them have dogmatically, but inconsistently, stated in recent publications like:

♦ Adams, Jay E. - *The Meaning & Mode of Baptism*. (Phillipsburg, NJ: Presbyterian & Reformed Publishing Company, 1975).

♦ Jordan, James B., ed, - *The Failure of the American Baptist Culture*. (Tyler, TX: Geneva Divinity School, 1982.)

♦ Spencer, Duane - *Holy Baptism*. (Tyler, TX: Geneva Divinity School, 1984).

Now this is new and, frankly, quite surprising, for so many men depended upon for their honesty and reputed for scholarship and historic orthodoxy. These new-age Pædobaptists claim to be followers of their Pædobaptist forefathers' confessions, their forefathers' catechisms, their forefathers' creeds, and their forefathers' practices, yet they have *departed* from their forefathers' honesty and their forefathers' words. How, you ask, have they *departed* from their forefathers' honesty and words? We state: They are not

PUBLISHER'S FOREWORD

honest to admit what their forefathers admitted about the basic, primary mode of baptism. What do we mean? Did not the Reformers practice infant-baptism via sprinkling and pouring? Did not the English Puritans and the Scottish Presbyterians practice the same? Does not the *Westminster Confession* read, "Baptism is rightly administered by pouring or sprinkling water upon the person." Chap. 28, III, p. 115? How then, you ask, have these modern Pædobaptists *departed* from their forefathers' honesty and their forefathers' words with regard to the mode of baptism? To follow the example of Christ, we answer your question with a question: What exactly did their forefathers admit about the basic, primary mode of baptism that the new Pædobaptists are not honest enough to admit? For brevity, let us examine what some of their forefathers have said. We will review: (1) some of the major Reformers, (2) some of the most well-known Puritans and Scottish Presbyterians, and (3) the Westminster Assembly of Divines. The following quotes are certainly not all that these individuals stated about the mode of baptism, but relative to what these modern Pædobaptists are saying, their honest confessions make enlightening reading. Consider:

Reformers on the basic, primary mode of baptism:

Theodore Beza — "Christ commanded us to be baptized, by which word it is certain immersion is signified." — Annotations on Matt. 7:4; "To be baptized in water signifies no other than to be immersed in water; which is the external ceremony of baptism." — Annotations on Acts 19:3; "Ye have put on Christ — this phrase seems to proceed from the ancient custom of plunging the adult in baptism." — Annotations on Gal. 3:27; *Annotations ad Novum Testamentum,* Geneva, 1582;

John Calvin — "The word baptize signifies to immerse and it is clear that the rite of immersion was observed by the ancient Church." *Institutes of the Christian Religion,* Book IV, Chap. 15, Section 19; "From these words (John 3:23) it may be inferred that baptism was administered by John and Christ, by plunging the whole body under the water." *Commentary on John 3,* p. 130; "Here we perceive (Acts 8:38) how baptism was administered among the ancients, for they immersed the whole body into the water." *Commentary on Acts 8*, p. 364;

Martin Luther — "The term baptism is Greek; in Latin it may be translated *immersio*; since we immerse anything into water that the whole may be covered with the water. And though that custom be quite abolished among the generality, (for neither do they entirely dip children, but only sprinkle them with a little water), nevertheless they ought to be wholly immersed and immediately to be drawn out again, for the etymology of the word seems to require it." *Works,* Vol. 1, p. 74, Wittenberg Edition;

Philip Melancthon — "When we are immersed in the water, this signifies that the old Adam and sin in us are dead. When we are drawn out of the water, this means that we are now washed." *Loci Communes,* 1555, Chap. 20, p. 206; "Baptism is immersion into water, which is performed with this accompanying [sic] benediction of admiration: I baptize thee." etc.; "Plunging signifies ablution from sin and immersion into the death of Christ." *Catechesis De Sacramentis, Opera Omnia,* Vol. I, p. 25;

Ulric Zwingli — "'Baptized into his death'. . .When ye were immersed into the water of baptism, ye were engrafted into the death of Christ; that is, the immersion of your body into water was a sign, that ye ought to be engrafted into Christ and his death, that as Christ died and was buried, ye also may be dead to the flesh." Annotations on Romans 6:3, *Opera,* Vol. VI, p. 420, Zurich, 1828.

Whatever else may be said about these Reformers and their teachings or their inconsistencies, they at least admitted the basic, primary meaning of the word *baptizo,* and they honestly confessed the practice of the Apostolic Church. Notice also, there is not the slightest hint that they considered sprinkling and pouring as the ONLY acceptable modes of baptism. Wherever Jay Adams, James Jordan, Duane Spencer, etc., got their idea that sprinkling and pouring are the ONLY acceptable modes, they did not get it from these Reformers.

Publisher's Foreword

Puritans and Scottish Presbyterians on the basic, primary mode of baptism:

Richard Baxter — "It is commonly confessed by us to the Anabaptists that in the Apostles' times the baptized were dipped over head in water, and that this signified their profession, both of believing in the burial and resurrection of Christ; and of their own present renouncing the world and the flesh, or dying to sin and living to Christ, as the Apostle expoundeth in the forecited text of Col. 2 and Rom. 6." *Disputation of the Right to Sacraments,* p. 58, London, 1658;

Thomas Boston — "The unlawfulness of dipping is not to be pretended since it is not improbable that it was used by John the Baptist, Matt. 3:6, and Philip, Acts 8:38; but seems to have been used in the ancient church." *Works,* Vol. II, p. 475;

Thomas Goodwin — "The eminent thing signified and represented in baptism is not simply the blood of Christ as it washeth us from sin; but there is a farther representation therein of Christ's death, burial and resurrection, in the baptized's being first buried under the water and then rising out of it. . .Therefore, it is said 'We are buried with him in baptism. . .wherein you are risen with him'. . .Upon the party himself who is baptized, is personally, particularly, and apparently reinacted the same part again in his baptism." *Works,* Vol. IV, Chap. 7, pp. 41-42;

John Lightfoot — "The baptism of John was immersion of the body. . .he baptized in the Jordan and in Enon, because there was much water; and that Christ being baptized came up out of the water; to which, that seems to be parallel in Acts 8:38, Philip and the Eunuch went down into the water." *Whole Works,* Vol. XI, Comments on Matt. 3:6, p. 63;

Thomas Manton — "We are buried with him in baptism." The like expression you have in Col. 2:12, 'Buried with him in baptism.' The putting the baptized person into the water denoteth and proclaimeth the burial of Christ and we by submitting to it are baptized." *Complete Works,* Vol. XI, p. 171;

Whatever else may be said about these Puritans and Scottish Presbyterians and their teachings, they plainly admitted the basic, primary meaning of the word *baptizo,* and they honestly confessed the practice of John the Baptist, Christ, the Apostles, and the Apostolic Church. There was not the slightest hint that these men considered sprinkling and pouring as the ONLY proper modes of baptism. Wherever Jay Adams, James Jordan, Duane Spencer, etc., got their idea that sprinkling and pouring are the ONLY acceptable modes, they did not get it from these Puritans and Scottish Presbyterians.

The Westminster Assembly on the basic, primary mode of baptism:

In the *Westminster Confession,* regarding baptism, Chap. 28, III, p. 115, we read: "Dipping of the person into the water is not necessary; but Baptism is rightly administered by pouring or sprinkling water upon the person." Notice, not one word states that sprinkling or pouring are the ONLY proper modes; rather, it was the Assembly's opinion that immersion was not absolutely necessary, and that baptism could be rightly administered by pouring or sprinkling. It is evident that the Assembly had no thought of hiding or denying the basic, primary meaning of the word *baptizo,* thereby denying the basic, primary mode of baptism. Instead, it was their voted decision to recognize immersion as an acceptable mode, but one that was not absolutely necessary, while at the same time espousing pouring or sprinkling as acceptable modes. Notice, there was no vote to deny immersion, nor to espouse sprinkling or pouring as the ONLY proper modes. Notice this was not the only thing the Westminster Assembly said about the mode of baptism. In their *Westminster Annotation upon all the books of the Old and New Testaments,* London, 1657, they stated: "In this phrase (Col. 2:12) the Apostle seemeth to allude to the ancient manner of baptism, which was to dip the parties baptized, and, as it were, to bury them under the water for a while, and then to draw them out of it, and lift them up, to represent the burial of our old man, and our resurrection to newness of life." (See also their statements on Matt. 3:6 and Rom. 6:4).

PUBLISHER'S FOREWORD

It is especially enlightening and extremely important to know how the doctrinal statements of the Presbyterians came to favor sprinkling and pouring over immersion as the preferred mode of baptism. When the Westminster Assembly met to frame a creed and government for the Presbyterian denomination, there arose quite a controversy over the mode of baptism. Dr. John Lightfoot was the presiding officer at the Assembly sessions and relates in his journal what happened at that session: "Wednesday, August 7, 1644, then fell we upon the work of the day, which was about baptizing...whether to dip...or to sprinkle...after a long dispute, it was at last put to the question and it was voted so indifferently, that we were glad to count names twice for so many were unwilling to have dipping excluded...and there arose a great heat upon it." *Lightfoot's Works,* Vol. 13, pp. 300-301. History goes on to relate that finally the issue passed, 25 to 24, Dr. Lightfoot casting the deciding vote. It is apparent that the Assembly just barely agreed for Presbyterianism to prefer sprinkling and pouring over immersion, and that by only one vote. See: D. Neal's *History of the Puritans,* Vol. 2, p. 295.

Whatever else may be said about the Westminster Assembly, they at least honestly admitted the meaning of the word *baptizo,* and confessed that immersion was the practice of the ancient church. They did not in any sense, as is evident from their actions and their statements, deny immersion as valid baptism, nor did they declare sprinkling and pouring to be the ONLY proper modes of baptism. Wherever Jay Adams, James Jordan, Duane Spencer, and company got their idea that sprinkling and pouring are the ONLY acceptable modes, they did not get it from the Westminster Assembly or the *Westminster Confession of Faith.*

Now, we appeal to the conscience of our readers: Did not some of the major Reformers, some of the most well-known Puritans and Scottish Presbyterians and the Westminster Assembly recognize and honestly concede that the basic, primary meaning of *baptizo* is to "dip, plunge and immerse," and that the practice of John the Baptist, Christ, the Apostles and the ancient churches was to baptize by dipping, immersing and plunging under water? Did they declare sprinkling or pouring to be absolutely the ONLY proper mode of baptism? We think not. The honest statements and concessions of the Pædobaptists' forefathers speak for themselves.

The admissions and confessions of the three groups of older Pædobaptists given above are worlds apart from what the new-age Pædobaptists like Jay Adams of Westminster Theological Seminary, Escondido, California, and James B. Jordan of the Geneva Divinity School, Tyler, Texas, and Duane Spencer (now deceased), formerly of the Grace Bible Church, San Antonio, Texas, have recently stated.

For example, **Jay Adams**, speaking of the mode of baptism, said: "It is not true that the word *(baptize)* means immerse and only immerse . . . it is significant that Biblical baptism, in its origin, was performed by sprinkling and not by immersion . . . immersion is not only foreign to the New Testament but, on the contrary, the mode was exclusively sprinkling or pouring. . .baptizing by immersion — has no Bible precedent — it must be rejected." *The Meaning & Mode of Baptism,* pp. 2, 11, 43, 44.

While we could not disagree more with these statements by Mr. Adams, we are profoundly thankful for the true things he admits in his book, as they have needed to be admitted for a long time by the Pædobaptists. He makes statements that clear away all the confusion, all the areas of murky gray, which have made it well-nigh impossible for people to see some of the basic issues involved in this controversy. Mr. Adams admits the position that Baptists have held all along. Listen to what he says: "Contrary to the opinion of those who maintain that the mode is of little significance, I believe it to be of real significance. The immersionists are correct in making something of the mode. This latter conclusion I base upon two facts. First of all, all things that pertain to the Word of God are important. But this is especially true of the only two sacraments our Lord left His Church. Obviously, unless the Apostles used BOTH immersion and pouring (or sprinkling), one or the other was the proper method. If it was pouring, we ought to pour; if immersion, we ought to immerse. . .Secondly, mode cannot be separated from meaning. The sacraments are symbolic. If so, then "mode" and "symbol" are one and the same. . .The symbol in the sacrament is either disclosed or destroyed by a true or false mode of observing the sacrament. Mode and symbol and, therefore, mode and meaning, cannot be divorced." *The Meaning & Mode of Baptism,* Intro., p. vi. Again, Adams says, "Correct meaning can be communicated only by the correct mode of baptism," Ibid., p. vii. And again he says, "The words 'one Lord, one faith, one baptism,' (Eph. 4:5) clearly indicate that just as there could be only one Christian faith, only one Lord, so there is only one baptism. As a consequence, the meaning is single, and the mode is single." Ibid., p. vii.

Please consider carefully a summary of what Jay Adams has said in these statements:

1. The immersionists are correct in making something of the mode.

2. The mode cannot be separated from meaning.

3. The sacraments are symbolic. If so, then mode and symbol are one and the same.

4. Mode and symbol and, therefore, mode and meaning, cannot be divorced.

These statements are true and Biblical. Historically, this has been the consensus opinion among Baptists. If you alter the mode, you pervert the symbol, and, therefore, you pervert the meaning. If you change the mode, you distort the central truth that baptism symbolizes. Ephesians 4:5 is plain. We totally agree with Mr. Adams on *these* points. You can no more have two Christian baptisms than you can have two Christian faiths or two Almighty Lords. It is impossible. Therefore, Baptists and Pædobaptists cannot both be right. It is either baptism by immersion or by sprinkling or pouring. There is no such thing as an optional mode. One is right, the other is wrong. But in striking contrast to the truthful statements Mr. Adams made above, he also erroneously said, "Immersion is not only foreign to the New Testament but, on the contrary, the mode was EXCLUSIVELY sprinkling or pouring." Ibid.,

Chap. 7, p. 43. This is plainly false and an obvious departure from what his Pædobaptist forefathers said.

For another example of what the new-age Pædobaptists are saying, **James B. Jordan**, writing the introduction to Duane Spencer's book *Holy Baptism,* states: "Spencer does not argue that sprinkling or pouring are acceptable modes of baptism; rather he argues that baptism is only properly administered when the water falls from above, and that immersion is simply wrong." Again, Jordan himself states, "Reformed and Presbyterian theologians seem content to argue that sprinkling is permissible. They want to allow for immersion. In fact, however, immersion as a mode grossly obscures the meaning of baptism." *Holy Baptism,* Introduction, p. x.

Duane Spencer provides another example of what the new-age Pædobaptists are saying about immersion. Spencer declared: "Only the untaught, or those blinded by denominational prejudice, still cling to the old notion that to baptize is to immerse." *Holy Baptism*, Chap. 7, p. 65.

We appeal again to the conscience of our readers: Are these men saying the same thing their forefathers said? Admittedly they are not. Jay Adams states in his book that he disagrees with anyone who asserts that "the original Christian method (of baptizing) was immersion." And then he says, "I believe them entirely wrong." *Meaning & Mode of Baptism,* Introduction, pp. v-vi. Take special note of Mr. Jordan's admittance of his deviation from the standard Pædobaptist opinion that we have already quoted. Jordan said, "Reformed and Presbyterian theologians seem content to argue that sprinkling is permissible. They want to allow for immersion." He goes on to say, however, that in his opinion, "Immersion grossly obscures the meaning of baptism." *Holy Baptism,* Introduction, p. x. Surely, we see how these new-age Pædobaptists have departed from their forefathers' honesty and their forefathers' words. There is a great difference. How drastically different! How obviously dishonest! How clearly wrong, either intentionally or ignorantly. Such statements, like the last one by Duane Spencer, that: "Only the untaught, or those blinded by denominational prejudice still cling to the old notion that to baptize is to immerse," are almost unbelievable! Untaught men are the only ones who believe that *baptizo* means to immerse? Does he mean untaught men like Beza, Calvin, Luther, Melancthon, Zwingli, Baxter, Boston, Goodwin, Lightfoot, Manton, Owen, and members of the Westminster Assembly? Untaught men, indeed! He said only men "blinded by denominational prejudice" believe that *baptizo* means to immerse? Does he mean prejudiced men like the major Reformers, Puritans, Scottish Presbyterians, and the Westminster Assembly? The denominational prejudice of all these men gave them every reason to hide the truth, but their scholarship and honesty before God made them admit the truth. We cannot say the same for the new-age Pædobaptists like Jay Adams, James B. Jordan, and Duane Spencer. Again we say, these modern Pædobaptists have *departed* from their forefathers' honesty, for they conceal what their forefathers admitted; and they have *departed* from their forefathers' words, for they most emphatically are not saying what their forefathers said.

Before leaving these particular assessments of the new-age Pædobaptists, we would make three observations in passing:

(1) We would **point out** to our readers that the new Pædobaptists are at least consistent in one thing: while they have departed from their forefathers' honesty and words, they have not completely departed from their forefathers' *ways*. They, like their forefathers, "say, and do not" (Matt. 23:3). Their forefathers honestly admitted that the basic, primary meaning of *baptizo* was immerse, dip, plunge or submerge under the water. Their forefathers also confessed that immersion was the practice of John the Baptist, Christ, the Apostles, and the ancient churches regarding the mode of baptizing. However, their forefathers refused to follow the ancient practice, adopting instead that part and pillar of Popery, infant-baptism. In a similar inconsistency, these modern Pædobaptists (Jay Adams, James B. Jordan, Duane Spencer, etc.) say they are followers of their forefathers' writings, yet in striking contrast to what their forefathers plainly wrote regarding the meaning and the mode of baptism, they advocate sprinkling and pouring as the ONLY proper

mode of baptism. Their forefathers advocated no such thing! Therefore, with regard to how well they follow their forefathers, we say that these new Pædobaptists "say, and do not." (Matt. 23:3).

(2) We would **warn** our readers to beware of the Protestant-Reformed teaching relative to "liberty of conscience" and the "separation of Church and State" found in such books as *The Failure of the American Baptist Culture* edited by James B. Jordan. While we recognize today's tendency toward anarchy, under the guise of Biblical liberty of conscience ("Every man doing that which is right in his own eyes." — Judges 21:25), we also recognize the unbiblical thinking of some Baptists about Church and State, which results in unbiblical pietism and/or political activism. Nevertheless, at the same time, we recognize a Biblical liberty of conscience ("Let every man be persuaded in his own mind." — Rom. 14:5), a Biblical private judgment ("Prove all things" — I Thess. 5:21), a Biblical dichotomy between the Church and the State ("My kingdom is not of this world" — Jn. 18:36 and "Render therefore, unto Caesar the things which are Caesar's and unto God the things which are God's"— Matt. 22:21). Therefore, we warn again about the "Protestant-Reformed" teaching about the relationship between Church and State and liberty of conscience, found in books like Mr. Jordan's. This type of Protestant thinking finds its roots in the teachings of: the National Mosaic Laws of Judaism, the canonized doctors of the Roman Catholics, *i.e.*, Augustine and Thomas Aquinas, Pope Innocent III of the Spanish Inquisition, and Pope Gregory XIII of the St. Bartholomew Massacre, and all the major Reformers, *i.e.*, Calvin, Luther, Bucer, Bullinger, Zwingli, Farel, Beza, Melancthon, and the Westminster Assembly. Why should you **beware?** Because Mr. Jordan and company, like the major Reformers and the Westminster Assembly, profess toleration and liberty of conscience when expedient, but are decidedly against true toleration and scriptural liberty of conscience. Their Pædobaptist forefathers, especially their Anglican and Presbyterian forefathers, whenever possible, propagated coerced uniformity, suppression, and persecution against all whose views differed from theirs. (See: Daniel

PUBLISHER'S FOREWORD

Neal's *The History of the Puritans,* London, 1837, Vol. 2, pp. 378-394, 436; pp. 505-506; Phillip Schaff's *History of the Christian Church,* Vol. 7, pp. 25-42; Vol. 8, pp. 320-330; 358-361; and W. K. Jordan's *The Development of Religious Toleration in England,* Harvard University Press, 1932-1940). All false religion seeks the aid of political government to suppress, persecute, and destroy all other faiths it deems heretical. Instead of relying upon the power of truth to propagate its views, false religion relies upon the power of the political sword, which, in itself, is a witness of its falsehood.

(3) We would **remind** our readers to be cognizant of the fact that, in reality, behind the religious veneer and philosophical jargon of James B. Jordan's Symposium, *The Failure of the American Baptist Culture,* lies the devilish, persecuting principle that motivated the likes of the sinister Archbishop William Laud, James II, John Graham of Claverhouse, and Robert Grierson of Lag, as well as the attempted, politically-enforced, absolute religious uniformity of "The Killing Times." See: J.C. Ryle's *Light From Old Times,* Chap. 10, pp. 258-302; J.D. Douglas' *Light From the North,* Chap. 10, pp. 153-167; Alexander Smellie's *Men of the Covenant,* Chap. 30, pp. 384-400; Jock Purves's *Fair Sunshine,* Banner of Truth, 1968; Perry Miller's *Orthodoxy in Massachusetts 1630-1650,* Boston, 1961; and Charles F. James' *Documentary History of the Struggle for Religious Liberty in Virginia,* J. P. Bell Co., 1900.

Now let us return to discuss the "peculiar circumstances" (mentioned earlier on page 3) which have once again drawn our attention to the infant-baptism controversy. Briefly and generally speaking, the times and circumstances (the demise of the testimony for and practice of Baptist ecclesiology and the vocal testimony against Pædobaptist ecclesiology) are these. Since the early 1800's the Baptist people in America, for the most part, have departed from the Bible-based Calvinistic theology and Baptist ecclesiology of their Baptist forefathers. We emphasize that the "majority" of professed Baptists have done this — certainly not all Baptists, for there is "at this present time also. . .a remnant." (Rom. 11:5). In their sincere desire to fulfill the Great Commission, the New School Baptists have plunged deeper and deeper into the labyrinth of

Arminianism and Pragmatism. Watered-down and corrupted by streams of modified Calvinism running from the Congregational New England Divinity movement, the Presbyterian New Measures movement, Andrew Fuller's unscriptural views of Imputation, Substitutionary Atonement, the natural abilities of fallen man, etc., and influenced by their own compassionate but erroneous evangelistic zeal, New School Baptists like Robert Hall, Jr., John Sutcliff, John Mason Peck, Luther Rice, Jonathan Maxy, W. B. Johnson, and a countless army of others, have been influenced to establish, without Biblical warrant, vast institutions (*i.e.*, conventions, annuities, foundations, seminaries, etc.) of tremendous wealth and prestige which have (in the public mind) usurped the identity, authority, and responsibility of the Lord's New Testament Churches. Hence, the New School Baptists have departed further and further from the ancient theology and ecclesiology their forefathers had observed. Even while professing and preaching an ecclesiology that demanded a separation between the regenerate and unregenerate, between the New Testament Church and the World, the New School Baptists devised and implemented nation-wide and world-wide pragmatic practices in evangelism and missions which guaranteed the very opposite. Ultimately, however, these vast institutions and new pragmatic practices have proven themselves to be nothing but huge engines of destruction tearing the heart out of the churches, devouring everything Bible and Baptist for the sake of growth and the accumulation of wealth and influence. In disdain for, and opposition to, their more numerous and popular New School counterparts, the Old School Baptists have recoiled more and more into criticism, Antinomianism, and Old-Line Conditionalism. Consequently, today both groups find themselves in a deplorable and disastrously effete condition doctrinally and practically, and at a loss with regard to defending their distinct identity in controversy. Even worse, in most cases both groups find that the historic Calvinistic theology and Baptist ecclesiology of their forefathers is often completely rejected in their congregations.

Publisher's Foreword

On the other hand, since the late 1950's and early 1960's, there has been an upsurge of interest in and publication of Puritan theology, for most of which, we might add, we are extremely grateful. But with the exposure to Puritan theology, there has also been an exposure to Puritan-Protestant-Pædobaptist ecclesiology, which basically is the same as Catholic ecclesiology, *i.e.*, both being without Biblical basis. With this upsurge in Puritan-Protestant-Pædobaptist publications, the Protestants have been strengthened, renewed, and emboldened. The circumstances with the Baptists have been far otherwise. With the passing of time, the death of the older defenders of the Baptist faith, the liberalizing of the Baptist schools, the decline in availability of the writings of the older Baptist authors upon the public bookshelves and the negligence in republishing the same, the almost complete turnover to Arminianism, the emphasizing of pragmatic methodology and glorification of the American goddess of size and success, the ancient theological and ecclesiological distinctives of the Baptist faith have all but disappeared from public memory. In this situation of the weakening and well-nigh silencing of the witness of Baptist ecclesiology, the Protestant Pædobaptists have renewed the ancient controversy between themselves and the Baptists. This is nothing new or strange, for as John Gill pointed out, "The Pædobaptists are ever restless and uneasy, always endeavoring to maintain and support, if possible, their unscriptural practice of infant-baptism; though it is no other than a pillar of Popery." *Infant Baptism, A Part and Pillar of Popery,* Boston, 1766. Consequently, strengthened by the multiplicity of Protestant Pædobaptist publications during the last 25 years (1960-1985) and emboldened by the timidity and inadequacy of the present-day Baptist rebuttal, the Protestant Pædobaptists have thrust forward their champions, who, assuming their invincibility like Goliath of old, hurl forth slander and reproach, while the Baptists, like the army of Israel, cower down fearfully in their trenches. Little wonder then, that multitudes of young men studying for the ministry and many members of Baptist churches have renounced their Baptist affiliations and joined Pædobaptist congregations. It appears to those who are ignorant of the issues that this

Baptist vs. Pædobaptist controversy is just a matter of disagreement about the amount of water used in baptism. This is far from the major issues involved. As far as the Publisher is concerned, in Protestant Pædobaptist ecclesiology there are at least the following Biblical errors and inconsistencies:

♦ A *Violation* of the basic laws of hermeneutics and the fundamental principle of *Sola Scriptura*;

♦ A *Defamation* of the Goodness and Wisdom of the Divine character;

♦ A *Confusion* of the Everlasting Covenant of Grace with the Abrahamic Covenant of Circumcision;

♦ A *Nullification* of the doctrines of original sin, total depravity, and inability;

♦ An *Abrogation* of the true nature and evidence of Sovereign saving grace and the doctrines of Regeneration and Conversion;

♦ An *Obliteration* and *Perversion* of the proper authority, subject, mode, and purpose of New Testament Baptism;

♦ A *Destruction* of the scripturally-required spiritual nature of Christ's New Testament Church (John 3:5-7; 15:19; 18:36; 2 Corinthians 6:14-18), because there is an amalgamation of the world with the saints, the lost with the saved, the believers with unbelievers, and the regenerate with the unregenerate by means of infant-baptism;

♦ An *Association* and *Integration* of the spiritual church with the political government, completely unjustified by the New Testament;

♦ A *Renunciation* and *Opposition* to true individual liberty of conscience and private judgment;

♦ A subtle *Repudiation* of the New Testament as the final authority in all matters of faith and practice, that is, of the New Testament as the Regulative Principle in all worship and, therefore,

Publisher's Foreword

♦ An *Invasion* and *Usurpation* of the crown rights and sole prerogatives of Christ as the only King and Lawgiver of the New Testament Church.

Therefore, as we see it, the practice of infant-baptism annuls the basic theological foundations of Christianity. In a word— "grace is no more grace." (Rom. 11:6).

Such obvious errors must be opposed. The differences between Baptists and Pædobaptists are no minor differences. No one, consequently, can ever properly understand this infant-baptism controversy without being aware of the opposing theologies behind it. In order for anyone to prepare adequately to deal with this controversy, we believe it is necessary that they become aware of following things about controversy in general, and this controversy in particular:

I. THE ANTIPATHY AND TIMIDITY TOWARD CONTROVERSY

II. THE INEVITABILITY OF THIS CONTROVERSY

III. THE THEOLOGY BEHIND THIS CONTROVERSY

IV. THE NECESSITY FOR THIS CONTROVERSY

I. THE TIMIDITY AND ANTIPATHY TOWARD CONTROVERSY

Why are the professed Christians of this generation so repulsed at the idea of religious controversy? What has brought about this timidity toward conflict in religious matters? What has begotten this timidity in Baptist people toward the baptism controversies? As a partial answer we propose three things:

First, the **dislike** of our natural heart toward exertion, especially in religious matters — By nature we all seek rest, comfort, and ease. Basically everything temporal is toward that goal. Anything that calls forth exertion, sacrifice, painstaking effort, the loss of time, goods, income, and especially reputation, the natural heart opposes. Anything that unsettles our lives, anything that searches our hearts or exposes our false hopes, we vehemently dislike. Controversy, especially religious controversy, is so un-nerving because we judge it so unnecessary.

Secondly, the **desire** of our natural heart for acceptance — By nature we like the praise of others; we shrink from collision and conflict. We love to be thought charitable. We all have a secret desire for the world's smile, approval, and applause. We greatly fear the world's frown, laughter, ridicule, and blame. We all have a secret wish to do as others in the world do, and not run to extremes. Controversial issues often convict us of not having gone far enough. Controversial issues most often mean we lose the world's approval and applause.

Before passing, let us consider that both the dislikes and the desires of the natural heart enter into this infant-baptism controversy. Jesus said that God had hidden some things "from the wise and prudent, and hast revealed them unto babes." (Matt. 11:25). John the Baptist said, "A man can receive nothing, except it be given him from Heaven." (John 3:27). If we know anything in the infant-baptism controversy that the Pædobaptists absolutely do not know, it is because of grace (I Cor. 4:7), and there is no cause for boasting with us. We honestly believe many of the Pædobaptists do not see the inconsistency of infant-baptism with free grace. However, we firmly believe that some of the more knowledgeable Pædobaptists reject believer's baptism and do everything they can to shore-up infant-baptism, not because they do not have enough information, but because they cannot face the implication. It is a case of not being willing to carry out this truth in its practical aspects that is the great hindrance to their understanding it; "If any man will do his will, he shall know of the doctrine, whether it be of God." (John 7:17). Some of the Pædobaptists understand the logical implications and the practical ramifications of admitting the invalidity of infant-baptism and accepting the solitary validity of believer's immersion. As an illustration consider the following:

> *"The Odious Ecclesiastical Consequences of the Immersionist Dogma. . .*All parties are agreed that baptism is the initiatory rite which gives membership

in the visible church of Christ. The great commission was: Go ye, and disciple all nations, baptizing them into the Trinity. Baptism recognizes and constitutes the outward discipleship. Least of all, can any immersionist dispute this ground. Now, if all other forms of baptism than immersion are not only irregular, but null and void, all unimmersed persons are out of the visible church. But if each and every member of a Pædobaptist visible church is thus unchurched, of course, the whole body is unchurched. All Pædobaptist societies, then, are guilty of an intrusive error, when they pretend to the character of a visible church of Christ. Consequently, they can have no ministry; and this for several reasons. Surely no valid office can exist in an association whose claim to be an ecclesiastical commonwealth is utterly invalid. When the temple is non-existent, there can be no actual pillars to that temple. How can an unauthorized herd of unbaptized persons, to whom Christ concedes no church authority, confer any valid office? Again: it is preposterous that a man should receive and hold office in a commonwealth where he himself has no citizenship; but this unimmersed Pædobaptist minister, so-called, is no member of any visible Church. There are no real ministers in the world, except the Immersionist preachers! The pretensions of all others, therefore, to act as ministers, and to administer the sacraments, are sinful intrusions. It is hard to see how any intelligent and conscientious Immersionist can do any act which countenances or sanctions this profane intrusion. They should not allow any weak inclinations of fraternity and peace to sway their consciences in this point of high principle. They are bound, then, not only to practice close communion, but to refuse all ministerial recognition and communion to these intruders. The sacraments cannot go beyond the pale of the visible Church. Hence, the same stern denunciations ought to be hurled at the Lord's Supper in Pædobaptist societies, and at all their prayers and preachings in public, as at the iniquity of 'baby-sprinkling.' The enlightened immersionist should treat all these societies just as he does that 'Synagogue of Satan,' the Papal church: there may be many good, misguided believers in them; but no church character, ministry, nor sacraments whatever." R.L. Dabney, *Lectures in Systematic Theology,* Lecture 64, pp.774-775.

Mr. Dabney, with his clear perception and forthright bravery, saw to the bottom of the practical ramifications. He saw that the Baptist position meant the loss of reputation, salaries, professorships, and positions along with the reorganization of churches, the new ordination of ministers, etc.. Therefore, he vigorously denounced the believer's immersion position. We believe other Pædobaptists see the implications also, but for whatever reasons, the dislikes and desires of their natural hearts keep them from admitting the truth. This is not our opinion alone. Consider: "We believe that it is their (Pædobaptist) unwillingness to face up to the implications of the radical difference between the old and the new covenant (Heb. 8:7ff) that prevents them from accepting our (Baptist) position." Erroll Hulse, *The Testimony of Baptism,* Carey Publications, Sussex, England, Foreword, p.5.

Thirdly, the **deception** of our natural heart about charity — *i.e.*, about the nature of true Biblical charity. This is another reason why people in general, and Baptists in particular, are so apathetic and timid toward controversy in religious matters. Now when we speak here of a deception about charity, we speak not of the natural "internal" deception which abides in the human heart described in Isaiah 44:20, "A deceived heart hath turned him aside, that he cannot deliver his soul," and in Jer. 17:9, "The heart is deceitful above all things." We speak rather about the "external" deception pawned off on many unsuspecting minds which is described in Romans 16:17-18, "Mark them which cause divisions and offenses contrary to the doctrine which ye have learned; and avoid them. For they that are such serve not our Lord Jesus Christ, but their own belly; and BY GOOD WORDS AND

Publisher's Foreword

FAIR SPEECHES DECEIVE THE HEARTS OF THE SIMPLE."

This specious charity is foisted upon the vast majority of professing Christian people. J.C. Ryle said, "There is a spurious charity, I am afraid, which dislikes all strong statements in religion, — a charity which would have no one interfered with, — a charity which would have everyone let alone in his sins, — a charity which, without evidence, takes for granted that everybody is in a way to be saved, — a charity which never doubts that all people are going to heaven, and seems to deny the existence of such a place as hell. But such charity is not of the New Testament, and does not deserve the name. Give me the charity which tries and hopes nothing that is not sanctioned by the Word. Give me the charity which St. Paul describes to the Corinthians (I Cor. 13:1, etc.); the charity which is not blind, and deaf and stupid, but has eyes to see and senses to discern between him that feareth and him that feareth Him not. Such charity will rejoice in nothing but 'the truth,' (I Cor. 13:6)." *Old Paths*, Cambridge, James Clarke Co., Ltd., 1977, Chap. 3, pp. 86-87.

It appears that Christians everywhere, and especially Baptist people, are suffering from this deceptive concept of Biblical charity. While on the one hand most Baptists are not even aware of any distinctive, identifying Baptist doctrines and practices, some Baptists on the other hand, because they are deluded by a false view of charity, are intimidated, regretful, and apologetic because Baptists ever believed such things. This false charity mistakes stretching the conscience for broadening the mind. It tolerates worldliness, wickedness, false doctrine, and negligent practice under the guise of Christian love. Nothing could be farther from the truth. False charity has helped to spawn, and especially to support twin serpents in the area of theology:

First, it is a part of the basis of that vague, dim, misty, hazy kind of theology which is most painfully apparent in the present age. It begets that kind of theology where there is something about Christ, something about grace, something about faith, and something about holiness, but it is not the real thing. Neither you nor its adherents can make it match the theology in the Scriptures. It will not aid you in life, nor comfort you in death.

Second, this false idea of Christian love is part of the foundation of that extravagantly broad and liberal theology which is so much in vogue in all modern religions. It is thought grand and wise to condemn no opinion whatsoever, and to pronounce all sincere, earnest preachers and people to be trustworthy, however unorthodox, unscriptural, heterogeneous, and mutually-destructive their opinions may be. Everything is true and nothing is false! Everybody is right and nobody is wrong! Everybody is likely to be saved, and nobody is to be lost. We are all going to the same place. The tendency of this modern thinking and bogus charity, according to the way most young seminary graduates act, is to reject confessions, creeds, doctrine, dogma, and every kind of authority in religion and to abhor everything that appears dogmatic or controversial as nothing but sheer bigotry or unprofessional, simple-minded, incompetent folly. Again we say, nothing could be further from the truth! "Love doth not behave itself unseemly. . .rejoiceth not in iniquity, but rejoiceth in the truth." (I Cor. 13:5,6). Yea, "Ye that love the Lord, hate evil." (Ps. 97:10). Speak "the truth in love," (Eph. 4:15). True Christian love always stands connected with the truth and cannot be separated from the truth.

This false conception of Christian love has chained this generation of Baptists. It hinders many from "earnestly contending for the faith which was once delivered unto the saints." (Jude 3). John the Baptist was not intimidated by specious charity, but was quick to point out to those that came to be baptized by him that their natural connection to Abraham did not qualify them for New Testament baptism (Matt. 3:7-10). They were the covenant nation, the covenant people, the covenant religion. They were the natural seed of believing Abraham, but this did not make them fit subjects for New Testament baptism. They certainly did not have a right to it by means of their connection to a believing parent. No, Jesus said, "The flesh profiteth nothing." (John 6:63). The Apostle John wrote, "Not of blood," (John 1:13). John the

Baptist said that circumcision entitles you to nothing. You must have a new heart. You must then give evidence of a new heart by the fruits of a new heart, *i.e.*, repentance and faith. These are the proper prerequisites to New Testament baptism. This is the same thing Paul said, "Circumcision is nothing," (I Cor. 7:19). "In Jesus Christ neither circumcision availeth anything, nor uncircumcision; but faith which worketh by love." (Gal. 5:6; see Gal. 6:15).

The author of the following works, Abraham Booth, has made it evident that he did not labor under any present-day hallucination or deception about Christian love, nor was he hindered by any inclination toward worldly approval or any intimidation about religious controversy; rather, Abraham Booth has given definitive answers to the infant-baptism controversy. He is an exemplary illustration of true Christian candor, charity, and courage. May the Lord of the harvest send forth more laborers of his kind into the harvest.

II. THE INEVITABILITY OF THIS CONTROVERSY

That man has a very superficial understanding of saving grace and of Christianity altogether who does not see that wherever real Christianity goes, controversy follows. That man is very shallow and immature in his reading and comprehension who has not observed this repeated testimony given in the Scriptures. Whenever God regenerates one of His children and begins to lead him by the Holy Spirit to "the knowledge of the truth," conflict, turmoil, and controversy inevitably follow. The Bible attests this to be so both internally and externally. For example, inwardly, after regeneration, there exists a "warring" in our members (Rom. 7:23). Paul explained that warring as: "the flesh lusting against the spirit, and the spirit against the flesh: and these are contrary the one to the other." (Gal. 5:17). Note that word, "contrary." The inward spiritual principle of grace implanted in us at regeneration, *i.e.*, the new man, here called "the spirit," is opposed to, contrary to, is an adversary to, "the flesh," the old natural, carnal man. The Amplified Bible renders this: ". . .these are antagonistic to each other — continually withstanding and in conflict with each other." (Gal. 5:17). It is not our purpose at this time to deal with the internal Spiritual warfare of the Christian, per se, but for those who are interested in this subject, we recommend, John Owen's "Mortification of Sin" *Works*, Vol..6, pp. 1-86; John Downame's *The Christian Warfare,* London, 1604; Christopher Love's *The Combat Between the Flesh and the Spirit,* London, 1650; and William Gurnall's *The Christian in Complete Armour,* London, Banner of Truth, 1974.

The real, born-again Christian has not only inward conflicts and internal controversy with his flesh, but he also has external conflict and controversy. He must "resist the devil" (James 4:7) for Satan is his "adversary" (I Pet. 5:8), and the whole world system "hateth" him (John 15:19). The "children of this world," the "children of the devil," (I John 3:10) are his implacable enemies. While we live after the world, we have peace with the world, but none with God. When we have peace with God, we have none with the world; "The friendship of the world is enmity with God. Whosoever, therefore will be a friend of the world is the enemy of God." (James 4:4; John 15:18-20). This has been true since the beginning. God put "enmity" between the serpent's seed and the woman's seed (Gen. 3:15). This enmity, *i.e.*, perpetual hatred (Ezek. 35:5), has always manifested itself between these two seeds in the form of controversy. Wicked men, ungodly men have fought against true Christians like the "world of the ungodly," (II Pet. 2:5) which ridiculed and opposed Noah. False religion, which is nothing but the world's religion, has continually given vent to this enmity by consistently being the greatest opponent of true Christianity through the ages. Samuel Ward said, "Religion is the greatest enemy to religion; the false to the true." *Sermons & Treatises of Samuel Ward,* London, 1636, p. 146. "He that is upright in the way is abomination to the wicked." (Prov. 29:27). "They hate him that rebuketh in the gate, and they abhor him that speaketh uprightly." (Amos 5:10). For example, Cain, who brought an unacceptable offering, rose up and slew righteous Abel. Why? "Cain, who was of that wicked one, and slew his brother. And wherefore slew he him? Because his own works were evil, and his brother's righteous. Marvel not, my brethren, if the world hate you ..." (I John 3:12-13). Jannes and Jambres, sorcerers of Egypt, withstood Moses (II Tim.

3:8). Balaam, the false prophet, who loved the wages of unrighteousness, withstood the progress of Israel (Num. 22:5 — 24:25). Hananiah, the false prophet, opposed Jeremiah (Jer. 28:1-17). Sanballat and Tobiah fought against the rebuilding work of Nehemiah (Neh. 2:10, 19, 20). The high priest, the Pharisees, the scribes and the doctors of law, all part of religious Judaism, constantly challenged and resisted John the Baptist and the Lord Jesus Christ. The very existence of true Christianity is a witness against false religion. Therefore, we should not be surprised or shocked to find controversy just as much a part of the Christian life today as it has always been and always will be (Acts 14:22; John 16:33). Did not the Lord Jesus say: "Suppose ye that I am come to give peace on earth? I tell you, Nay: but rather division." (Luke 12:51-53); and, "I am come to set a man at variance against his father and the daughter against her mother." (Matt. 10:35-36)? Does not the Scripture say: "There was a division among the people because of him." (John 7:43)? And did not the Apostle Paul state: "Persecutions, afflictions ... came unto me at Antioch, at Iconium, at Lystra... yea, and all that will live godly in Christ Jesus SHALL suffer persecution." (II Tim. 3:11-12)? Why were the Jews always stirring up the people and the political rulers against Paul? Why have false religions always worked hand-in-hand with political governments? Obviously, to suppress any and every view that differed from theirs (John 11:40-48) in order to preserve their worldly situations. Why have false religions always opposed and persecuted true Christians? "As then he that was born after the flesh [Ishmael] persecuted him that was born after the Spirit [Isaac], even so it is now." (Gal. 4:29). Conflict, turmoil, and controversy will inevitably be a way of life for Christians. We, as Baptists, certainly need not be surprised, then, when controversy rages around us and our distinctive Baptist doctrines, nor when old enemies like the Pædobaptists renew old controversy. The infant-baptism controversy with Pædobaptists is inevitable for true Baptists because our principles of ecclesiology are diametrically opposed and mutually exclusive. The Pædobaptists realize that they cannot let us alone. The false religionists of Jesus' day said, "If we let him alone, all men will believe him: and the Romans shall come and take away both our place and nation."

(John 11:48). Similarly, the Pædobaptists see that if the Baptists are left alone, the teaching and practices of the Baptists would be spread abroad, many would believe and be immersed becoming Baptists, and the Pædobaptists would lose "their place." Our controversy with the Pædobaptists over infant-baptism is inevitable unless we are unfaithful to our principles. They cannot let us alone. Therefore, what we need to do is prepare for the inevitable, and there can probably be no better preparation than the book by Abraham Booth, now in the reader's hand. This inevitable conflict between principles leads to the discussion of our next point: What are the principles involved in the infant-baptism controversy?

III. THE THEOLOGY BEHIND THIS CONTROVERSY

> "Ideas in general do have consequences and theological ideas have tremendous consequences." C. Gregg Singer, *A Theological Interpretation of American History,* Nutley, NJ: The Craig Press, 1976, p. 1.

This is true because every man lives according to the way he thinks. The Scripture states, "As he thinketh in his heart so is he." (Prov. 23:7). Whatever we think, our basic concepts, thoughts, ideas, philosophies, and theologies establish our values and determine the course we pursue in life. Theological ideas about God, the soul, salvation, judgment, heaven, and hell are some of the most deeply-rooted ideas in our naturally religious natures. Therefore, theological ideas are going to have a strong influence, a tremendous sway upon the behavior of men, and while religious controversy may appear to be nothing to most people but a strife about "words and names," it is far otherwise. In reality, it is a conflict of souls about issues of eternal significance. Make no mistake, behind every religious controversy there are distinct ideas, concepts, and theologies grappling over the weightiest matters—the concerns of the soul. As we have pointed out before in this Foreword, the differences between the Baptists and Pædobaptists are no minor differences. Doctrine establishes practice, and practice confirms doctrine. Baptist ecclesiology is diametrically opposed to Pædobaptist ecclesiology. Therefore, understanding the theologies involved in this controversy means everything with regard to understanding the controversy itself. For example, there has always been opposition against those who consistently advocate the Baptist distinctives. There has been opposition, first by Judaism, then by Catholicism, then by Popery and Protestantism alike. Since the first century, the Baptist people have been that "sect that everywhere is spoken against." (Acts 28:22). The reason is not hard to find: "If ye were of the world, the world would love his own: but because ye are not of the world, but I have chosen you out of the world, therefore the world hateth you." (John 15:19). The Lord Jesus Christ stated emphatically, "My Kingdom is not of this world." (John 18:36). In the light of these two Scriptures, it is no wonder that Popery and Protestantism unite against their common enemy, the Baptists, for they recognize that strict Baptist theology and ecclesiology, properly defined and defended, means the exposure and dissipation of their worldly religious empires. For what other reason would Protestantism unite with Popery against the Baptists when, outwardly, Protestantism is supposed to be so historically and theologically opposed to Catholicism? It is a good question. It demands an answer. We propose two:

First - Strict Baptist Ecclesiology Exposes the Similarity of the Protestant Pædobaptists to the Roman Catholics.

Jesus said, "If I had not come and spoken unto them, they had not had sin; but now they have no cloke for their sin." (John 15:22). The same thing is true regarding the Baptist view of the nature of saving grace and the nature of the New Testament Church. If it didn't exist, if it was never declared and exposed to view, Popery, Prelacy, and Presbytery alike would have a cloak for their errors. But by comparison with Baptist ecclesiology, it becomes clearly evident that Catholic ecclesiology and Protestant Pædobaptist ecclesiology are actually two arms of the same beast, two faces on the same head, two walls of the same prison. Strict Baptist ecclesiology exposes them both as built upon, and sustained by, the same unscriptural practice of infant-baptism—and therefore, at the root, based upon the same unscriptural principle, *i.e.*, salvation by works. Consider for a moment their similarity:

A. The **ROMAN CATHOLIC** belief in the saving efficacy of infant-baptism:

1. "Whoever shall affirm that baptism is indifferent, that is, not necessary to salvation; LET HIM BE ACCURSED. Whoever shall affirm that children are not to be reckoned among the faithful by the reception of baptism, because they do not actually believe; and therefore that they are to be re-baptized when they come to years of discretion; or that, since they cannot personally believe, it is better to omit their baptism, than that they should be baptized only in the faith of the church: LET HIM BE ACCURSED." Decree No. 24, Session VII of the Council of Trent, March 3, 1547, John Dowling, *History of Romanism,* New York, 1846, Book 7, Chap. 4, p. 510.

2. "Infants, unless regenerated unto God through the grace of baptism. . .are born to eternal misery and perdition. Catechism of the Council of Trent, quoted by Loraine Boettner, *Roman Catholicism,* Philadelphia, 1979, Chap. 8, p. 190.

3. "Baptism cleanses man from Original Sin and from all personal sins, gives him rebirth as a child of God, incorporates him into the Church, sanctifies him with gifts of the Holy Spirit, and, impressing [sic] on his soul an indelible character..." *Instructions in the Catholic Faith* by Parish Priests, p. 192, No. xl.

B. The **PROTESTANT PAEDOBAPTIST** belief in the saving efficacy of infant-baptism:

1. **James Bannerman** of the Free Church of Scotland, said, "In such a case of infants regenerated in infancy, the sign is meant to be connected with the thing signified that the moment of its baptism is the appointed moment of its regeneration too. . .when the infant carries with it to the tomb the sign of the covenant, administered in faith, shall we not say that with the sign, and mysteriously linked to it, there was

also the thing signified; and that in such a case of a dying babe regenerated in infancy, the laver of Baptism was the laver of regeneration, too."' *The Church of Christ,* Banner of Truth, Edinburgh, 1974, Vol. 2, pp. 119-120.

2. **R.L. Dabney**, an Old School Southern Presbyterian, said, "Many collateral advantages are gained by this minor citizenship of the baptized in the Church. They are retained under wholesome restraints. Their carnal opposition to the truth is greatly disarmed by early association. The numerical and pecuniary basis of the Church's operations is widened. And where the duties represented in the sacrament of baptism are properly followed up, the actual regeneration of children is the ordinary result." *Lectures in Systematic Theology,* Lecture 66, pp. 798-799.

3. **Charles Hodge**, an Old School Northern Presbyterian, exhorting parents to fulfill their duty to have their children baptized, said: "Do let the little ones have their names written in the Lamb's Book of Life, even if afterwards they choose to erase them. Being thus enrolled may be the means of their salvation." Again, he said, "Baptism is an act in which and by which a man receives and appropriates the offered benefits of the redemption of Christ. . .it is a means in the hands of the Spirit of conveying to believers the benefits of redemption. . .Baptism signs, seals and actually conveys its benefits to all its subjects, whether infants or adults, who keep the covenant." *Systematic Theology,* Vol. 3, pp. 588, 589, and 590.

4. **Herman Hoeksema** of the Protestant Reformed Church, quoting Abraham Kuyper, said, "At the very moment when the minister administers the water of baptism, your Mediator and Saviour performs a work of grace in the soul of the baptized child." *Believers and Their Seed,* Chap. 3, p. 36.

5. **John Murray**, of the Orthodox Presbyterian Church, said, "Baptized infants are to be received as the children of God and treated accordingly." *Christian Baptism,* Chap. 4, p. 56.

We freely admit that the quotes cited above are not all these men have said about baptism. But when a man has heard all that the Pædobaptists have to say about baptism, he is either confused about what they believe, or convinced that they have confused the Abrahamic Covenant with the Everlasting Covenant of Grace, or convinced that they believe in grace being conveyed by baptism. From the multitude of testimonies given above, we feel clearly justified in saying that there is a clear similarity between Catholic Pædobaptists and the Protestant Pædobaptists. The existence and witness of a sound Baptist Ecclesiology will bring this similarity to the forefront along with the inconsistencies and errors of both. Little wonder all Pædobaptists oppose the Baptists and believer's baptism. The author of the following books, Abraham Booth, has shown himself fully competent in defending the Baptist position and exposing the inconsistencies of Pædobaptism. May the Great Shepherd of the sheep send more undershepherds of this kind into the sheepfolds. Let us now consider our next point.

Second – Strict Baptist Ecclesiology Exposes the Inconsistency of the Protestant Pædobaptists Toward the Catholics.

As we have already shown before in this Foreword, the Protestant Pædobaptists "say, and do not." (Matt. 23:3), and little do people realize how much. Obviously, most of them do not see that while they promise "liberty, they themselves are slaves." (II Peter 2:19). Protestantism was born as an avowed "protest" against the heresies and corruptions of Popery. The first reformers received their infant-baptism from Catholicism and never renounced it. John Gill said, "Infant-baptism is no other than a part & pillar of Popery. . .nor can there be a full separation of the church from the world, nor a thorough reformation in religion, until it is wholly removed." *Infant-Baptism, A Part & Pillar of Popery,* Boston, 1746, p. 3. The great Protestant denominations separated from Roman Catholicism, but they still retain the Roman Catholic practice of infant-baptism. Hence, even though these great denominations have separated from Roman Catholicism— Roman Catholicism has not separated from them. This is a grave inconsistency.

PUBLISHER'S FOREWORD

There are other great inconsistencies in Calvinistic Pædobaptism besides this renouncing of Catholicism's ways while espousing Catholicism's baptism. Let us now consider two of these grave inconsistencies, especially in connection with our infant-baptism controversy.

John Murray, in writing about the Reformation, stated: "It (the Reformation) might be summed up in the re-discovery of salvation by grace. . . *Sola Gratia* and *Sola Scriptura* were its fundamental principles. By one line of logical connection or another, all Reformation doctrine and practice are dependent upon, and traceable to, these two principles." *Collected Writings,* Vol. I, p. 292. *Sola Scriptura* means that the Scriptures are the only infallible guide of faith and practice. Everything Christians need doctrinally and practically is revealed in the Scriptures. Nothing they need is left out. Nothing with infallible authority exists beyond them in this world. The sufficiency, finality, and authority of the Scriptures are found in II Tim. 3:16, 17 and Isaiah 8:20. *Sola Gratia* means that salvation is solely by free grace, without any mixture of works whatsoever. Salvation begets works, but salvation is not because of works. Hence, we read: "by grace are ye saved through faith; and that not of yourselves," (Eph. 2:8). Salvation is "by grace; to the end the promise might be sure to all the seed;" (Rom. 4:16) and salvation is "according to his own purpose and grace, which was given us in Christ Jesus before the world began." (II Tim. 1:9). According to John Murray's testimony (and those of a multitude of others), *Sola Scriptura* and *Sola Gratis* are the two most basic Reformation, *i.e.*, Protestant principles. In fact, R.C. Sproul said, "The Reformation principle of *Sola Scriptura* was given the status of the formal cause of the Reformation by Melancthon and his Lutheran followers." *The Foundation of Biblical Authority,* Chap. 4, p. 103.

We declare plainly that all Protestant Pædobaptists (Reformed, Presbyterian, etc.) inconsistently violate BOTH of these Reformation principles by their practice of infant--baptism. Consider:

A. They profess *Sola Scriptura* and the absolute necessity for Scriptural warrant in all matters of faith and practice. They also admit the New Testament contains no Scriptural example of infant-baptism nor any command for practicing infant-baptism. Yet, in contradiction to what they profess on both these issues, they inconsistently practice infant-baptism anyway.

B. They profess *Sola Gratia* and denounce salvation by works as being totally without Scriptural warrant, yet they profess to believe and administer, inconsistently, sprinkling or pouring for baptism in order to "convey the benefits of redemption" to its subjects, whether infants or adults.

Where, you ask have they professed *Sola Scriptura* and admitted no Scriptural example or precept for infant-baptism, yet practiced it anyway? Where have they professed *Sola Gratia* and yet professed faith in the saving efficacy of baptism? Consider:

1. Pædobaptist Confessions of *Sola Scriptura* and the Absolute Necessity for Scripture Warrant in Matters of Faith and Practice:

Let us be perfectly clear, first, on what this concept is. **John L. Girardeau**, Old School Southern Presbyterian, Professor of Systematic Theology, Columbia Theological Seminary, Columbia, South Carolina, clarified this principle when he wrote, "A divine warrant is necessary for every element of doctrine, government and worship in the church; that is, whatsoever in these spheres is not commanded in the Scriptures, either expressly or by good and necessary consequence from their statements, is forbidden. . .This principle is deducible by logical inference from the great truth — confessed by Protestants — that the Scriptures are an infallible rule of faith and practice, and therefore supreme, perfect and sufficient for all the needs of the church. . .This truth operates positively to the inclusion of everything in the doctrine, government and worship of the church which is commanded, explicitly or implicitly in the Scriptures, and negatively to the exclusion of everything which is not so commanded." *Instrumental Music,* Chap. 1, p. 9-10. Again he said, "We are not at liberty to use our own judgment and to act without a divine warrant in regard to things of God's appointment." Ibid., p. 19. Again he said, "It is not permissible to worship Him in any way not prescribed in the Scriptures." Ibid., p. 129. Finally, he remarked, "Whatever others may think or do, Presbyterians cannot forsake this principle without guilt of defection from their own venerable standards," Ibid., p. 25, 26. This principle professed by Pædobaptists is simply: "We must have precept and example from the Scriptures for everything we do in God's worship and in faith and practice." Let us now look at some of those "venerable standards" of the Protestant faith regarding this principle.

The Thesis of Berne (1528):

The Church of Christ makes no laws or commandments without God's Word. Hence all human traditions, which are called ecclesiastical commandments, are binding upon us only insofar as they are based on and commanded by God's Word (Sect. II).

The Geneva Confession (1536):

First we affirm that we desire to follow Scripture alone as a rule of faith and religion, without mixing with it any other things which might be devised by the opinion of men apart from the Word of God, and without wishing to accept for our spiritual government any other doctrine than what is conveyed to us by the same Word without addition or diminution, according to the command of our Lord (Sect. I).

The French Confession of Faith (1559):

We believe that the Word contained in these books has proceeded from God, and receives its authority from him alone, and not from men. And inasmuch as it is the rule of all truth, containing all that is necessary for the service of God and for our salvation, it is not lawful for men, nor even for angels, to add to it, to take away from it, or to change it. Whence it follows that no authority, whether of antiquity, or custom, or numbers, or human wisdom, or judgments, or proclamations, or edicts, or decrees, or councils, or visions, or miracles, should be opposed to these Holy Scriptures, but on the contrary, all things should be examined, regulated, and reformed according to them (Art. V).

The Belgic Confession (1561):

We receive all these books, and these only, as holy and confirmation of our faith; believing, without any doubt, all things contained in them, not so much because the church receives and approves them as such, but more especially because the Holy Ghost witnessed in our hearts that they are from God, whereof they carry the evidence in themselves (Art. V).

Therefore we reject with all our hearts whatsoever doth not agree with this infallible rule (Art. VII).

Second Helvetic Confession (1566):

Therefore, we do not admit any other judge than Christ himself, who proclaims by the Holy Scriptures what is true, what is false, what is to be followed, or what is to be avoided (Chap. II).

(All the above quoted from *Reformed Confessions of the 16th Century,* A.C. Cochrance, editor, Philadelphia, 1966.)

Westminster Confession (1646):

"The Old Testament in Hebrew and the New Testament in Greek, being immediately inspired by God, and, by His singular care and providence, kept pure in all ages, are therefore authentical; so as, in all controversies of religion, the Church is finally to appeal unto them." Chap. 1, Sect. 8, p. 23.

"The supreme judge by which all controversies of religion are to be determined, and all degrees of councils, opinions of ancient writers, doctrines of men, and private spirits, are to be examined, and in whose sentence we are to rest, can be no other but the Holy Spirit speaking in the Scriptures." Chap. 1, Sect. 10, p. 24.

PUBLISHER'S FOREWORD

"God alone is Lord of the conscience, and hath left it free from the doctrines and commandments of men which are in any thing contrary to his Word, or beside it in matters of faith and worship." Chap. 20, Sect. 8, p. 23.

"The acceptable way of worshipping the true God is instituted by himself, and so limited by his own revealed will, that he may not be worshipped according to the imaginations and devices of men, or the suggestions of Satan, under any visible representation, or any other way not prescribed in the Holy Scripture." Chap. 21, Sect. 1, pp. 90, 91.

(Quoted from *The Westminster Confession of Faith*, Edinburgh, 1973 edition.)

In these confessions the Pædobaptists have very gallantly and clearly stated the principles of *Sola Scriptura* and the absolute necessity for Scriptural warrant. They speak for themselves. Individual statements from the Reformers, Puritans, and modern Pædobaptists by the score could now be presented espousing the same principle; for brevity we will only present two more, seeing we have already given John L. Girardeau's belief—then we will have our "two or three witnesses" (Deut. 19:15).

John Murray, Professor of Systematic Theology, Westminster Theological Seminary, Philadelphia, said: "We all believe the Bible to be the Word of God, the only infallible rule of faith and practice." *Collected Writings*, Vol. 1, p. 2. Again he said, speaking of *Sola Scriptura*, "If any other canon (rule) is permitted to regulate our polemic, then our witness has the seeds of compromise and of failure from the outset." *Collected Writings*, Vol. 1, p. 293. Even more clearly, he said, "For all modes and elements of worship there must be authorization from the Word of God. . .The Reformed principle is that the acceptable way of worshipping God is instituted by Himself, and so limited by His revealed will, that He may not be worshipped in any other way than that prescribed in the Holy Scripture, that what is not commanded is forbidden. This is in contrast with the view that what is not forbidden is permitted. There are some texts in the New Testament that bear directly on this question: Mark 7:7, 8; John 4:24; Col. 2:20-23; I Peter 2:5. In the Orthodox Presbyterian Church there is general agreement on this. But in application it is not observed." *Collected Writings,* Vol. I, p. 168.

Thomas Manton, scribe of the Westminster Assembly, said: "It (Scripture) containeth all things which are necessary for men to believe and do. . .Yea, it doth contain not only all the essential but also the integral parts of the Christian religion; and nothing can be any part of our religion which is not there. The direction of old was. . .(Isaiah 8:20), and everything must now be tried by the 'prophets and apostles' which is our foundation of faith, worship, and obedience (Eph. 2:20)." *Morning Exercises at Cripplegate,* Vol. 5, p. 603.

We appeal to our readers on the basis of the quotations given above. Do not the Pædobaptists have it as a historic principle that they **will not** believe or practice anything except what they find in precept and example in the Word of God? Let one of their own answer: "Nothing is lawful in the worship of God, but what we have precept or precedent for; which whoso denies, opens a door to all idolatry and superstition, and will-worship in the world." Mr. Copings, in *Jerubbal,* p. 487, quoted in *Pædobaptism Examined,* Vol. 1, Part 2, Chap. 1, p. 316. However, consider now what they admit about precept and example for infant-baptism:

2. Pædobaptist Admission about the Total Lack of Express Scriptural Precept or Plain Scriptural Example for Infant-Baptism:

Martin Luther — "It cannot be proved by sacred Scripture that infant-baptism was instituted by Christ or begun by the first Christians after the Apostles." *Vanity of Infant-Baptism,* Part 2, p. 8, quoted in *Pædobaptism Examined,* by Abraham Booth, Vol. 1, Part 2, Chap. 1, p. 303.

John Calvin — "As Christ enjoins them to teach before baptizing, and desires that none but believers shall be admitted to baptism, it would appear that baptism is not properly administered unless when preceded by faith." *Harmony of the Evangelists,* Vol. 3, p. 386.

Publisher's Foreword

Herman Witsius — "We readily acknowledge that there is no express and special command of God, or of Christ, concerning infant-baptism." *Economy of the Covenants,* Vol. 3, p. 385.

Richard Baxter — "I know of no one word in Scripture, that giveth us the least intimation that any man was baptized without the profession of saving faith." *Disputation of the Right to Sacraments,* p. 149-151.

Thomas Boston — "There is no example of baptism recorded in the Scriptures, where any were baptized but such as appeared to have a saving interest in Christ, *i.e.*, repentance." *Works,* Vol. 6, p. 127.

James Bannerman — "Nothing but the most violent injustice done to the language of Scripture by a bold and unscrupulous system of interpretation can suffice to get rid of the evidence which, in the case of the Baptism of converts mentioned in Scripture, connects the administration of the rite with a profession of faith in Christ on the part of the person who was the recipient of it. The association of the person's profession, faith, repentance, or believing, with Baptism, appears in a multitude of passages; while not one passage or example can be quoted in favor of the connection of Baptism with an absence of profession." *The Church of Christ,* Banner of Truth, Edinburgh, 1974, Vol. 2, p. 64. See also William Cunningham's, *The Reformers and the Theology of the Reformation,* Banner of Truth, Edinburgh, 1967, Chap. 5, p. 263-265.

Even the new-age Pædobaptists like Jay Adams, James Jordan, etc., mentioned earlier, are willing to admit the same thing. Duane Spencer, in his book, *Holy Baptism,* Geneva Ministries, 1982, Chap. 16, p. 167, while trying to promote his new ideology that sprinkling or pouring are the ONLY proper modes of baptism confesses: "Admittedly there is no direct evidence, either in principle or in practice, that the New Testament Church administered Christian baptism to infants." An abundance of further testimony upon this point may be found in Abraham Booth's *Pædobaptism Examined,* Vol. 1, Part 2, Chap. 1, pp. 303-367.

We ask our readers — Is there not here a most glaring inconsistency? Pædobaptists, both old and new, admit there is no precept nor example in the Word of God for infant-baptism. At the same time they profess, as a standing principle, "Nothing is lawful in the worship of God, but what we have precept or precedent for." But in spite of these two basic truths, they still administer sprinkling or pouring to unconsenting, unrepentant, and unbelieving infants in order to "convey the benefits of redemption" to their souls. If this is not inconsistency, we confess we do not know what it is. We close this point with Richard Baxter's question: "What man dare go in a way which hath neither precept nor example to warrant it, from a way that hath a full current of both?" *Plain Scripture Proof,* p. 24.

We plainly declare again, that all Protestant Pædobaptists (Reformed, Presbyterian, Anglican, etc.) inconsistently violate BOTH of their own Reformation principles of *Sola Scriptura* and *Sola Gratia* by their practice of infant-baptism. We have now given proof of their violation of the former, *Sola Scriptura*. It only remains for us to prove their violation of the latter, *Sola Gratia*.

Because of lack of time and space, we will condense. We ask our readers to do some research. Check Phillip Schaff's *The Creeds of Christendom*. Read for yourself and see if the Protestant Pædobaptists do not profess *Sola Gratia*. See if they do not, almost without exception, denounce salvation by works and decry man's ability to save himself. They profess salvation by Christ alone, grace alone, and faith alone. Yet, inconsistently, they still administer sprinkling or pouring to unconsenting, unbelieving infants to "sign, seal and convey the benefits of redemption to their souls." We have given their own confessions on this point before. See: Pages 30-31 — B. The **PROTESTANT PÆDOBAPTIST** belief in the saving efficacy of infant-baptism — Nos. 1-5. Considering these confessions, beyond a doubt, Pædobaptists "say, and do not."

Plainly, there are glaring, obvious inconsistencies with the Pædobaptists' theology surrounding infant-baptism. A thorough examination of Pædobaptist doctrine and practice in the light of strict Baptist ecclesiology makes the similarity between Catholics and Pædobaptist stand out in bold relief. Little wonder, then, that the Pædobaptists fight against the Baptists. Consistent Baptist ecclesiology is a witness against the Pædobaptists, Popish, and Protestant. When the fog is cleared from our eyes, we come to see that the controversy is between two religious groups who both profess *Sola Scriptura* and *Sola Gratia*. However, strict Baptists put both those principles into practice. Pædobaptists do not. If there was no one to implement those principles consistently, then the real character of Pædobaptism would be concealed, the authority of the Scriptures would be neglected, and the real nature and evidence of saving grace obscured. Surely there is a real necessity for this controversy, in order to maintain pure grace and the fact that "if of grace, then it is no more of works." (Rom. 11:6). The author of the following book, Abraham Booth, has shown himself to be a "father in Israel" in handling these issues.

IV. THE NECESSITY FOR THIS CONTROVERSY

C. H. Spurgeon said, "I need not say that conflict has done much mischief — undoubtedly it has; but I will rather say, that it has been fraught with incalculable usefulness; for it has thrust forward before the minds of Christians, precious truths, which but for it, might have been kept in the shade... I believe there is a needs-be for controversy in the finite character of the human mind, while the natural lethargy of the churches require a kind of healthy irritation to arouse their powers and stimulate them to exertion. . .I glory in that which at the present day is so much spoken against — sectarianism, for 'sectarianism' is the cant phrase which our enemies use for all firm religious belief. I find it applied to all sorts of Christians; no matter what views he may hold, if a man be earnest, he is a sectarian at once. Success to sectarianism; let it live and flourish. When that is done with, farewell to the power of godliness. When we cease, each of us, to maintain our own views of truth and to maintain those views firmly and strenuously, then truth shall fly out of the land, and error alone shall reign: this indeed, is the object of our foes: under the cover of attacking sects, they attack true religion, and would drive it, if they could, from off the face of the earth." *Metropolitan Tabernacle Pulpit,* Vol. 8, Sermon #442, pp. 181-192.

Richard Baxter said, "The servants of God do mind the matter of religion more seriously than others do; and therefore their differences are made more observable to the world. They cannot make light of the smallest truth of God; and this may be some occasion of their differences; whereas the ungodly differ not about religion, because they have heartily no religion to differ about. Is this a unity and peace to be desired? I had rather have the discord of the saints than such a concord of the wicked." *The Golden Treasury of Puritan Quotations,* Moody Press, 1975, p. 62.

John Milton said, "There is no learned man but will confess that he hath much profited by reading controversies — his senses awakened, his judgment sharpened, and the truth which he holds more firmly established. All controversy being permitted, falsehood will appear more false, and truth the more true." *The Golden Treasury,* Ibid., p. 63.

I Cor. 11:19 states, "There must be also heresies among you, that they which are approved may be made manifest among you." Divisions, strife and heresies are but trials and opportunities for God's people; yea, blessings to those who have the grace to be properly "exercised thereby" (Heb. 12:11). By controversy, falsehood appears more false, and truth more true. In Abraham Booth's following presentation of Baptist ecclesiology and theology, that which is true will be made apparent because he was willing to face the infant-baptism controversy in his generation. Are we? Without doubt, our response to the heresies, conflicts, trials, etc., that confront us in life is indicative of the grace we profess to have, and it is always a manifestation of who is "approved among us."

CONCLUSION:

We realize that the charges of bigotry, sectarianism, and narrow-mindedness will be leveled against us after this

PUBLISHER'S FOREWORD

publication becomes available to the public. Some will say we are mean, sour, vindictive, and hateful. No doubt we can be legitimately charged with many faults but consider — "Then came his disciples, and said unto him, knowest thou that the Pharisees were offended, after they heard this saying? But he answered and said, every plant, which my Heavenly Father hath not planted shall be rooted up." (Matt. 15:12, 13). — Christ's conduct here shows us that:

> "We are not from fear of giving offence. . .to refrain from speaking the truth, especially with regard to doctrines and usages, unsanctioned by Divine authority, which men endeavor to impose as articles of faith and religious observances, and by which they cast into the shade doctrine plainly revealed, and substantially make void ordinances clearly appointed by the Lord. The 'teaching for doctrine the commandments of men' — the 'making void God's commandment by men's traditions' we must clearly expose and strongly condemn, undiverted from our course by the fear of shocking the prejudices of even those genuine Christians who have been entangled in the snares of any of those systems where man holds the place of God, however much we may love their persons, and value what is genuine in their Christian faith and character. This is kindness to them, as well as justice to truth. With regard to everything in the shape of religious doctrine, which we cannot find in the Bible — with regard to everything in the shape of religious institutions, unsanctioned by divine authority — we must lift up our voices like a trumpet, and proclaim, whosoever may be offended, 'Every plant which our Heavenly Father hath not planted, should — must — shall be rooted up.'" John Brown, *Discourses and Sayings of Our Lord,* Vol. 1, p. 499f.

So, in final analysis, this infant-baptism controversy is the age-old battle of truth versus error, the Word of God versus the will of man, consistency versus inconsistency, and grace versus works. It is a matter of our walk being consistent with our talk, our submission being consistent with our profession, and our practices being consistent with our principles. In the end, it is a matter of real, complete, consistent recognition and submission to Christ as King and only Lawgiver over the New Testament Church; whether we will obey His laws, or implement our own; or whether we will come finally under the indictment of Luke 6:46, "Why call ye me, Lord, Lord, and do not the things which I say?" Regarding "whether or not" we should be involved in this age-old battle, we believe we shall always prefer the thoughtful, enthusiastic "shout of controversy" over the fearful, apathetic "silence of consent." Regarding "how" we should be involved, we believe that a Scriptural bravery is always to be chosen over a hypocritical charity, and a genuine manly honestly is always better than a polished, effeminate duplicity, even at the risk of the charge of bigotry! There is a time to keep silence and there is "a time to speak"! The author of the following book, as far as we can discern, believed exactly the same thing.

THE BAPTIST STANDARD BEARER, INC.
(Ps. 60:4-5; Is. 59:19; 62:10-12)
Stonehaven,
Paris, Arkansas
June 17, 1985

MEMOIR OF THE LIFE AND WRITINGS OF ABRAHAM BOOTH

Mr. Abraham Booth was born at Blackwall, in Derbyshire, on the 20th of May, 1734, Old Style. Before he was a year old, his parents removed to Annesley-wood House, a hamlet in Northamptonshire, for the purpose of occupying a farm under the Duke of Portland. Abraham was the eldest of a numerous family, and when able, he assisted his father in the farm, and continued thus employed till he was sixteen years old. At this period he had never spent six months at school: his father taught him to read, making it a daily practice to hear him say his lesson after dinner. He owed it almost entirely to his own industry that he acquired the art of writing, and a knowledge of arithmetic. To prosecute these studies, he cheerfully gave up his hours of recreation, and even of repose.

He was brought up in the church of England, but when about ten years of age, some General Baptist ministers visited the neighbourhood, and through the blessing of God upon their labours, his mind was awakened to a permanent concern about the salvation of his soul. When he was about the age of twenty-one, in the year 1755, he was baptized by one of these ministers, Mr. Francis Smith, of Barton, and became a member of the General Baptist Society.

When Mr. Booth left the farming business, he learned the trade of stocking weaving. At the age of twenty-four he married Miss Elizabeth Bowman, the daughter of a neighbouring farmer, who proved a most excellent wife, and with whom, till within a few years of his own death, he enjoyed much domestic felicity.

To provide for an increasing family, they opened a school at Sutton Ashfield; Mrs. B. instructing the female scholars in useful branches of needle-work, and Mr. B. continuing to work at his loom, in connection with the school.

It was not long after his joining the society, that he was encouraged to preach, which he did as an itinerant, throughout the neighbouring districts. In 1760, the pious people at Kirkbywood House, having been formed into a church, Mr. Booth was appointed their minister. He laboured among them about six or seven years, but never became their regular pastor; the reason of this, doubtless, was the change which about this time took place in his theological sentiments. He had hitherto held the Armenian doctrine of universal redemption, and, as a strenuous advocate for the universality of divine grace, he printed a poem in reproach of the doctrines of personal election, and particular redemption. He was at this time twenty-six years of age. When he, about seven years afterwards, published his Reign of Grace, he thought it proper to make all the atonement in his power for having written in such a spirit, and for having published such errors. He thus speaks of his performance: "As a poem, if considered in a critical light, it is despicable; if in a theological view, detestable; as it is an impotent attack on the honour of divine grace, in respect to its glorious freeness, and a bold opposition to the sovereignty of God, and as such I renounce it." At a future period of his life, he thus alludes to these circumstances:— "The doctrine of sovereign and distinguishing grace, as commonly and justly stated by Calvinists, it must be acknowledged, is too generally exploded. This the writer of these pages knows by experience, to his grief and shame. Through the ignorance of his mind, the pride of his heart, and the prejudice of his education, he in his younger years often opposed it with much warmth, though with no small weakness; but after an impartial inquiry, and many prayers, he found reason to alter his judgment; he found it to be a doctrine of the Bible, and dictate of the unerring Spirit. Thus convinced, he received the obnoxious sentiment, under a full conviction of its being a divine truth."

Mr. Booth always acted upon the principle of integrity and uprightness, and therefore having fully made up his mind, he did not conceal his change of sentiments. This ultimately led to a separation from his people, and Mr. Booth preached his farewell sermon to the General Baptist congregation, from the parable of the unjust steward. In this he remarked, "that fraud and concealment, of various kinds, may obtain the favour of men;—that when favour is gained by such means, he who gains it, and they who grant it, are chargeable with injustice peculiarly censurable;—and that scripture, reason, and conscience, unite their authority in recommending universal fidelity to accountable creatures, and especially to the ministers and professors of religion, in the view of the great day of account, when they must all give up their stewardship."

He was for a short time silent as a minister, but having procured a room at Sutton Ashfield, called Bore's Hall, it was registered as a preaching house, and he recommenced his labours as a Calvinistic preacher of the gospel. It was during these five or six years of labour, that his invaluable treatise *The Reign of Grace,* the substance of which he delivered in a series of discourses to his small congregation, and afterwards at Nottingham and Chesterfield, at both of which places he was in the habit of preaching on alternate sabbaths, in connection with his charge at Sutton Ashfield.

When Mr. Booth had finished his manuscript, one of his friends, who had perused it, spewed it to the Rev. Henry Venn, an evangelical clergyman, the author of *The Complete Duty of Man.* After perusing it, this gentleman took a journey from Huddersfield, in Yorkshire, to Sutton Ashfield, to see and converse with the author, who was working at his stocking-loom. Mr. Venn strongly urged Mr. Booth to publish this work, which he accordingly did. "When I had got it printed," said Mr. B. to the writer, "my good friend, Mr.

Venn, took as many copies as enabled me to pay the printer, leaving me the remaining copies for sale." This was said not long before his death, and with strong feelings of gratitude towards his clerical friend. It was the circumstance of this work being published, as before observed, that introduced Mr. Booth to the knowledge of the destitute church in Preston Street.

Thus furnished with a mature and disciplined judgment, and having given the most convincing proofs of an inflexibly honest mind, and uncompromising principles, Mr. Booth undertook, at the age of thirty-four years, the difficult and responsible station of pastor of that church, which the great Samuel Wilson had planted, and the good Samuel Burford had watered; and which it had pleased God by his blessing abundantly to increase.

Up to this period Mr. Booth's acquirements were confined, or nearly so, to a knowledge of the English grammar. He felt his deficiencies in this respect, and having a strong desire for acquiring a knowledge of the languages, he resolved to improve the opportunities afforded him for obtaining an acquaintance with the Latin and Greek. He accordingly put himself under the tuition of a Roman Catholic priest, who was an eminent classical scholar. This gentleman, of whose erudition Mr. Booth always spoke in very high terms, used to breakfast with his pupil; they retired together to his study to attend to business. With this exception, Mr. Booth might be considered as a self-taught scholar.

Having obtained a familiar acquaintance with Latin, he gained access to the writings of eminent foreign divines; such as Witsius, Turretine, Staplerus, Vitringe, and Venema. He was also intimately acquainted with the best writers on ecclesiastical history; viz. Dupont, Cave, Bingham, Venema, Spanheim, and the Magdeburg Centuriators. On the article of Jewish antiquities, he had read Lewis, Jennings, Reland, Spencer, Ikenius, Carpzovivus, and Fabricius of Hamburgh. Among the English writers he preferred Dr. John Oven, whose evangelical and learned works he was very frequently quoted, and to whom he in various ways acknowledged his obligations.

Mr. Booth's attention to reading was subordinated to his work as a minister, and his duties as a pastor. He was generally at home and in his pulpit every Lord's day. To the writer of this, not long before his death, he remarked, "I have never left my people, since I first settled with them, more than two Lord's days at a time." He added, "Had I left them so much as some pastors have left theirs, I have no doubt my people would have left me as theirs have left them."

Notwithstanding the eminence of his learning, and the strength of his mental powers, **he at one period of his ministry felt greatly embarrassed in his preaching.** "I wondered much," said he, "that those persons who had heard me preach in the morning, should come again in the afternoon. I really thought for some time that I must have given up the ministry; and I felt more thankful then, than for any other temporal blessing, that I had a trade to which I could return for the support of my family."

When, about the year 1792, the subject of the African Slave Trade very greatly engaged the attention of the nation, and petitions from every part of the kingdom were presented to the legislature for its abolition, Mr. Booth took a very active and lively interest in promoting a petition to express his abhorrence, and that of his congregation, of that infernal traffic. He also preached a sermon, founded on Exodus XXI, 16: "And he that stealeth a man, and selleth him, or if he be found in his hand, he shall surely be put to death." This was published at the request of the church, and extensively circulated. They also made a pecuniary collection towards the expenses which attended the application to parliament. This horrid trade was not suppressed till eight years afterwards, but there is no doubt that he essentially contributed towards it; at least, this is the opinion of the most competent judge on the subject, the celebrated antislavery advocate, Clarkson. In his work entitled, *The Abolition of the Slave Trade,* &c. that inestimable philanthropist has given a list of names of the principal benefactors, who by their writings, money, and influence, assisted in this enterprise of mercy; and among them, to his immortal honour, is found that of our never-to-be-forgotten, and still lamented, Abraham Booth.

It was the privilege of the writer to become acquainted with this excellent minister about a year and a half before he was called to his reward. He hopes never to forget his affectionate counsels, and he has a strong and lively recollection of the ardent piety he evinced, while he laboured under the violence of an asthmatic complaint. "I have never," said he, "thought so much of the words of Daniel to Belshazzar, as since I have been thus afflicted, The God in whose hand thy breath is! — The writer observed, "What a mercy, Sir, the last part of the sentence, "Thou halt not glorified," is not applicable to your character." He replied with great energy, "I hope it is not, in its most awful meaning; but in a very great degree it is true of me." He added, "And yet I trust I can say, to the honour of divine grace which has assisted me, that since I first professed religion, I have been so much preserved from every evil way, that if the secrets of my life were written by one who was not an enemy to me, there would be nothing to tell the world of which I should be ashamed to hear." His emphatic and devout aspirations in blessing God for the good hope through grace which he enjoyed, were most remarkable. His conversation was evidently in heaven, and his affections set supremely on things above. It was most edifying to hear his spiritual conversation and godly exhortations; he appeared

> "Like a bird that's hampered,
> Which struggles to get loose."

A few months before his death, Mr. Booth, on returning from a meeting of his ministering brethren in the city was taken suddenly ill, and from that time, in September 1805, was almost wholly laid aside from public labour, which now entirely devolved upon his esteemed and respectful assistant, the Rev. William Gray. He administered the Lord's supper on the first Lord's day in January, 1806, and, notwithstanding his extreme weakness, he attended the monthly meeting for sermon and prayer, held at his place on Thursday, the 23d of January. His brethren in the ministry present, who very highly revered his character, and others of his old friends, took an affectionate and last farewell of this good minister of Jesus Christ.

It was pleasing for those friends who visited him at this period, to find that the doctrines of reigning grace, which he had so fully stated, and so ably defended nearly forty years before, were now the support of his mind, and the consolation of his heart. To many anxious inquiries he would say, "I have no fears about my state, I now live upon what I have been teaching to others."

> "The gospel bears my spirit up;
> A faithful and unchanging God
> Lays the foundation for my hope
> In oaths, and promises, and blood."

On the Saturday preceding his death, January 25, 1806, he requested to see a much esteemed friend, that he might communicate to him his last instructions, and to whom, among other things, he said, "I am peaceful, but not elevated." On the next day, the son of his friend called at the house of Mr. Booth, and inquired after his health. After replying to his inquiry, he added, "Young man, think of your soul; if you lose that, you lose your all. Your father is my especial friend. Be not half a Christian. Some people have religion enough to make them miserable, but not enough to make them happy. The ways of religion are good ways; I have found them thus sixty years." This was on the Lord's day, during which he for some time was enabled to sit up in his study. Many of his friends, supposing his dissolution was at hand, called to see him; as they rightly conjectured, for the last time. Though scarcely able to converse, he spoke a few words to them, especially to some of his young friends, who were anxious to take their leave of him. To one of these he said, "But a little while, and I shall be with your dear father and mother." To another, "I have borne you on my heart before the Lord, you now need to pray for yourself." To a third, in reference to a Socinian minister, he said with deep solemnity, "Beware of _____'s sentiments." It should seem, that on this day he had no expectation that he should so soon die. Mr. Gutteridge, a deacon of the church, when he parted with him in the afternoon, said, "The Lord be with you, and if I do not see you again, I trust we shall meet in the better world." Mr. Booth replied, "I expect to see you again in this." He went to bed about nine o'clock. On the next morning he was speechless, though apparently in possession of his reason. About nine in the evening, his son-in-law, Mr. Granger, and his assistant, Mr. Gray, who were in the room, remarking they did not hear him breathe, drew near to the bed-side just in time to see him lie back on the pillow, when he almost instantly expired without a sigh or groan.

The leading traits of his character may be judged of from the following extracts from his last will and testament, written not long before his death:— "I, Abraham Booth, Protestant Dissenting Minister, in the parish of St. Mary's, Whitechapel, reflecting on the uncertainty of life, do make this may last Will and Testament, in manner following:

"Being firmly persuaded that the doctrines which have constituted my public ministry for a long course of years, are divine truths; being deeply sensible that all I have, and all I am, are the Lord's, and entirely at his disposal; and being completely satisfied that his dominion is perfectly wise and righteous; I, in the anticipation of my departing moment, cheerfully commend my departing spirit into his hands, in expectation of everlasting life, as the gift of sovereign grace, through the mediation of Jesus Christ; and my body I resign to the care of Providence in the silent grave, with the pleasing hope of its being raised again at the last day, in a state of perpetual vigour, beauty, and glory."

He directed in his will that not more than twenty pounds should be expended on his funeral, which was carefully attended to.

Memoir of the Life and Writings of Abraham Booth

The estimation in which Mr. Booth was held by the church, appears by an extract from a narrative entered in their records:

"He possessed a noble disinterestedness of spirit; he sought not ours but us; he was truly the servant of this church, for Jesus" sake. A pastor, in the language of Jeremiah, according to God's heart; who fed his people with knowledge and understanding. There are, perhaps, but few instances in the church of Christ, of one who has better exemplified the character of a Christian bishop, as drawn by the apostle Paul, Tit. i. 7-9.

Mr. Booth was interred in the burying ground behind Maze-Pond meeting house, where a plain head-stone stands, to perpetuate the place which received, and, it is hoped, retains his mortal remains.

In the meeting-house where he had so long and so ably maintained the doctrines of grace; and the scriptural discipline of the church, a neat marble tablet is placed over the vestry door, with the following honourable inscription:

THIS TABLET
was erected by the Church in grateful Remembrance
of their beloved and venerable Pastor
ABRAHAM BOOTH:
who, with unremitted Fidelity, discharged his ministerial Labours
in this place, thirty-seven Years.
As a Man, and as a Christian, he was highly and deservedly esteemed:
As a Minister he was solemn and devout:
His addresses were perspicuous, energetic, and impressive:
they were directed to the Understanding, the Conscience, and the Heart.
Profound Knowledge, sound Wisdom, and unaffected Piety,
were strikingly exemplified
in the Conduct of this excellent Man.
In him, the poor have lost a generous and humane Benefactor;
the Afflicted and the Distressed, a sympathetic and wise Counsellor;
and this Church,
a disinterested, affectionate, and faithful Pastor:
nor will his name, or writings, be forgotten,

Memoir of the Life and Writings of Abraham Booth

while Evangelical Truth shall be revered, Genius admired,
or Integrity respected.
He departed this Life on the 27th January, 1806,
In the 73d year of his Age.

The following accurate description of Mr. Booth's character, was written and published soon after his death, by his friend, the Rev. Dr. Newman. All who knew the original will pronounce it a most finished full-length portrait.

"**As a Christian,** he was pre-eminent, facing the Lord above many. Called by divine grace when about twelve years of age, he experienced, no doubt, in the long course of threescore years, many changes of trials and temptations, many alternations of hope and fear, of joy and sorrow. Yet, with respect to his personal interest in the divine favour, he seems to have been carried on in an even tenor, without many remarkable elevations or depressions. His common conversation breathed much of a devotional spirit, and discovered the strong sense he had of his own sinfulness before God, and the simplicity of his dependence on the influences of the Holy Spirit. Firm in his attachment to his religious principles, he despised the popular cant about charity, and cultivated genuine candour; which is alike remote from the laxity of latitudinarians, and the censoriousness of bigots. He was conspicuous for self-denial, and contempt of the world; walking humbly with God. His moral character was pure and unblemished. Perhaps there never was a man of more stem, unbending integrity: he would have been admired and revered by Aristides the Just. Sincerity clear as crystal, consistency with himself, and unbroken uniformity of conduct, were always to be seen by the ten thousand eyes that were continually fixed upon him. He was temperate, even to abstemiousness: in fortitude bold as a lion." Caution was interwoven with the texture of his mind; yet he would sometimes say, "We have need of caution against caution itself, lest we be over-cautious." He once observed, that in morals, integrity holds the first place, benevolence the second, and prudence the third. Where the first is not, the second cannot be; and where the third is not, the other two will often be brought into suspicion. In his attendance on public worship, he was remarkable for an exemplary punctuality. In the weekly meeting of ministers, and the monthly meeting of ministers and churches, if he were not with them precisely at the appointed hour (which very rarely happened), they did not expect him at all. His manners were simple, grave, and unaffected; frequently enlivened with an agreeable pleasantry. It was edifying and delightful to observe how he perpetually breathed after more conformity to Christ—more heavenly-mindedness. That man must either have been extremely wise or extremely foolish, who could spend an hour in his company without being made wiser and better.

"**As a divine**, he was a star of the first magnitude. A Protestant, and a Protestant Dissenter, on principle, and one of the brightest ornaments of the Baptist denomination, to which he belonged. A Calvinist, and in some particulars approaching what is called High Calvinism; but he has sometimes declared, as many other great men have done, that he never saw any human system, which he could fully and entirely adopt. From the pulpit, his sermons were plain and textual, not systematic; highly instructive, always savoury and acceptable to persons of evangelical taste; for, the glory, the government, and the grace of Christ, were his favourite themes. He aimed to counteract, with equal care, self-righteous legality on the one hand, and on the other, Antinomian licentiousness. Such was the excellence of his personal character, that he needed not the arts of the orator, and the graces of elocution, to gain attention. His audience listened with profound veneration, and hung upon his lips. He had the gift of prayer in a very high degree, and whoever heard him was powerfully impressed with the idea that he was a man who prayed much in secret. From the press, he appeared to the greatest advantage. Nor will it be denied by any, that his writings are very elaborate and exquisitely polished. No bagatelles, no airy speculations all solid and useful. His **Reign of Grace,** and, indeed, all his works, will continue to instruct and delight the Christian world till the end of time.

"**As a Christian pastor,** he shone with distinguished lustre. Every member of the church in which he presided, had a share in his affection. The poor were as welcome to his advice and assistance as the rich: and his faithful reproofs were given without partiality to either, as occasion required. It was justly remarked at his grave, that he has unintentionally drawn his own picture, in his sermon, entitled, *"Pastoral Cautions."* He was not a lord over God's heritage. It has been said, he appeared always willing to give up almost every thing to the decision of the church; and the consequence was, the church gave up almost every thing to his decision. His attention to the poor and the afflicted of his congregation, was highly exemplary. Nor did he content himself with saying, "Be ye warmed, and be ye filled," but liberally contributed to the supply of their wants, according to his ability. The economical system he established at home, furnished him with a considerable fund for charitable uses abroad. His charity was never ostentatious-none but the omniscient eye knew the extent of it, and therefore it is impossible to say how many of the sons and daughters of affliction have lost, by his death, a most generous benefactor.

"**As a literary man,** he was generally acknowledged to belong to the first class among Protestant Dissenters. Without the advantages of a liberal education, he had cut his own way, by the force of a strong, keen mind, through rocks and deserts. His memory was amazingly tenacious; his reasoning powers acute; his apprehension quick; his deliberation cool and patient; his determination slow and decided. His application must have been very intense; to which his vigorous and robust constitution of body was happily subservient. Though he perused a prodigious multitude of books, and respected the opinions of wise and learned men, he ever maintained a sublime independence of mind, and thought for himself. His knowledge of languages was very considerable. Not many of the literati of this country have had so intimate an acquaintance with the grace and force of words, or have written with such correctness and energy united. Yet he has been heard to say, that he had a wife and family before he knew anything of the theory of English grammar. He was not unacquainted with the Greek and Roman classics; they were, however, by no means his favourite authors. It would surprise the public to know what loads of ponderous Latin quartos he read, of French, Dutch, and German divines! The Greek Testament he went through nearly fifty times, by the simple expedient of reading one chapter every morning, the first thing, not so much for the purpose of criticism as of devotion. General science and literature claimed a share of his attention, and every one was astonished to observe the fund of information he possessed on all subjects: In history, civil and ecclesiastical—in antiquities, Jewish and Christian—in theological controversy, and the creeds of all denominations, he was equalled by few, and excelled by none. It is pleasing to recollect, that all his learning was solemnly consecrated to the cross of Christ; and that, while he was disgusted, as he often was, with the illiteracy and ignorance of books which he perceived even among educated preachers in many instances, he was very far from supposing human literature to be essential to the gospel ministry.

"**As a universal friend and counsellor**, he was exceedingly beloved. His extensive and diversified knowledge, his well-tried integrity, his penetration, prudence, and benevolence, occasioned numberless applications for his counsel, not merely from the Baptists, but from Christians of almost all parties. Difficult texts of scripture, knotty points of controversy, disputes in churches, and private cases of conscience, were laid before him in abundance. Seldom was there an appeal made to the judgment of any other man. It was like faking counsel at Abel, and so they ended the matter." Yet he was no dictator. When he had patiently heard the case, and candidly given his opinion, he would usually say, Consult other friends, and then judge for yourself." Such a degree of majesty attended him, plain as he was in exterior, that if he sat down with you but a few minutes, you could not help feeling that you had a prince or a great man in the house. It would sometimes appear to strangers that he was deficient in that winning grace which accompanies softness and sweetness of manner; but those who were most intimately acquainted with him, are fully prepared to say, there was in general, the greatest delicacy of genuine politeness in his conduct. Many young ministers will long deplore their loss. Never surely can they forget how readily he granted them access to him at all times—how kindly he counselled them in their difficulties—how faithfully he warned them of their dangers! With a mournful pleasure they must often recollect his gentleness in correcting their mistakes—his tenderness in imploring the divine benediction upon them—his cordial congratulations when he witnessed their prosperity!"

Mr. Booth left five children; two sons and three daughters; and some small property to each of them.

In addition to *The Reign of Grace,* Mr. Booth published, after he came to London, the following works. In 1770, the *Death of Legal Hope, the Life of Evangelical Obedience;* or, an Essay upon Gal. ii. 19. In 1777, he reprinted a work, which had been translated from the French by Dr. James Abbadie, Dean of Killaloe, in Ireland, entitled, *The Deity of Christ essential to the Christian Religion.* In 1778, he published his work entitled, *An Apology for the Baptists;* in which they are vindicated from the imputation of laying an unwarrantable stress on the Ordinance of Baptism. In 1784, he published his *Pœdobaptism Examined,* on the Principles, Concessions, and Reasonings of the most learned Pædobaptists. In the year 1787, a second and enlarged edition of this work was printed; and in 1792, *A Defence of Pœdobaptism Examined;* or, Animadversions on Dr. Edward Williams" Antipædobaptism Examined. In 1788, he published his *Essay on the Kingdom of Christ.* In 1786, he published a work, entitled, *Glad Tidings to perishing Sinners; or, The Genuine Gospel* a complete Warrant for the Ungodly to believe in Jesus Christ. A second edition, much improved, was published in 1790. In this year he published a most valuable sermon, which he had preached at the Baptist monthly meeting, entitled, *The Amen to Social Prayer,* from the word Amen. In 1803, he published another monthly meeting sermon, entitled, *Divine Justice essential to the Divine Character.* In 1805, the last year of his life, he published a work entitled *Pastoral Cautions;* the substance of which, twenty years before, he delivered as a charge to Mr. Thomas Hopkins, when he was ordained as pastor over the church in Eagle Street.

Several of his addresses at funerals, and some funeral sermons, were also published. After his death two essays, which he had employed his last days in revising were published, entitled, *An Essay on the Love of God to his Chosen People;* and *On a Conduct and Character formed under the Influence of Evangelical Truth.* Some other of his manuscripts were not published.

It is not part of the writer's design to attempt a description of these excellent publications. It will be seen from their titles how deeply impressed was their author's mind with the most exalted views of the riches of divine grace in man's salvation; and of the constraining influence of grace, to produce the most exact regard to the divine law of God, in universal holiness of life. Mr. Booth was certainly one of the most eminent ministers who has belonged to the Particular Baptist denomination. To his exalted usefulness, in the formation of holy and benevolent purposes in the minds of people, the Baptist Fund owes its chief endowments; and the Academical Institution, at Stepney, its entire foundation. The Baptist Fund sent his publications, *On the Kingdom of Christ, and Pastoral Cautions,* in every grant of books made to young ministers. If they would resolve to do this also in regard to his *Pœdobaptism Examined,* &c. it might lead to its republication. It is not to the credit of the denomination, that a work of so much labour and research should be out of print. It will be an evidence of great laxity, and want of evangelical zeal, when the Baptists overlook and forget the excellence of the works and character of Abraham Booth.

MEMOIR OF THE LIFE AND WRITINGS OF ABRAHAM BOOTH

*NOTE: This memoir taken from "A History of the English Baptists" by Joseph Ivimey, London, 1830; Volume 3; pp. 365.379.

BOOK I

AN
APOLOGY
FOR
THE BAPTISTS

An
Apology
for
The Baptists

IN WHICH THEY ARE
VINDICATED FROM THE IMPUTATION
OF LAYING AN
UNWARRANTABLE STRESS
ON THE
ORDINANCE OF BAPTISM:
AND AGAINST THE
CHARGE OF BIGOTRY
IN REFUSING COMMUNION AT THE
LORD'S TABLE TO PÆDOBAPTISTS

By Abraham Booth

There is—one Baptism. Ephes. 4:5.
They who are not rightly baptized, are, doubtless, not baptized at all. —Tertullian
No unbaptized Person communicates at the Lord's Table. —Theophylact

LONDON
Printed, and Sold by E. and C. Dilly, in the *Poultry;*
G. Keith, *Grace-Church-Street;*
and J. Johnson, *St. Paul's Church-Yard.*
MDCCLXXVIII.

The Baptist Standard Bearer, Inc.
NUMBER ONE IRON OAKS DRIVE • PARIS, ARKANSAS 72855

Thou hast given a *standard* to them that fear thee;
that it may be displayed because of the truth.
— *Psalm 60:4*

PUBLISHER'S NOTES

The original title of this book is "AN APOLOGY FOR THE BAPTISTS." Today's readers should not be confused about what the author meant when he used the word "Apology" in the title. While the word "Apology" can be legitimately used as an expression of regret or admission of error, Abraham Booth did not write this book as such an expression or admission on the part of Baptists. We believe that Booth meant the book to be a "Defense" for the Baptists. Consider the following facts —

1. THE SUB-TITLE OF THE BOOK.

This makes it evident that the book was originally intended to be a vindication and defense of Baptist principles and practice.

2. THE CONTENTS OF THE BOOK.

The preface and body of the book clearly verifies that it is not an expression of regret or admission of error on the part of Baptists.

3. AUTHOR'S USAGE OF THE WORD APOLOGY IN THE BOOK.

The word "Apology" can be used to describe an admission of error or a confession of guilt or an expression of regret. Abraham Booth did not write this book for such purposes and we believe a thorough reading and careful consideration of the way Booth used the word "Apology" in this book will dispel any lingering doubts in the reader's mind.

4. THE DEFINITION OF APOLOGY.

   A. *American Dictionary of the English Language.* 1st Edition. Noah Webster. (G. & G. Merriam Co., 1828). — "Apology—something said or written in defense of what appears to others wrong."

B. *Oxford English Dictionary.* Compact Edition. 2 vols. (Oxford University Press, 1981). -- "Apology—a defense of a person or vindication of an institution, etc., from accusation or aspersion."

C. *Klein's Comprehensive Etymological Dictionary of the English Language.* Ed. Ernest Klein. (Elserier Publishing Co., 1966). — "Apology —defense; justification."

5. CHANGES BY THE PUBLISHER

This edition of Abraham Booth's, AN APOLOGY FOR THE BAPTISTS has been re-typeset in order to modernize the antiquated type style and to make the text more legible. However, old English spellings have been retained.

Table of Contents

	Page
The Preface	1
Section I. *The Baptists not chargeable with laying an unwarrantable stress on the Ordinance of Baptism*	3
Section II. *The general Grounds on which we proceed, in refusing Communion at the Lord's Table to Pædobaptist believers- Novelty of the Sentiment and Practice of our Brethren, who plead for Free Communion; and the Inconsistency of such a Conduct with their Baptist Principles.*	21
Section III. *Arguments against Free Communion at the Lord's Table.*	33
Section IV. *Several Passages of Scripture considered, which our Brethren produce in favour of their Sentiments.*	73

SECTION V.
The Temper required by Christians one towards another, not contrary to our Practice—Our Conduct freed from the Charge of Inconsistency—No Reason to exalt the Lord's Supper, in point of Importance, as greatly superior to the Ordinance of Baptism. 91

SECTION VI.
Reflections on the distinguishing Character, STRICT BAPTISTS, which our Brethren apply to us. 137

THE PREFACE

It was not a fondness for controversy, but a desire to vindicate the honour of Christ, as lawgiver in his own kingdom; to assert the scriptural importance of a positive institution in the house of God; and to exculpate himself, together with a great majority of his brethren of the Baptist persuasion, from charges of an odious kind, that excited the author to compose and publish the following pages. If these designs be answered, the writer obtains his end; and if not, he has the testimony of his own conscience to the uprightness of his intentions.

As we are expressly commanded to "contend earnestly for the FAITH once delivered to the saints;" it can hardly be questioned, whether a sincere concern for the purity and permanence of our LORD'S APPOINTMENTS in the gospel church, be not an indispensable duty. For they are no less the expressions of his *dominion over us,* than of his love to us; no less intended as means of his *own glory,* than of our happiness. The subject, therefore, that is here presented to the reader's notice, though not of the *greatest,* yet is far from being *of little* importance in the Christian religion.

It is entirely on the *defensive* that the author takes up his pen; for had not the principles and practice of those professors who are invidiously called, STRICT BAPTISTS, been severely censured, by many that maintain, and by some who deny, the divine authority of Infant Baptism, these pages would never have seen the light.

That HE who is King in Zion may reign in the hearts and

regulate the worship of all his professing people; that the Spirit of wisdom, of holiness, and of peace, may dwell in all the churches of Christ; and that the same divine Agent may direct the reader's inquiries after truth, engage his affections in the performance of duty, and enable him to "walk in all the commandments and ordinances of the Lord blameless;" is the sincere desire and fervent prayer of his willing servant in the gospel of Christ.

GOODMAN'S FIELDS
March 3, 1778
A. BOOTH

AN APOLOGY FOR THE BAPTISTS

SECTION I.

The Baptists not chargeable with laying an unwarrantable Stress on the Ordinance of Baptism.

Many reflections are cast on the Baptists, and various charges are laid against them; reflections and charges of such a kind, as greatly impeach the truth of their doctrinal principles, and the candor of their Christian temper. They are frequently represented by their Pædobaptist brethren, as *uncharitably rigid,* as *incorrigible bigots* to a favourite opinion, and as putting baptism in the place of our Lord's *atoning blood* and the *sanctifying agency* of the divine Spirit. To give them epithets and load them with charges of this kind, the generality of their opponents agree; whether they be members of our National Establishment, or in the number of Protestant Dissenters.

But why such unfriendly surmises and bold accusations? What is there in our principles or conduct that lays a foundation for such hard suspicions and such severity of censure? As to making baptism a substitute for *the atonement* of Jesus Christ, and the *sanctifying agency* of the Holy Spirit, it is manifestly contrary to our avowed sentiments; so contrary, that all the world, one would have thought, must agree to acquit us of such a charge.[1] For it is

---

[1] I speak of the *Particular* Baptists. How far any of those who are called

too notorious to admit a plea of ignorance in any of our opponents, that we consider no one as a proper subject of that institution, who does not profess repentance towards God, and faith in our Lord Jesus Christ; who does not, in other words, appear to be in a state of salvation. Nay, so far from making baptism *a saving* ordinance, we do not, we cannot consider any one as a proper subject of it, who looks upon it in that light.

Yet were an imputation of this kind as just and pertinent, as it is groundless and ungenerous; did we really ascribe a regenerating efficacy and saving effects to that sacred appointment; we should hardly forbear concluding, that these complaints and charges came with an ill grace from our brethren of the Establishment; especially from the clergy, who have solemnly declared their assent and consent to all that is contained in the book of Common Prayer. For they, immediately after baptizing an infant, address first the people, and then the omniscient God, in the following remarkable words; "Seeing dearly beloved brethren, that this child IS REGENERATE and grafted into the body of Christ's church, let us give thanks to Almighty God for these benefits—We yield thee hearty thanks, most merciful Father, that it hath pleased thee to REGENERATE this infant with thy Holy Spirit, to receive him for THINE OWN CHILD by adoption, and to incorporate him into thy holy church"—. Thus the clergy most solemnly profess to believe, when they administer baptism to infants. And, when giving catechetical instructions to children, they inculcate on their tender minds the same things, as truths and facts of great importance. For thus they interrogate each young catechumen, and thus they teach him to answer. "Who gave you this name? My Godfathers and Godmothers in my baptism, WHEREIN I WAS MADE, a member of Christ, a child of God, and an inheritor of the kingdom of heaven. How many sacraments hath Christ ordained in his church? Two only, as GENERALLY NECESSARY TO SALVATION, that is to say,

---

General Baptists, may have given occasion for such imputations, I neither take upon me to affirm nor deny.

baptism and the supper of the Lord. What is the inward and spiritual grace? [*i.e.* of baptism.] A death unto sin, and a new birth unto righteousness; for, being by nature born in sin, and the children of wrath, we are HEREBY MADE the children of grace."[2] Thus children are taught by the parish minister; and in the firm persuasion of these things they are *confirmed* by the bishop. For, immediately before he lays upon them his episcopal hand, he recognizes, in a solemn address to God, the great blessings supposed to be conferred and received by them at the time of their baptism. Thus he prays; "Almighty and ever living God, who hast vouchsafed to REGENERATE THESE THY SERVANTS by water and the

---

[2] See the Office for *Public Baptism of Infants,* and *the Catechism.* Whether the doctrine here advanced be consistent with the sentiments of Protestant Pædobaptists in general, or calculated to instruct the ignorant and edify believers, I must leave the reader to judge. I will take the liberty, however, of subjoining a quotation from the celebrated WITSIUS, and another from the no less excellent Dr. OWEN, relating to this point. The former thus expresses himself: "Communion with Christ and his sacred body is thought to precede baptism in chosen infants; surely by a dispensation of grace. To be sure, it has been established as a foundational principle to perform pædobaptism; (*i.e.,* at a later age, as a young boy or girl). From time to time this has been contested, by the orthodox, on the following grounds: that it behooves those, to whom the covenant of grace extends, and the communion of Christ, and (the communion) of the congregation, whose kingdom is in heaven, to be baptized. Notwithstanding, all these things befit chosen infants, and befit the established body proper. Bodius asserts that the learned members of the Roman ecclesia have engaged in a most grievous error, when they determine that baptism ought to be performed before the marking of this sign (*i.e.,* circumcision); that they are not members of Christ's body, that his body and communion do not extend to them, but that then only are they freed from the power of the devil, and pass over into the family of Christ." *Miscel Sac.* Tom. II. Exercit. XIX § XXI.—The latter thus: "Not sound is that pernicious doctrine, and because he would set poison with evil foresight, before the souls of sinners, indeed the father of lies might have contrived it himself. For in fact wretched men, wholly ruined by their sins, are complacent because they have been reborn in baptism, and thus they sleep soundly although they see the absolute and indispensible necessity of the renovation of the whole spiritual man, they neglect to acknowledge their own most wretched state and to flee to the quickening grace of Christ. And thus they lie in a most destructive security, forever doomed." *Theologoum, 1. vi. c.v.* p. 477, 478.

Holy Ghost, and hast given unto them FORGIVENESS OF ALL THEIR SINS."— And, after imposition of hands; "We make our humble supplications unto thee [the divine Majesty] for these thy servants, upon whom (after the example of thy holy apostles) we have now laid our hands, to CERTIFY THEM (by this sign) OF THY FAVOUR AND GRACIOUS GOODNESS TOWARDS THEM" —Once more; As the church of England suggests, *a painful doubt,* relating to the final happiness of such infants as die without baptism; so she *absolutely forbids* her Burial Service to be read over *any* who die unbaptized; placing them, in this respect, on a level with those that die under a sentence of excommunication for the most enormous crimes, or are guilty of *selo de se.* For thus she instructs her members and thus she directs her ministers: "It is certain by God's word, that children which are *baptized,* dying before they commit actual sin, are *undoubtedly saved* —Here it is to be NOTED, that the office ensuing [*i.e.* the burial office] is not to be used for any that die UNBAPTIZED, OR EXCOMMUNICATE, or HAVE LAID VIOLENT HANDS UPON THEMSELVES."[3] Nay, so confident is our National Church of these things being agreeable to the word of God, that she boldly pronounces the following sentence on all who dare to call them in question. Whosoever shall hereafter affirm, that the "form of God's worship contained in the book of Common Prayer, and administration of the sacraments, containeth ANY TIIING in it that is repugnant to the scriptures, let him be excommunicated *ipso facto,* and not restored but by the bishop of the place, or archbishop, after his repentance and public revocation of such his wicked errors."[4] Thus our

---

[3] *Order for Confirmation, Rubrick,* at the conclusion of the *Office for Publick Baptism of Infants,* and *Rubrick* prefixed to Order for *Burial of the Dead.*

[4] *Constitutions and Canons,* No. IV.—While hearing the thunder of this Canon Ecclesiastical, I am reminded of that anathematizing decree established by the Council of Trent: *Si quis dixerit baptismum liberum esse, hoc est, non necessarium ad salutem, anathema sit.* Sess. VII. Can. V. That is, If any one shall assert, that baptism is free, or *not necessary to salvation,* let him be accursed.

An Apology for the Baptists

National Church teaches, and thus her clergy profess, most solemnly profess to believe. Consequently, were we really chargeable with representing baptism as *a saving* ordinance, our brethren of the establishment could not, consistently, lodge a complaint against us on that account.

If we consult the writings of the most eminent preachers among the Methodists we shall find, that their sentiments harmonize with the doctrine of the National Church, in regard to the efficacy and absolute necessity of baptism. The late pious and extensively useful Mr. GEORGE WHITEFIELD, thus expresses his views of the subject before us; "does not this verse: JOHN iii. 5 urge the ABSOLUTE NECESSITY of water baptism? Yes, where it may be had; but how God will deal with persons unbaptized we cannot tell. What have we to do to judge those that are without."[5]— Our ministering brethren of the Tabernacle have sometimes taken the liberty of making reflections upon us, as if our opinion relating to baptism greatly intrenched on the offices and honour of Jesus Christ. Had they met with language and sentiments like these in any of *our* publications, especially in those of the late Dr. GILL; they would, undoubtedly, have thought themselves fully warranted in using their utmost efforts to expose the dangerous error; and to guard their hearers against us, as making *a saviour* of baptism. But while *some* of them, being Conformists, have solemnly professed their cordial consent to the various articles contained in the book of Common Prayer and administration of the sacraments, and while they *all* unite in revering the character of the late Mr. WHITEFIELD; they could not be either candid or consistent in condemning us, were we really chargeable with representing baptism as necessary to salvation. What, then, must we think of their conduct, when there is no proof, nor the least shadow of proof, that we have ever done any such thing? —As I have a sincere and high regard for many who preach the gospel and unite in public worship at the Tabernacle, and as it is my earnest prayer

---

[5] Works, Vol. iv. p. 355, 356.

that a divine blessing may attend them; so it would give me real pleasure to find, that they who fill the pulpit in that place, are more cautious in censuring the Baptists, and more consistent with their *loud professions* of candour and a catholic spirit; lest, through mistake, they be still culpable of bearing false witness against their brethren.

Mr. JOHN WESLEY, enumerating the benefits we receive by being baptized, speaks in the following language: "By baptism we *enter into covenant with God,* into that *everlasting* covenant, which he hath commanded for ever. By baptism we are admitted into the church, and consequently *made members* of Christ, its head. —By baptism we, who were by nature children of wrath, *are made the children of God.* And this regeneration is more than barely being admitted into the church. —By *water,* then, as a means, the water of baptism, we are *regenerated* or *born again.* Baptism doth now save us, if we live answerable thereto; if we repent, believe, and obey the gospel. Supposing this, as it admits us *into the church here, so* INTO GLORY HEREAFTER. —If infants are guilty of original sin, in the *ordinary* way, THEY CANNOT BE SAVED, unless this be WASHED AWAY BY BAPTISM."[6] —So Mr. WESLEY *teaches;* so, says a learned cardinal, the church has *always believed*;[7] and the Council of Trent *confirms* the whole. In the firm persuasion of this doctrine, Mr. WESLEY is also desirous of *settling* the members of his very numerous societies. For these positions are contained in a book professedly intended to preserve the reader from UNSETTLED NOTIONS *in religion.* Now, as I cannot suppose this author imagines, with DODWELL, that infants who die without baptism, are not immortal; I know not whether he chooses to lodge them in the *limbus puerorum* of the Papists[8]; or whether, with AUSTIN, he consigns them over to eternal damnation; though the one or

---

[6] Preservative, p. 146-150.
[7] "The church has always believed that infants perish if they depart from this life unbaptized." BELLARM. apud AMESIUM, *Bell. Enervat.* Tom. III. p. 67.
[8] FORBESII Instruct. Hist. Theolog. p. 493.

the other must be their case. For, that millions die without baptism, is an undoubted fact; and that God in favour of such, should be *frequently departing* from the *ordinary* method of his divine procedure, *much oftener* departing from, than acting according to it, is hard to conceive; is absolutely incredible, as it involves a contradiction. Yet, on Mr. WESLEY's principles, it must be so, if the generality of those that have died, since baptism was instituted, be not excluded the kingdom of heaven. For he who considers what multitudes of Jews and Heathens have peopled the earth, ever since the Christian dispensation commenced; what an extensive spread Mahomet's imposture has had for more than eleven hundred years; and what numbers of infants die without baptism, even in Christian countries, cannot but conclude, even admitting Pædobaptism to have been practised by the apostles, that a vast majority of deceased infants have left the world without being baptized.[9] Now who could suppose an author and a preacher, that affects the efficacy and exalts the importance of baptism at this extravagant rate, should charge the Baptists with placing an unlawful dependance on that ordinance? Yet, that he has frequently done so, in his pulpit discourses, if not in his numerous publications, is beyond a doubt; is known to thousands. Where, then, are his consistency, his candour, his catholic spirit!

Nor are we conscious of attributing any degree of importance to Baptism, which our Pædobaptist Dissenting brethren do

---

[9] Mr. WESLEY, it is well known, is a very warm defender of general redemption. He must, consequently, believe, that those infants who die without baptism, were as really redeemed by the death of Christ, as those that have the ordinance administered to them. In regard, therefore, to all that perish for want of baptism, it should seem, on his principles, as if our divine Lord were less careful to provide *an administrator* to confer an ordinance, than to *offer a propitatory sacrifice;* and more sparing of a *little water,* than of his *own blood:* even though he knew the latter would be of no avail, in millions of instances, without the former. But whether such sentiments be agreeable to the scriptures, or honourable to our Lord's atonement, the reader will be at no loss to determine.

not allow, and for which they do not plead. Do we consider it as a divine appointment, as an institution of Christ, the administration and use of which are to continue to the end of the world? So do they. Do they consider it as an ordinance which, when once rightly administered to a proper subject, is never to be repeated? So do we. Do we look upon it as indispensably necessary to communion at the Lord's table? So do they. Do we actually refuse communion to such whom we consider as unbaptized? So do they. No man, I presume, if considered by them as not baptized, would be admitted to break bread at the Lord's table, in any of their churches; however amiable his character, or how much soever they might esteem him, in other respects.

Nor is this a new opinion, or a novel practice: for such has been the sentiment and such the conduct of the Christian church in every age. *Before* the grand Romish apostasy, in the *very depth* of that apostasy, and *since* the Reformation, both at home and abroad; the general practice has been, to receive none but baptized persons to communion at the Lord's table. The following quotations from ancient and modern writers, relating to this point, may not be improper. JUSTIN MARTYR, for instance, when speaking of the Lord's supper says; "This food is called by us, the EUCHARIST; of which it is NOT LAWFUL for any to partake, but such as believe the things that are taught by us to be true, and have been BAPTIZED."[10] —JEROM; "Catechumens cannot communicate;" *i.e.* at the Lord's table, they being *unbaptized*.[11] —AUSTIN, when asserting the absolute necessity of infants receiving the Lord's supper, says; "Of which, certainly, they cannot partake, UNLESS THEY BE BAPTIZED."[12] —BEDE informs us, that three young princes among the eastern Saxons, seeing a bishop administer the sacred supper, desired to partake of it, as their deceased and royal father had done. To whom the bishop answered; "If ye

---

[10] *Apolog.* II, p. 162. Apud SUICERUM, *Thef. Ecclesi.* Tom. II. col. 1135.
[11] Catechumeni-communicare non poffunt. In cap. VII. *Epist. II. ad Corinth.*
[12] Quod nifi baptizati non utique poffunt. *Epist. ad Bonifacium,* Epist. CVI.

will be washed, or baptized, in the salutary fountain, as your father was, ye may also partake of the Lord's supper, as he did: but if you despise the former, YE CANNOT IN ANY WISE receive the latter. They replied, We will not enter into the fountain, or be baptized; nor have we any need of it; but yet we desire to be refreshed with that bread." After which the historian tells us, that they importunately requesting, and the bishop resolutely refusing them admission to the holy table, they were so exasperated, as to *banish both him and his out of their kingdom.*[13]—THEOPHYLACT; "NO UNBAPTIZED PERSON partakes of the Lord's supper."[14]—BONAVENTURE; Faith, indeed, is necessary to all the sacraments, but especially to the reception of baptism; because baptism is THE FIRST among the sacraments, and THE DOOR of the sacraments.[15]

Quotations of this kind might, no doubt, be greatly multiplied: but that none were admitted to the sacred supper in the first ages of the Christian church, before they were baptized, we are assured by various learned writers, well versed in ecclesiastical antiquity. For instance: FRID. SPANHEIMIUS asserts, "That *none but baptized* persons were admitted to the Lord's table."[16] —Lord Chancellor

---

[13] If you wish to be cleansed at that fountain, (and) to be saved, where your father was cleansed, you are able to partake of the sacred bread, of which he partook. But if you condemn the bath of life, by no means whatever are you able to share in the bread of life. But, they say, we do not wish to enter the fountain, because we do not think there *is* a need for this, but we wish to be made whole again by that bread. And when they were warned by him, carefully and often, that it was not possible that anyone should share in the sacred gift without first undergoing a sacred cleansing, moved to a pitch of anger they spoke: If you can not assent to us in this simple matter which we seek, you shall never be able to dwell in our province. And they expelled him, and ordered him to leave with his belongings. *Hist. Eccles.* lib. II. cap. V. p. 63.

[14] *No one unbaptized shall be admitted. In cap. XIV.* Matt. p. 83.

[15] Fidem quidem esse necessariam omnibus sacramentis, sed specialiter appropriari baptismo: quoniam baptismus est primum inter sacramenta et janua sacramentorum. Apud FORBESIUM, *Instruct. Historic. Theolog.* lib. X. cap. IV. § 9.

[16] Subject ad eucharistiam admissa, foli baptizati. *Hist. Christian.* col. 623.

KING; "Baptism was *always precedent* to the Lord's supper; and *none* were admitted to receive the eucharist, till they were baptized. This is so obvious to every man, that it needs no proof."[17] —Dr. WALL; *"No church* ever gave the communion to *any persons* before they were baptized— AMONG ALL THE ABSURDITIES THAT EVER WERE HELD, none ever maintained THAT, that any person should partake of the communion *before* he was baptized."[18] —Dr. DODDRIDGE; "It is certain that Christians in general have always been spoken of, by the most ancient Fathers, as baptized persons: —and it is also certain, that as far as our knowledge of primitive antiquity reaches, NO UNBAPTIZED person received the Lord's supper."[19]

That the Protestant churches in general have always agreed in the same sentiment and conduct, is equally evident. Out of many eminent writers that might be mentioned, the following quotations may suffice. URSINUS, for instance, asserts; "That they who are not yet baptized, SHOULD NOT BE ADMITTED TO THE SACRED SUPPER."[20] — RAVENELLIUS, when speaking of the Lord's supper, says; Baptism OUGHT TO PRECEDE; nor is the holy supper to be administered to any, EXCEPT THEY BE BAPTIZED."[21] — ZANCHIUS; "We believe that Baptism, as a sacrament appointed by Christ, is ABSOLUTELY NECESSARY in the church."[22] —HOORNBEEKIUS; *"No one is* admitted to the sacred supper, UNLESS HE IS BAPTIZED."[23] — TURRETTINUS; "It is one thing to have a right to those

---

[17] *Enquiry,* Part II. p. 44.
[18] *Hist. Infant Bap.* part II. chap. IX.
[19] Lectures, p. 511.
[20] Nondum baptizati, ad coenam non funt admittendi. *Corp. Doct. Christ.* p. 566.
[21] Baptismus debet praecedere; coena vero nonnifi baptizatis est danda. *Bibliotheca Sacra,* Tom. I. p. 301.
[22] Credimus baptismum in ecclesia omnino necessarium esse tanquam sacramentum a Christo institum, nisi baptizatus. *Socin. Consut.* Tom. III. p. 416.
[23] Nemo ad coenam admittitur, nifi baptizatus. *Socin. Confut.* Tom. III. p. 416.

external ordinances of the church, which belong to a profession; and it is another to be interested in the internal blessings of faith. Unbaptized believers have actually a right to *these,* because they are already partakers of Christ and his benefits; though they have not yet a right to *those,* except in observing the appointed order, *by baptism.*"[24] MASTRICHT; As no *uncircumcised* male was admitted to the typical supper, that is the passover; so, under the New Testament, no *unbaptized* person is admitted to the Lord's table.[25] — LEYDECKER: "Baptism is necessary, not only in a way of expediency, but by virtue of a *divine precept.* They, therefore, who reject it, REJECT THE COUNSEL of GOD AGAINST THEMSELVES."[26] —BENEDICT. PICTETUS; The supper of our Lord ought not to be administered to persons that are *unbaptized:* for before baptism, men are not considered as members of the visible church."[27] —MARCKIUS; "The dying, and the *unbaptized,* are not to be admitted to communion."[28] —Dr. MANTON; "*In foro ecclesia,* before the church, *none but baptized persons* have a right to the Lord's table."[29] —Mr. BAXTER; "If any should be so IMPUDENT as to say, it is not the meaning of Christ, that *baptizing* should IMMEDIATELY, WITHOUT DELAY, follow *discipling,* they are confuted by the constant example of scripture. So that I dare say, that this will be out of doubt with all *rational,*

---

[24] Aliud jus habere ad sfacra ecclesi, auæ ad prosessionem referuntur: Aliud ad interna fides. Catechumens credentes actu jus habent ad ifta, quia jam participes funt Christi et beneficiorum ejus; licet non dum habænt jus ad illa, nifi ordine servato et posito baptismo. *Institut. Theolog.* Tom, III, Loc. XVIII. Quest. IV. §. 10.

[25] Ad coenam *typicam,* h.e. ad pascha, non admittebatur ullus— *præputiatus,* Exed. xii. 40 sicut sub N.T. non admittitur *nonbaptizatus,* Act. ii. 41, 42, *Theolog.* lib. VII. cap. V. §. s9.

[26] Baptismus necessarius est necessitate præcepti, non solum expedientiar. Quare, qui eum rejiciunt, concilium Dei adversus se ipsos rejiciunt. *Idea Theolog.* p. 225.

[27] Non debet administrati coena-non baptizatis; nam ante baptismum non censentur homines esse in ecclesia. *Theolog. Christiana,* p. 959, 960.

[28] Ad communionem hanc admittendi Bunt, non-expirantes, aut non-baptizati. *Christ. Theolog. Medulla,* p. 406.

[29] Supplem. Morn Exercis. p. 199.

considerate, impartial Christians."[30] —Once more: Dr. DODDRIDGE, thus expresses his views of the subject. "The law of Christ requires that ALL who believe the gospel should be *baptized*—For any to abstain from baptism, when he knows it is an institution of Christ, and that it is the will of Christ that he should subject himself to it, is such an act of disobedience to his authority, as IS INCONSISTENT WITH TRUE FAITH. —How EXCELLENT SOEVER any man's character is, he must be *baptized* before he can be looked upon as completely a member of the church of Christ."[31]

Perfectly conformable to these testimonies, are the *Catechisms* and *Confessions of faith,* that have been published at any time, or by any denomination of Christians: for, if the positive institutions of Christ be not entirely omitted, *baptism is* not only always mentioned first; but generally mentioned in such a way, as intimates that it is *a prerequisite* to the Lord's table. And so, even in our common forms of speaking, if we have occasion to mention both those solemn appointments of our Lord, baptism still has the priority. Thus *generally,* thus *universally, is* it allowed, that baptism is necessary to communion at the Lord's table. — Nay, many of our Protestant Dissenting brethren consider the ordinance in a more important light than we. For they frequently represent it, as *a seal of the covenant of grace; as a mean of bringing their infant offspring into covenant with God;* and some of them severely censure us, for leaving our children to the *uncovenanted mercies of the Most High, merely because we do not baptize them. Expressions and sentiments these, which we neither adopt nor approve; because they seem* to attribute more to the ordinance, than the sacred scriptures, in our opinion, will warrant.

It appears, then, to be a fact, a stubborn, incontestable fact, that our judgment and conduct, relating to the necessity of baptism *in order to communion,* perfectly coincide with the sentiments and practice of our National Church, and with all

---

[30] Plain Scripture Proof. p. 126.
[31] *Lectures,* p. 508, 512. *Discourse on Regan.* Postscript to Pref. p. 12, 13.

An Apology for the Baptists

Pædobaptist churches in these kingdoms. Nor have I heard of any such church now upon earth, with which we do not, in this respect, agree: for none, of whom I have any intelligence, be their sentiments or modes of worship whatever they may, in regard to other things, admit any to the sacred supper, who have not, in their opinion, been baptized. —And, on the other hand, when the *importance* of baptism comes under consideration between us and them, it is manifest, that both Conformist and Nonconformist Pædobaptists in general, ascribe more to it than we, and place a greater dependence upon it. Consequently, neither candour, nor reason, nor justice will admit, that we should be charged, as we have frequently been, with laying an unwarrantable stress upon it.

The point controverted between us and our Pædobaptist brethren is not, Whether *unbaptized believers* may, according to the laws of Christ, be admitted to communion; for here we have no dispute: but, *What is* baptism, and *who* are the proper subjects of it? In the discussion of these questions there is, indeed, a wide and a very material difference; but in regard to the former we are entirely agreed. —Why, then, do our brethren censure us as *uncharitably rigid,* and *incorrigible bigots?* The principal reason seems to be this: They, in general, admit, that *immersion* in the name of the triune God, on a profession of faith in Jesus Christ, is *baptism, real baptism;* while our fixed and avowed persuasion will not permit us to allow, that *infant sprinkling,*[32] though performed with the greatest solemnity, is worthy of the name. Consequently, though they, consistently with their own principles, may receive us to communion among them, yet we cannot admit *them* to fellowship with us at the Lord's table, without contradicting our professed sentiments. For it appears to us, on the most deliberate inquiry, that immersion is not *a mere*

---

[32] The reader is desired to observe, that when I make use of the phrase *infant sprinkling,* or any expression of a similar import, it is merely by way of *distinction;* without annexing any secondary, or obnoxious idea to it.

circumstance, or *a mode* of baptism, but *essential* to the ordinance; so that, in our judgment, he who is not immersed, is not baptized. This is the principle on which we proceed, in refusing communion to our Pædobaptist brethren; whom, in other respects, we highly esteem, and towards whom we think it our duty to cultivate the most cordial affection. — Nor can we suppose but they would act a similar part, were they in our situation. Were they fully persuaded, for instance, that the great Head of the church had not commanded, nor any way authorized, his ministering servants to require a profession of faith *prior* to baptism; and were they equally certain that the ordinance never was administered by the apostles to any but *infants,* nor in any other way than that of *aspersion,* or *pouring;* would they not look upon the *immersion of professing believers* as a quite different thing from baptism? And, were this the case, would they not consider us an unbaptized, and refuse to have communion with us on that account? I am persuaded they would, notwithstanding their affection for any of us, as believers in Jesus Christ. Consequently, if we *be* really culpable in the eyes of our brethren, it is for *denying the validity* of infant baptism; not because we *refuse communion* to Pædobaptists—for an error in our *judgment,* which misleads the conscience; not for perverseness of *temper,* or a want of *love* to the disciples of Christ.

Nor was the Lord's supper appointed to be *a test* of brotherly love among the people of God; though several objections that are made against us, seem to proceed on that supposition. It must, indeed, be allowed, that as it is a sacred feast and an ordinance of divine worship, mutual Christian affection, among communicants at the same table, is very becoming and highly necessary; and so it is in all other branches of social religion. But that sitting down at the holy supper should be considered as *the criterion* of my love to individuals, or to any Christian community, does not appear from the word of God. No, the supper of our Lord was designed for other and greater purposes. It was intended to teach and exhibit the most interesting of all truths, and the

An Apology for the Baptists

most wonderful of all transactions. The design of the Great Institutor was, that it should be a memorial of God's *love to us,* and of IMMANUEL'S DEATH FOR US: *that,* the most astonishing favour ever displayed; *this,* the most stupendous fact that angels ever beheld. Yes, the love of God, in giving his dear, his only Son; and the death of Christ, as our divine substitute and propitiatory sacrifice, are the grand objects we are called to contemplate at the Lord's table. —As to *a proof, a substantial proof* of our love to the children of God, it is not given at so cheap and easy a rate, as that of sitting down with them, either occasionally or statedly, at the holy table. Numbers do that, who are very far from loving the disciples of Christ, for the truth's sake. To give real evidence of that heavenly affection, there must be the exercise of such tempers, and the performance of such actions, as require much self-denial; and without which, were we to commune with them ever so often, or talk ever so loudly of candour and a catholic spirit; we should, after all, be destitute of that *charity,* without which we are *"nothing."* The reader, therefore, will do well to remember, that the *true test* of his love to the disciples of Christ, is, not a submission to any particular ordinance of public worship; for that is rather an evidence of his love to God and reverence for his authority; but, sympathizing with them in their afflictions; feeding the hungry, cloathing the naked, and taking pleasure in doing them good, whatever their necessities may be. For this I have the authority of our final Judge, who will say to his people; "Come ye blessed of my Father, for" —what? Ye have manifested your love to the saints and your faith in me, by holding free communion at my table with believers of all denominations? No such thing. But, "I was an hungred, and ye *gave me meat;* I was thirsty and ye *gave me drink; I* was a stranger and ye *took me in;* naked, and ye *clothed me;* I was sick, and ye *visited me;* I was in prison, and ye *came unto me."*[33]

Our opponents often insinuate, that we are more zealous to

---

[33] Matt. xxv. 34-40. Luke xiii. 25, 26, 27.

establish a favourite mode and make proselytes to our own opinion and party, than to promote the honour of Jesus Christ and the happiness of immortal souls. Were this the case, we should, indeed, be much to blame, and greatly disgrace our Christian character. But why are the Baptists to be thus represented? Do they affirm that the kingdom of Christ is confined to them? that they only have the true religion among them? and that, unless men are of their party, they will not be saved? Do they wish success to none that are employed in the vineyard, but themselves? or say of others, engaged in the same common cause, Master forbid them, because they follow not with us? On the contrary, do they not profess a warm esteem and affection for all those of whatever communion, who love the Lord Jesus Christ, and aim to promote his cause in the world? and do they not give proof of this, by holding a friendly correspondence with them as opportunities offer; and by cordially joining them in occasional exercises of publick worship? It is not the distinguishing tenet of Baptism, how much soever they wish it to prevail, that is the main band that knits them in affection to one another: it is the infinitely nobler consideration of the relation they stand in to Christ as his disciples. They hope therefore, to be believed when they declare, that they most cordially embrace in the arms of Christian love the friends of Jesus, who differ from them in this point; and to be further believed when they add, that they hold the temper and conduct of the furious zealot for Baptism, who fails in his allegiance to Christ, and in the charity he owes his fellow Christians, in sovereign contempt.[34]

Nor are they who plead for infant baptism the only persons under whose censure the generality of us have the unhappiness to fall. So very peculiar is our situation, that some even of our Baptist brethren, charge us with being *too strict* and *rigid,* because we do not receive Pædobaptists into communion; a practice which they have adopted and warmly defend. Nay, some of them have boldly declared, that our

---

[34] Dr. STENNETT's *Answer* to Mr. ADDINGTON, Part II p. 284, 285.

conduct by refusing so to do, is *"greatly prejudicial* to the honour and interest of true religion, and NOT A LITTLE CONTRIBUTING TO THE CAUSE OF INFIDELITY."[35] This, it must be allowed, is a *home thrust*. We have need, consequently, to be provided with armour of proof; with *Robur et AEs triplex*. Especially, considering, that this charge is laid against us, by two of our brethren, under those respectable characters, THE CANDID, and THE PEACEFUL. For when such amiable and venerable personages as CANDOUR and PEACE, unite in prefering a bill of indictment against a supposed offender, the grand jury can hardly forbear prejudging the cause, by finding it *a true bill,* before they have examined so much as one witness of either side. —Mr. BUNYAN also, who zealously pleaded the cause of free communion, when it was yet in its infancy, and who intitled one of his publications in defence of his favourite hypothesis, *Peaceable principles and true;* did not fail to charge his Baptist brethren, who differed from him in that particular, in a similar way. Yes, notwithstanding Mr. BUNYAN's candid, catholic, peaceable principles; and though he was, at that very time, pleading for candour, Catholicism, and peace, in the churches of Christ; he draws up a long list of hateful consequences, and charges them to the account of his brethren's conduct, merely because they did not admit Pædobaptists into communion with them. The design of the following pages, therefore, is to show that we cannot receive Pædobaptists into communion at the Lord's table without doing violence to our professed sentiments, as Baptists; and to answer the principal objections which these our brethren have started against us. In doing of which, I shall argue with them on their *own principles,* as Protestant Dissenters and Antipædobaptists; which kind of argumentation is always esteemed both fair and forcible, when rightly applied.

My reader will not here expect a discussion of the mode and subject of Baptism; for it is not that ordinance, considered in itself, or as detached from other appointments of Jesus

---

[35] CANDIDUS and PACIFICUS, *in their Modest Plea for free Communion.*

Christ; but the *order* in which it is placed, and the *connection* in which it stands with the Lord's supper, that are the subject of our inquiry. Nor will my Pædobaptist brethren be offended, if I assume, as truths and facts, things which are controverted between them and us: because I do not here dispute with *them,* but with such as profess themselves Baptists, yet practice free communion. And though I look upon the *former* as under a mistake, in regard to baptism; I consider them as acting, not only conscientiously but *consistently* with their own principles, in respect of that ordinance: while I view the conduct of the *latter,* not only as contrary to the order of the primitive Christian churches, but as *inconsistent* with their own avowed sentiments; which disorder and inconsistency I shall now endeavour to prove.

SECTION II.

The general Grounds on which we proceed, in refusing Communion at the Lord's Table, to Pædobaptist believers—Novelty of the Sentiment and Practice of our Brethren, who plead for Free Communion; and the Inconsistency of such a Conduct with their Baptist Principles.

The following positions are so evidently true, and so generally admitted by Protestant Dissenters, that they will not be disputed by those of our brethren who plead for free communion.

Our divine Lord, in whom are hid all the treasures of wisdom and knowledge, is perfectly well qualified to judge, what ordinances are proper to be appointed, and what measures are necessary to be pursued, in order to obtain the great design of religion among mankind—Being head over all things to the church, he possesses the highest authority to appoint such ordinances of divine worship, and to enact such laws for the government of his house, as are agreeable to his unerring wisdom and calculated to promote the important objects he has in view; which appointments and laws must bind the subjects of his government in the strictest manner —Having loved the church to the most astonishing degree, even so as to give himself a ransom for her; he must be considered, as having made the wisest and the best appointments, as having given the most salutary and perfect laws, with a view to promote her happiness, and as means of his own glory—These laws and ordinances are committed to writing and contained in the Bible: which heavenly volume is the rule of our faith and practice, in things pertaining to religion, our complete and ONLY rule, in all things relating to the instituted worship of God and the order of his house. So that we should not receive any thing, as an article of our creed, which is not contained in it; do nothing, as a part of divine worship, not commanded by it; neither omit, nor alter any thing that has the sanction of our Lord's appointment— Nor have we any reason to expect, that our divine Lawgiver and sovereign Judge will accept our solemn services, any further than we follow those directions which he has given, without addition, alteration, or diminution. "What thing soever I command you, observe to do it: thou shalt not add thereto, nor diminish from it;" were the injunctions of JEHOVAH to the ancient Israelitish church. "Teaching them to observe all things, whatsoever I have commanded you;" is the requisition of JESUS CHRIST, to all his ministering servants.[1]

In the worship of God there cannot be either obedience or faith, unless we regard the divine appointments. Not *obedience;* for that supposes a precept, or what is equivalent to it. Not *faith;* for that requires a promise, or some divine declaration. If, then, we act without a command, we have reason to apprehend that God will say to us, as he did to Israel of old, "Who hath required this at your hand?" And, on the contrary, when our divine Sovereign enjoins the performance of any duty, to deliberate is disloyalty; to dispute is rebellion. — "Believers, who really attend to communion with Jesus Christ," says a judicious author, "do labour to keep their hearts chaste to him in his ordinances, institutions, and worship. They will receive nothing, practise nothing, own nothing, in his worship, but what is of his appointment. They know that from the foundation of the world he never did allow, nor ever will, that in any thing the *will* of the creatures should be the *measure* of his honour, or the *principle* of his worship, either as to matter or manner. It was a witty and true sense that one gave of the second

---

[1] Deut. xii. 32. Matt, xxvii. 20. —SMITH's *Compend. Acc. of the Form and Order of the Church,* p. 15, 16.

commandment; *Non imago, non simulachrum prohibetur; fed, non facies tibi.* It is *a making to ourselves,* an inventing, a finding out ways of worship or means of honouring God, not by him appointed, that is so severely forbidden."[2] — "To serve God otherwise than he requireth," says another learned writer, "is not to *worship,* but to rob and *mock* him. In God's service, it is a greater sin to do that which we are not to do, than not to do that which we are commanded. This is but a sin of omission; but that a sin of sacrilege and high contempt. In this we charge the law only with difficulty; but in that with folly. In this we discover our weakness to do the will, but in that we declare our impudence and arrogancy to control the wisdom of God. In this we acknowledge our own insufficiency; in that we deny the all-sufficiency and plenitude of God's own law—We see the absurdity and wickedness of will-worship, when, when the same man who is to perform the obedience, shall dare to appoint the laws; implying a peremptory purpose of no further observance than may consist with the allowance of his own judgment. Where as true obedience must be grounded on the *majesty* of that power that commands, not on the *judgment* of the subject, or *benefit* of the precept imposed. Divine laws require obedience, not so much from the *quality* of the things commanded (though they be ever holy and good) as from the *authority* of him that institutes them."[3]

That the gospel should be preached in all nations for the obedience of faith; and that, under certain restrictions, they who receive the truth should be formed into a church state, few can doubt: and it is equally clear, from the foregoing positions, that it belongs to the supreme, royal prerogative of Jesus Christ, to appoint the terms and conditions on which his people shall have a place in his house and a seat at his table. For we cannot suppose, with any appearance of reason, that these conditions are *arbitrary;* or such as every distinct community may think fit to impose. No; a gospel church has

---

[2] Dr. OWEN *on Communion with God,* p. 170.
[3] Bp. REYNOLD's *Works,* p. 163, 422.

no more power to fix the terms of communion, or to set aside those prescribed by Jesus Christ, than to make a rule of faith, or to settle ordinances of divine worship. This is one characteristic of *a church,* as distinguished from *a civil society;* the terms of admission into the *latter* are discretional; provided they do not interfere with any divine law; but those of the *former* are fixed by him who is King in Zion. No congregation of religious professors, therefore, has any authority to make the door of admission into their communion, either straiter, or wider, than Christ himself has made it.[4] — "The original form of this house, [*i.e.* the church of Christ] was not precarious and uncertain; to be altered, and changed, and broke in upon by man, or by any set of men, at pleasure. This would reflect on the wisdom and care, as well as on the steadiness of Christ; who is in his house, as well as in the highest heavens, the steady and the faithful Jesus; the same yesterday, to day, and for ever, and not in the least given to change: but its form is fixed, particularly in the New Testament. Had not Moses, nor any of the elders of Israel, so much power over the tabernacle as to alter or change a pin thereof? and with what face can man pretend to a power to model and alter at pleasure gospel churches? As if Christ, the true Moses, had forgot, or neglected, to leave with us the pattern of the house."[5]

Baptism and the Lord's supper are positive appointments in the Christian church, about which we cannot know any thing, relating to their mode of administration, subjects, or design, except from the revealed will of their Great Institutor. For, as a learned writer observes, "All *positive* duties, or duties made such by institution alone, depend entirely upon the will and declaration of the person, who institutes or ordains them, with respect to the real design and end of them; and consequently, to the due manner of performing them." It behoves us, therefore, well to consider the rule which our Lord has given relating to these

---

[4] Dr. RIDGLEY's *Body of Divinity,* p. 343. Glasgow Edit.
[5] Mr. BRAGGE, *on Church Discipline,* p. 9.

ordinances. "Because we can have *no other* direction in this sort of duties; unless we will have recourse to mere invention, which makes them our OWN INSTITUTIONS and not the institutions of those who first appointed them."[6]

That there is a connection between the two positive institutions of the New Testament, is manifest from the word of God; and that one of them must be prior to the other, in order of administration, is evident from the nature of things: for a person cannot be baptized and receive the sacred supper at the same instant. Here, then, the question is, (if a doubt may be moved on a point so evident, without affronting common sense) which of them has the previous claim on a real convert's obedience? *Baptism,* or the *Lord's Supper?* If we appeal to the persuasion and practice of Christians in all nations and in every age it will clearly appear, That the *former* was universally considered, by the churches of Christ,[7] as *a divinely appointed* prerequisite for fellowship in the *latter,* till about the middle of the last century, here in England; when some few of the Baptists began to call it in question, and practically to deny it. This our brethren now do, who defend and practise *free communion.* For they admit Pædobaptists to the Lord's table; though, on their OWN PRINCIPLES, infant sprinkling is not baptism.

This appears from hence. That only is baptism which Christ

---

[6] Bp. HOADLY's *Plain Account*, p. 3.

[7] That there were people of different denominations in the second and third centuries, who pretended a regard to the name of Jesus Christ, and yet rejected baptism, is readily allowed; but then, it may be observed, that many of them had as little esteem for the Lord's supper. Nay, as a learned writer asserts, the generality of them renounced the scriptures themselves. Nor am I ignorant that SOCINUS, in the latter end of the sixteenth century, considered baptism as an indifferent thing, except in reference to such as are converted from Judiasm, Paganism, or Mahometanism; but our brethren with whom I am now concerned will hardly allow, that societies formed on the principles of those ancient corrupters of Christianity, not yet on those of SOCINUS, are worthy to be called, CHURCHES OF CHRIST. Vid. SUICERUM, *Thesaur. Eccles.* sub voce Cf. Baptism; and Dr. WALL's *Hist. Inf. Bap.* Part II. Chap. V.

appointed as such. That, therefore, which essentially differs from what he appointed, cannot be baptism. But they believe, as well as we, that Pædobaptism, as now practised, essentially differs from the appointment of Christ, both as to mode and subject: yet a mode of administration, and a subject to whom it should be administered, are necessary to existence of baptism, as an ordinance of Christ; for without these it is only an abstract notion. If, then, the proper subject be *a professing believer,* and the appointed mode *immersion* in water, which they maintain as well as we; it is not real baptism where these are wanting. Agreeable to that saying, of an ancient writer: "They who are not rightly baptized, are, doubtless, not baptized at all?"[8] —But that our brethren do not consider infant sprinkling as having the essentials of Christian baptism in it, is put beyond a doubt by their own conduct. For they no more scruple to baptize professing believers, who have been sprinkled in their infancy, than we do: and yet, I presume, they are not very fond of being considered, or called, ANABAPTISTS; which, notwithstanding, is their proper character, if they allow that the aspersion of infants has the essentials of baptism in it.

This, then, is a fact, a notorious, undeniable fact, that our brethren practically deny the necessity of baptism in order to communion at the sacred supper: for they do not, they cannot believe the aspersion of infants to be Christian baptism, without rendering themselves obnoxious to the charge of *Anabaptism.* A sentiment so peculiar, and a conduct so uncommon as theirs are, in regard to this institution, require to be well supported by the testimony of the Holy Ghost. For were all the Christian churches now in the world asked, except those few that plead for free communion; whether they thought it lawful to admit *unbaptized* believers to fellowship at the Lord's table? there is reason to conclude they would readily unite in that declaration of Paul; "WE HAVE NO SUCH CUSTOM, NEITHER THE CHURCHES OF GOD" that went before us. Yes, considering the *novelty* of

---

[8] Baptismum quum rite non habeant, sine dubio non habent. TERTULL, *de Baptismo, cap. xv.* pg. 230.

An Apology for the Baptists

their sentiment and conduct, and what *a contradiction* they are to the faith and order of the whole Christian church; — considering that it never was disputed, so far as I can learn, prior to the sixteenth century, by orthodox or heterodox, by Papists or Protestants, whether *unbaptized* believers should be admitted to the Lord's table; they all agreeing in the contrary practice, however, much they differed in matters of equal importance, it may be reasonably expected, and is by us justly demanded, that the truth of their sentiment and the rectitude of their conduct, should be *proved, really proved* from the records of inspiration. A man may easily shew his fondness for novelty, and the deference he pays to his own understanding, by boldly controverting and resolutely opposing the practice of the wisest and the best of men in every age; but, if he would avoid the imputation of arrogance, he must demonstrate, that the things he opposes are *vulgar errors,* which have nothing to recommend them but great antiquity and general custom. Our persuasion, therefore, concerning the necessity of baptism as a term of communion, having had the sanction of universal belief and universal practice for almost sixteen hundred years, it lies on our brethren to prove that it is false and unscriptural; and to shew, from the New Testament, that theirs has the stamp of divine authority.

But is it not strange, strange to astonishment, if the scriptures contain their sentiment and vindicate their conduct, that it never was discovered by any who acknowledged the proper Deity, the eternal dominion, and the complete satisfaction of Jesus Christ, till the later end of the last century? seeing, long before then, almost every principle of the Christian faith, almost every branch of Christian worship, had been the subject, either of learned, or unlearned controversy, among such as thought themselves the disciples of Jesus Christ. The Quakers arose, it is well known, about the time when this new sentiment was first adopted in England; and they entirely renounced baptism, as well as the Lord's supper. But, so far as appears, the people of that denomination never supposed, that they who thought it their duty to celebrate the sacred supper, were at liberty to do it *before* they were baptized. —Here I cannot but remark, with how little affection and reverence the positive institutions and the authority of Christ were treated, in this island, in the last century. The ingenious author of the *Pilgrim's Progress* was one of the first, in this kingdom, who dared to assert, that the want of baptism *is no bar to communion,* and acted accordingly. The Quakers arising a little before him, proceeded a step further, and entirely cashiered both baptism and the supper of our Lord; looking upon them, as *low, carnal, temporary* appointments. Much respect, I allow, is due to the character of BUNYAN. He was an eminent servant of Jesus Christ, and patiently suffered in his Master's cause. Many of his writings have been greatly useful to the church of God, and some of them, it is probable, will transmit his name, with honour, to future ages. But yet I cannot persuade myself, that either his judgment or piety appeared in this bold innovation. The disciples of GEORGE FOX, though less conformable to the word of God, acted more consistently with their own principles, than did the justly celebrated DREAMER then, or our brethren who practise free communion now.

But I forget myself. The last century was the *grand ara* of improvement in this nation; of prodigious improvement in light and liberty. *In light;* as well divine, as philosophical. In *real* philosophical science, by the labours of a BACON, a BOYLE, and a NEWTON. In *pretended* theological knowledge, by those of a JESSEY and a BUNYAN. Did the *former,* by deep researches into the system of nature, surprise and instruct the world by discoveries, of which mankind had never before conceived? The *latter,* penetrating into the gospel system, amused mankind, by casting new light on the positive institutions of Jesus Christ, and by placing baptism among things of little importance in the Christian religion; of which no ancient theologue had ever dreamed —none, we have reason to think, that loved the Lord Redeemer. *In liberty;* not less religious than civil; in the church as well as the state. Did the struggles of real patriotism, and the Abdication of a Popish Prince, make way for true liberty in the *latter?* The repealing of Christ's positive laws by FOX and BARCLAY, and the practical claim of a dispensing power by JESSEY and BUNYAN, made way for the *inglorious* liberty of treating positive institutions in the house of God just as professors please.

Some of the Popish missionaries among the Indians have been charged, by respectable authorities, with concealing the doctrine of *the cross* from their hearers, lest they should be tempted to despise the great Founder of the Christian religion, because he made his exit on a gibbet; and with making it their principal aim, to persuade the poor ignorant creatures to be *baptized;* imagining that they would be sufficiently christianized, by a submission to that ordinance. As if being baptized and conversion to Jesus Christ, were one and the same thing! What a destructive delusion this! What an impious exaltation of a positive institution, into the place of redeeming blood, and the regenerating power of the Holy Spirit! —But were one of our ministering brethren, who plead for free communion, to be sent as a missionary into those parts of the world; he, I presume, would not be in the least danger of thus over-rating baptism, and of depreciating its great Institutor. No; he would boldly preach *a crucified* and risen Jesus, as the only foundation of hope for his hearers; and, if the energy of God attended his labours with considerable success, he would think it his duty to lay before such as believed in Christ, what he had learned from the New Testament, relating to a gospel church —its nature and ordinances, its privileges, duties, and great utility. In doing of which, he could hardly forbear to mention *baptism,* as an appointment of his divine Master: but though he might *mention* it, yet, on his hypothesis, he could not, *require a* submission to it, as previously necessary to their incorporating as a church, and their having communion together at the Lord's table. He might, indeed, *recommend* it to his young converts, as having something agreeable in it; but if they did not see its propriety; or if, on any other account unknown to him, they did not choose to comply, and yet were desirous of being formed into a church state, and of having communion at the Lord's table; he could not refuse, though not one of them was, or would be baptized. For if it be lawful to admit *one* believer to communion, purely *as a believer,* and without baptism; it cannot be criminal to admit *all* such, if they desire it: that which is proper and right for *one,* being so to *a million,* if they be in the same circumstances. Thus he would gather a church in perfect contrast with those formed by his fellow missionaries. For, while they put baptism in the place of the Saviour, he would reject his command and lay the ordinance entirely aside: they make it ALL, and he make it NOTHING. —And were a narrative of such proceedings to fall into the hands of a Pedobaptist, who had never heard of any that practised, or pleaded, for free communion, what a singular figure it would make in his view! "A minister of Jesus Christ," he would say, "gathering a church among the Indians, and administering the sacred supper, yet all his communicants *unbaptized!* Strange, indeed! —A Christian minister, called a BAPTIST, entirely omitting that *very ordinance* from which he takes his denomination! This is stranger still! For the BAPTISTS, of all men, are said to love *water* and to be fond of *baptism.* It exceeds the bounds of credibility: but, if it be a fact, he is the oddest mortal and the most unaccountable Baptist that ever lived. For he does violence to his own distinguishing sentiment, and is guilty of *Felo de se.* Like Job's leviathan, he has not his equal on earth: an unheard-of phenomenon in the religious world, and will probably be the wonder of ages yet unborn. But the ambiguity of his character is such, that I fear the pen of ecclesiastical history will always be doubtful what to *call* him, or under what denomination of religious professors he claims a place?" —Such would be the surprise and such the reflections of the learned and the vulgar, who had not heard of Baptists that plead for free communion; they being the only Christians now in the world, for aught appears, that are capable of realizing such a report.

But were such a singular conduct warranted by the laws of Christ, or agreeable to the truly primitive pattern; the surprise and the censure of weak, fallible mortals, would be of little importance. For it is not the approbation of men, but the revelation of God, that is our only rule in the administration of divine institutions. To that revelation, therefore, we must appeal, and by it the sentiment and practice, now in dispute, must stand or fall.

SECTION III.

Arguments against Free Communion at the Lord's Table.

It must, I think, be allowed, that the *order* and *connection* of positive appointments in divine worship, depend as much on the sovereign pleasure of the great Legislator, as the appointments themselves: and if so, we are equally bound *to regard* that order and connection, in their administration, as to observe the appointments at all. Whoever, therefore, objects to that order, or deviates from it, opposes that sovereign authority by which those branches of worship were first instituted. —For instance: Baptism and the Lord's supper, it is allowed on all hands, are *positive* ordinances; and, as such, they depend for their very existence on the sovereign will of God. Consequently, which of them should be administered *prior* to the other, (as well as, to what *persons,* in what *way,* and for what *end)* must depend entirely on the will of their divine Author. His determination must *fix* their order; and his revelation must *guide* our practice.

Here, then, the question is, Has our sovereign Lord revealed his will, in regard to this matter? "To the law and to the testimony—How readest thou?"—To determine the query, we may first consider the order of *time,* in which the two positive institutions of the New Testament were appointed. That baptism was an ordinance of God, that submission to it was required, and that it was administered to multitudes, before the sacred supper was heard of, or had an existence, are undeniable facts. There never was a time, since the ministry of our Lord's forerunner commenced, in which it was not the duty of repenting and believing sinners to be baptized. The venerable JOHN, the twelve APOSTLES, and the SON OF GOD incarnate, all united in recommending baptism, at a time when it would have been impious to have eaten bread and drank wine as an ordinance of divine worship. Baptism, therefore, had the *priority,* in point of institution; which is presumptive evidence that it has, and ever will have, *a prior claim* on our obedience. —So, under the ancient œconomy, *sacrifices* and *circumcision* were appointed and practised in the patriarchal ages; in the time of Moses, the *paschal feast* and *burning incense* in the holy place, were appointed by the God of Israel. But the two former, being prior in point of institution, always had the priority in order of administration.

Let us now consider the order of *words,* in that commission which was given to the ambassadors of Christ. He who is king in Zion, when asserting the plenitude of his legislative authority, and giving directions to his ministering servants, with great solemnity says; "ALL POWER is given to me in heaven and in earth. Go ye, therefore, and teach all nations, BAPTIZING them in the name of the Father, and of the Son, and of the Holy Ghost: teaching them to OBSERVE ALL THINGS WHATSOEVER I HAVE COMMANDED YOU."[1] Such is the high commission, and such the express command, of Him who is LORD OF ALL, when addressing those that were called to preach his word, and administer his institutions. —Here, it is manifest, the commission and command are, first of all *to teach;* then what? To *baptize?* or to *administer the Lord's Supper? I* leave common sense to determine. And, being persuaded she will give her verdict in my favour, I will venture to add; A limited commission includes *a prohibition* of such things as are not contained in it; and positive laws imply their *negative.* For instance: When God commanded Abram to circumcise all his *males,* he readily concluded, that neither circumcision, nor any rite of a similar nature, was to be administered to his *females.* And,

---

[1] Matt. xxviii. 18, 19, 20.

as our brethren themselves maintain, when Christ commanded that *believers* should be baptized, without mentioning any others; he tacitly prohibited that ordinance from being administered to *infants;* so, by parity of reason, if the same sovereign Lord commanded, that believers should be baptized—baptized *immediately* after they have made a profession of faith; then he must intend, that the administration of baptism should be *prior* to a reception of the Lord's supper: and, consequently, tacitly *prohibits* every unbaptized person having communion at his table.

The order of administration in the *primitive* and *apostolic practice,* now demands our notice. That the apostles, when endued with power from on high, understood our Lord in the sense for which we plead, and practised accordingly, is quite evident. For thus it is written; "Then they that gladly received his word were"—what? admitted to the Lord's table? No; but "BAPTIZED. And the same day there were added unto them about three thousand souls. And they continued stedfastly in the apostles doctrine and fellowship, in breaking of bread and in prayer."[2] —Now, in regard to the members of this first Christian church, either our opponents conclude that they were all baptized, or they do not. If the latter, whence is their conclusion drawn? Not from the sacred historian's narrative. For thence we learn, that they whose hearts were penetrated by keen convictions, were *exhorted* to be baptized—that they who gladly received the truth were *actually* baptized—and that they who were baptized, and they only, for any thing that appears to the contrary, were *added* to the church. Either, therefore, our brethren must, in this case, infer without premises and conclude without evidence; or they must have recourse to some divine declaration, not contained in this context. But, in what book, in what chapter, in what verse, is any declaration found, relating to this church at Jerusalem, that can warrant such a conclusion? —If, on the other hand, our brethren allow, that

---

[2] Acts ii. 41, 42.

all the members of this truly apostolic church were baptized; then, either they consider the constitution of it, in that respect, as expressive of the mind of Christ, and as a model for succeeding churches, or they do not. If the former, either Jesus Christ discovered some defect in that plan of proceeding, and, in certain cases, countermanded his first order, or the conduct of our brethren must be wrong; they admitting persons to communion, who, on their own principles, are not baptized. But if they do not look upon this apostolic precedent, as expressive of the mind of Christ, and as a pattern for future imitation to the end of the world; they must consider the apostles, either as ignorant of our Lord's will, or as unfaithful in the performance of it.

Consequences these, which cannot be admitted, without "greatly prejudicing the honour and interest of true religion, and not a little contributing to the cause of infidelity:" for which reason they will, no doubt, be abhorred by all our brethren.

Again: It is manifest from that first and most authentic history of the primitive Christian church, contained in the Acts of the apostles; that after sinners had received the truth and believed in Jesus Christ, they were exhorted and commanded, by unerring teachers to be baptized without delay. For thus we read; "Repent and BE BAPTIZED every one of you" —When they believed Philip, preaching the things concerning the kingdom of God, and the name of Jesus Christ, they were *baptized,* both men and women —And Philip said, "If thou believest with all thy heart, thou mayest. And he answered and said, "I believe that Jesus Christ is the son of God. And he commanded the chariot to stand still: and they went down both into the water, both Philip and the eunuch, and he *baptized* him—And was *baptized,* he and all his straightway—Many of the Corinthians, hearing, believed, and were *baptized*—And now, why tarriest thou? ARISE AND BE BAPTIZED—Can any man forbid water, that these should not be baptized, which have received the Holy Ghost, as well as we? And he COMMANDED them to be *baptized* in the name of The Lord."³ —Hence it is abundantly evident, that baptism, in those days, was far from being esteemed an indifferent thing; and equally far from being deferred, till the Christian converts had enjoyed communion at the Lord's table for months and years. Yes, it appears with the brightest evidence, that a submission to baptism was the *first,* the very *first* public act of obedience, to which both Jews and Gentiles were called, after they believed in Jesus Christ. And it is equally clear, from the last of those passages here transcribed, that the highest evidence of a person's acceptance with God, though attended with the baptism of the Holy Spirit in the bestowal of miraculous gifts, was so far, in the account of Peter, from superseding the necessity of a submission to the ordinance of baptism; that he urged the consideration of those very facts, as a reason why they who were so blessed and honoured should submit to it *immediately.* Consequently, while our brethren revere the authority by which the apostles acted, and while they believe that infant sprinkling is not baptism; they are obliged, in virtue of these ancient precedents, and by all that is amiable in a consistent conduct, to admit none to communion at the Lord's table, whom they do not consider as really baptized according to the command of Christ. —Nor have we the least reason to believe, that the apostles were invested with *a discretional* power, to alter our Lord's institutions as they might think proper; either as to mode, or subject, or their order and connection one with another. No; they never pretend to any such power; they utterly disclaim it. Let us hear the declaration of one, as the language of all, and that in regard to the sacred supper. "I have RECEIVED OF THE LORD, that which also I delivered unto you." And again, relating to his doctrine in general, when writing to the same people and in the same epistle, he says: "I delivered unto you THAT WHICH I ALSO RECEIVED."⁴ The apostles, being only *servants* in the house of God, had no more authority to

---

³ Acts ii. 38, viii, 12, 37, xvi, 33, xviii, 8, xxii, 16, x, 47.
⁴ I Cor. xi. 23, xv. 3.

alter or dispense with an ordinance of Jesus Christ, than any other minister of the word. Their apostolic gifts and powers did not at all invest them with a right of *legislation* in the kingdom of their divine LORD. They were still but *stewards;* as *such* they claimed regard from the churches, in which they laboured and to which they wrote: at the same time freely acknowledging, that it was their indispensable duty to "be found faithful" in the whole extent of their office; they being accountable to the great Head of the church. They acted, therefore, in the whole compass of their duty, under the command, and by the direction of the ascended Jesus. Nay, the more they were honoured and blessed by him, the more were they bound to obey the least intimation of his will.

Once more: If we regard *the different signification* of the two institutions it will appear, that baptism ought to precede. In submitting to baptism, we have an emblem of our union and communion with Jesus Christ, as our great representative, in his death, burial and resurrection: at the same time declaring, that we "reckon ourselves to be dead indeed unto sin, but alive to God;" and that it is our desire, as well as our duty, to live devoted to him. And as, in baptism, we profess to have *received* spiritual life; so in communicating at the Lord's table, we have the emblems of that heavenly food by which we *live,* by which we *grow,* and in virtue of which we hope to *live for ever.* And as we are born of God but once, so we are *baptized* but once: but as our spiritual life is maintained by the *continued* agency of divine grace and the comfort of it enjoyed by the *habitual* exercise of faith on the dying Redeemer, so it is our duty and privilege *frequently* to receive the holy supper. Hence theological writers have often called baptism, the sacrament of *regeneration,* or of *initiation;* and the Lord's supper, the sacrament of *nutrition.* —Whether, therefore, we consider the order of *time,* in which these two institutions were appointed; or the order of *words,* in the great commission given by our Lord to his ministering servants; or the order of administration in the *apostolic practice;* or the *different signification* of the two solemn appointments, a submission to baptism ought ever to *precede a* reception of the Lord's supper. Or, should any one question the validity of this inference, I would only ask; Whether, in regard to the sacred supper he might not as well deny the necessity of always *blessing* the bread, before it be broken; or of *breaking* the bread, before it be received; or of receiving the *bread,* before the *wine?* Or, by what *better* arguments, he would prove the opposite conduct, either unlawful or improper? Nay, if these *declarations,* and *facts,* and *precedents,* be not sufficient to determine the point in our favour; it will be exceedingly hard, if not impossible, to conclude with certainty, in what order any two institutions that God ever appointed, were to be administered. For, surely, that order of proceeding which agrees with the *time* in which two institutions were appointed; with the *words* in which the observation of them was enjoined; with the *first administration* of them by unerring teachers; and with their *different signification,* must be the order of *truth,* the order of *propriety,* and the order of *duty,* because it is the order of GOD. And our brethren will do well to remember, that when Paul commends the Corinthians for "keeping the ordinances AS THEY WERE DELIVERED TO THEM;" it is plainly and strongly implied, that divine ordinances are given us to *keep;* that they who keep them *as they were instituted,* are to be commended; and that they who do not *keep* them at all, or observe them in *a different order* or *manner* from that at first appointed, are worthy of censure. Nor is the order in which the two positive institutions of Jesus Christ should be administered, less clearly expressed in the New Testament, than the mode and subject of baptism. This, however, is a notorious fact, that while the *latter* have been much and warmly disputed, the *former* does not appear to have been ever called in question by the real disciples of Christ; except in the conduct of those few that plead for free communion. They, indeed, practically deny that which appears clear as the sun, to all other Christians; by frequently admitting persons to the Lord's table, and baptizing them afterwards: for they do not refuse to baptize their Pædobaptist members, if they desire it, though they may have been in fellowship with them for ten, or twenty, or fifty years. —But have not—

I appeal to the understanding and the conscience of my brethren themselves;—have not the Pædobaptists as good a warrant for their practice, as you have for inverting the *plain,* the *established,* the *divinely appointed* order, in which the two positive institutions ought to be administered? They baptize and then teach; you administer the sacred supper and then baptize. They baptize thousands whom they never admit to the Lord's table; you receive to that sacred ordinance numbers who, on your own principles, never were, nor ever will be baptized. Do they argue in defence of their practice and endeavour to prove their point, not by express commands, or plain facts, recorded in the New Testament; but by *inferences,* and that, sometimes, from such passages of holy writ, as have not, in our opinion, any relation at all to the subject? so do you. For it is not pretended, that there is any *express command* to receive unbaptized believers into communion; and as to *a plain precedent,* our brethren are equally silent. The *whole* of their arguing, therefore, must be either analogical or inferential. Yet the design of it is to shew, what is our duty in regard to *a positive* institution; an appointment about which we cannot know any thing at all, but from revelation. But what can that be in divine revelation, relating to *a positive* ordinance, which is neither commanded in a precept —a precept relating to the *ordinance* in question; nor exhibited in an example? What, I demand, can it be, or how should it direct our conduct? If our brethren's way of arguing be just, we may turn Pædobaptists at once; for it is impossible to stand our ground in a contest with them.

It would, no doubt, have been highly offensive to God, if the priests or the people of old had inverted the order appointed by him, for the administration of his own solemn appointments. For instance; first admit to the *passover,* afterwards *circumcise; burn incense* in the holy place, then offer the *propitiatory sacrifice.* This, I conceive, our brethren must allow. Have they any reason, then, to imagine, that a similar breach of order is not equally displeasing to God, under the New Testament œconomy? If not, it must be supposed, that the Most High has not so great a regard to the purity of his own worship, is less jealous of his honour, and does not so much insist on his eternal prerogative now, as he did under the former dispensation: suppositions these, which they who acknowledge his universal dominion and absolute immutability, will hardly admit.

It must, I think, be acknowledged, even by our brethren themselves, that we have as good a warrant for omitting an *essential branch* of an ordinance, or to reverse the order in which the *constituent parts* of an ordinance were originally administered; as we have to lay aside a different institution, or to change the order in which two different appointments were first fixed. And if so, were a reformed and converted Catholic, still retaining the Popish tenet of communion in *one kind* only, desirous of having fellowship with our brethren at the Lord's table; they must, if they would act consistently on their present hypothesis, admit him to partake of the *bread,* though, from a principle of conscience, he absolutely refused the *wine,* in that sacred institution. —Or, supposing, which is quite the reverse, that any of those who are in actual communion with them, finding the mastication and swallowing of solid food a little difficult, should conscientiously approve the condescending indulgence of Pope PASCHAL, in the twelfth century; who ordered, that such persons should partake only of the wines:—[5] Or, if any of their people should imagine, that the wine ought always to be administered *before* the bread; and should, from an erring conscience declare, that if the ordinance were not so administered they could not partake of it; they must, according to the tenour of their arguing, comply. They could not refuse; because the persons in question are considered, as *real believers* in Jesus Christ, and *sincerely desirous* to be found in the way of their duty, to the best of their knowledge.

The sentiment which our brethren adopt, if suffered to operate in its full extent, would exclude both baptism and the

---

[5] Dr. PRIESTLY, *on giving the Lord's Supper to Children,* page 25, 26.

Lord's supper from the worship of God. As to *baptism,* whether infant or adult, it ought never to be made a term of communion in the house of God, on the principle espoused by our opponents. For, according to them, the grand, the *only* query, that is really necessary relating to a candidate for communion, is; Has GOD received him? Is he *a believer* in Jesus Christ? And, so certain are they of this being an unerring rule, that if we dare to question a believer's right of communion, because we think he is not baptized; we might almost as well deny the doctrine of transubstantiation in the face of the Council of Trent: for we immediately expose ourselves to the dreadful censure of acting in a way, "GREATLY PREJUDICIAL to the honour and interest of true religion, and NOT A LITTLE CONTRIBUTING to the cause of INFIDELITY."[6] I think myself happy, however, that the *anathema fit* of the one, is destitute of power to enforce it; as the *opprobrious charge of* the other, wants evidence to prove it.

If, then, our brethren's grand rule of proceeding be right, we are bound to receive believers, *as such,* and have communion with them at the Lord's table, though they do not consider themselves as baptized. And here I would beg leave to ask; Whether they would receive a candidate for communion, whom they esteem as a believer in Jesus Christ, who has not been baptized in infancy; nor, looking on baptism as a temporary institution, is willing to be baptized at all? The supposition of a person, in such circumstances, applying for fellowship at the Lord's table, is far from being improbable; nay, I have known it a real fact. What, then, would our

---

[6] When I read the title of a certain publication a few years ago, I was ready to say; If the title page do not promise more than the author performs, we are now in a fair way to have INFIDELITY RUINED FOR EVER. But alas! I have since found that my expectations were too sanguine. For infidelity still exists; and the principles of it lurk in every breast, that will not allow unbaptized believers to have a right of communion at the Lord's table: of which obnoxious sentiment, almost the whole of the Christian church now is and has ever been. PACIFICUS, I presume, knows the book to which I refer; and *verbum sat sapienti.*

brethren do in such a case? As to PACIFICUS, he has informed us plainly enough what would be *his* conduct in such an instance; he pleading expressly for admitting believers of ALL *denominations* to communion at the Lord's table. Yes, the very *title* of his piece, is; "*A modest Plea for Free Communion at the Lord's table, between true believers of* ALL *denominations.*"

Nor is the title of the same plea, under the signature of CANDIDUS, any way different in its real import, for it runs thus: "A *modest Plea for Free Communion at the Lord's table;* PARTICULARLY *between the Baptists and Pœdobaptists.*" For it is manifest that the emphatical word, PARTICULARLY, if not quite impertinent, must signify, that though CANDIDUS *chiefly* defends free communion between *Baptists* and *Pœdobaptists;* yet that he is far from denying, nay, that he *really pleads* for the same free communion, with those that are neither the one nor the other. And who can they be but *Katabaptists,* or those in the same circumstances with the person in the case here supposed? So that whether they be *Quakers,* or *Catholics;* whatever their distinguishing sentiments or modes of worship may be; they consider themselves as bound to admit them to the sacred supper, if they look upon them as true believers, and they request communion with them. But as all our opponents are not entirely of their mind in this respect, I shall proceed with the argument. —If, then, they receive a person, in the supposed case, they avowedly reject baptism, as unnecessary to fellowship in a church of Christ; for if it be not requisite in *every* instance, it is not so in *any.* If they refuse him, it must be because he is not baptized; for, according to the supposition, they consider him as a partaker of divine grace and a believer in Jesus Christ. But if they reject him purely on that ground, they ought, on their Anti-Pædoptist principles, to reject *all* who have had no other than infant baptism; because they consider it as a very different thing from the appointment of Christ. Yet, they declare to all the world, every time they administer baptism on a profession of faith, to any of their Pædobaptist friends, that they do not believe infant sprinkling to be an ordinance of Christ.

It may, perhaps, be objected; "The two cases are not parallel: because the supposed candidate for communion, is not only unbaptized, but opposes the ordinance itself." True: but, admitting a small disparity, he acts on a principle of conscience: for he supposes, with the Quakers, that baptism was not intended, by Jesus Christ, as a standing ordinance in his church; though he has a very different view of the Lord's supper. And, to adopt a method of arguing used by our brethren, when pleading for free communion; What have you to do with another man's conscience, in a matter that is nonessential? To his own Master he stands or falls. He considers the Lord's supper as a very important ordinance, and longs to partake of it. And have not you told us, repeatedly, that it was designed for ALL believers; that ALL believers are capable of improvement by it; and that they have a right of communion, entirely *independent* of our judgment? Is he to be refused *one* ordinance, in the enjoyment of which he has reason to expect the presence of Christ and the blessing of heaven; merely because a sovereign God has not been pleased to shew him his duty and privilege in regard to *another?* And though you may not pay so great a regard to the reasoning of one whom you call a RIGOROUS BAPTIST, yet you cannot be deaf to the arguing of a friend, an ally, and one of the first advocates for free communion. Hear, then, I beseech you, what MR. BUNYAN says, who speaks to the following effect. None can, *"render a bigger reason than this,"* for not submitting to baptism, "I HAVE NO LIGHT THEREIN." Such a person has *an invincible* reason, *"one that all the men upon earth, and all the angels in heaven, are not able to remove. For it is* GOD *that creates light; and for him to be baptized without light, would only prove him unfaithful to his own conscience, and render him a transgressor against God."*[7] What, will you keep him from celebrating the death of his Lord, in the sacred supper, only because he does not see baptism with *your* eyes!

---

[7] BUNYAN's *Works,* Vol. I, p. 135, 136, 8vo. edit. † p. 143

An Apology for the Baptists

Consider, I beseech you, that he is, in your own judgment, a sincere, a conscientious man; that he is born of God, and fervently loves our dearest Lord. Yes, the sincerity of his heart and his disposition to obedience are such, that, could he be once persuaded of baptism being a permanent ordinance in the Christian church, he would not hesitate a moment to be baptized. Nay, he would rejoice in an opportunity of so manifesting his cordial subjection to Jesus Christ, were he convinced, that he is under an equal obligation to be baptized, as he is to receive the Lord's supper, and *that* prior to *this*. And must, after all, the bare want of a *little water* be an insurmountable bar to his having communion with you? Shall this one circumstance of water "DROWN *and* SWEEP AWAY all his excellencies; not counting him worthy of that reception that, with hand and heart, shall be given to a novice in religion, because he consents to WATER? — "Nay," NO MAN can reject him; he cannot be A MAN if he object against him; not a man in Christ; not a man in understanding.'—How unreasonable it is to suppose, that he must not use and enjoy what *he knows,* because he knows *not all!"* And it will appear yet more unreasonable when it is considered, that "baptism gives neither being nor "WELL-BEING to a church."[8] Is this your kindness to a Christian brother! Is this your charity, your candour, your catholic spirit! Away with such rigid and forbidding notions; with such an unreasonable attachment to an external rite, and let your communion be FREE INDEED? UNIVERSALLY FREE, for Quakers, for Papists, for whomsoever appears to be born of God and desires fellowship with you. For though a converted Quaker may happen to be no friend to *baptism;* and though a reformed Catholic may still be prejudiced against *wine,* at the Lord's table; yet, as both may have communion with you, in other respects, why should you object against it? Besides, do you not hope to have communion with them in heaven? On the same principle, you might refuse communion to ENOCH, or ELIJAH, or PAUL,

---

[8] BUNYAN's *Works,* Vol. I, page 134, 169, 174.

were any one of them now upon earth, if he would not submit to baptism! Were you aware how much this uncharitable and dividing spirit has a tendency to "INJURE REAL RELIGION," and how much it "CONTRIBUTES TO THE CAUSE OF INFIDELITY;" such is your veneration for the revelation of God, and such your affection for Jesus Christ, that, I am persuaded, you would *never say a word* about baptism, nay, you would *wish it out of the world,* rather than give such occasions of scandal and mischief, as you unwittingly do. For the author to whom I have just appealed assures us, and lays it down as a maxim, which you ought never to violate; that in such cases baptism, though an *ordinance* of God, "IS TO BE PRUDENTLY SHUNNED. *"Let the cry be never so loud,* CHRIST, ORDER, THE RULE, THE COMMAND, or the like; CARNALITY is but the bottom, and they are but BABES that do it; *their zeal is but a* PUFF. What shall we say? ALL THINGS must give place to the profit of the people of God; yea, sometimes *laws* themselves, for their outward preservation, MUCH MORE for godly edifying."[9] —Further; Though, in the case supposed, the candidate for communion *opposes* baptism, yet there is not so great a difference between the two instances as may, at the first view, be imagined. For, on our brethren's Baptist principles, infant baptism not being an appointment of Christ, they who have had no other are unbaptized. In this respect, therefore, the cases are parallel. Besides, they are equally unwilling to submit to what our opponents consider as the only true baptism; and are equally conscientious in their refusal. The genuine, the necessary consequence, therefore, is, (if our brethren would act consistently) they must either accept both, or neither; for, in the judgment they form of each, God has received the one, as well as the other. But, as before hinted, by the same rule that we receive *one* to communion, who *is* not baptized; who does not *consider* himself as baptized; who does not *pretend* to be baptized; we may receive *all:* for as there is but one *Lawgiver, so* there is

---

[9] BUNYAN's *Works,* Vol. I. page 136, 141, 144.

but one *law,* relating to this matter; and he who has a right to dispense with it *once,* may do so *as often* as he pleases. Consequently, the principle adopted, by those who plead for free communion, has a natural tendency to *exclude baptism* from the worship of God.

Again: Though our brethren plead, that the persons whom they receive and continue in communion with them, are, in their *own judgment,* baptized; yet we may venture to query, whether this be *always* the case. The following is a well authenticated fact. Several persons, being convinced of believers baptism, and wishing for fellowship with the people of God, related their Christian experience to a church and her pastor who practice free communion. It was agreed to receive them. But when the time appointed for their being baptized came, and the pastor was ready to administer the ordinance to them, one of them was absent; and, consequently, was not baptized with his brethren. The stated season for celebrating the death of Jesus at his own table quickly approaching, he was, notwithstanding, received into fellowship, had communion at the Lord's table, and was baptized afterwards.[10] —Now this person was *not* a Pædobaptist; this person was *not,* even in his *own judgment,*

---

[10] If I be not greatly deceived, the pastor of this church has pleaded the cause of free communion, under the name of PACIFICUS. A character, no doubt, very happily chosen, to express that peculiarly peaceful temper and admirably condescending conduct, which are so clearly displayed in this little anecdote. But, as a perfectly consistent character is hard, exceedingly hard to be found among mortals, my reader will not be much surprised if I observe; That PACIFICUS himself has failed, in *one* particular, to answer his name. Yes, he and his coadjutor CANDIDUS have, in a very *unpeaceful, uncandid* manner, charged a vast majority of their Baptist brethren, with "NOT A LITTLE CONTRIBUTING TO THE CAUSE OF INFIDELITY;' merely because they do not practise this REMARKABLY FREE COMMUNION. *Peace* and *Candour* are, indeed, very excellent things, as PACIFECUS and CANDIDUS are most amiable names; yet I would take the liberty of hinting, that *peace* and *unity,* without *truth* and *righteousness,* are an illicit combination; a wicked conspiracy against both God and man. *Amicus* PACIFICUS, *amicus* CANDIDUS, *sed magis arnica* VERITAS.

baptized, when he took a seat at the Lord's table. No; by desiring to be immersed on a profession of faith, he *declared* that he was unbaptized; *as such* he approached the holy table; and *as such* the pastor, in the name of the church, gave him the right hand of fellowship. Hence we see, that our opponents can admit such persons to the sacred supper, as *confess* themselves to be unbaptized, if occasion require; that is, if their Christian friends do not approve of the old, established mode of proceeding. —Besides, as it is not uncommon for the Pædobaptists members of those churches that practise free communion, to desire baptism upon a profession of faith, after they have been in fellowship many years; so it is probable, that some such members may be convinced, that infant sprinkling is not a divine appointment, and, consequently, that they themselves are not baptized; yet live in the neglect of baptism for months and years, having communion at the Lord's table all the while. We will, therefore, suppose an instance of this kind in that Christian community of which PACIFICUS is pastor; and that he and the church in general are acquainted with it. What, then, must be done in the case? Done? why PACIFICUS will undoubtedly remonstrate against the shameful neglect. But if his remonstrances do not produce the desired effect, what then? What? why things must remain *in statu quo*. Because PACIFICUS cannot move to have him excluded, with any appearance of candour or consistency; he openly pleading for communion with believers of all denominations. Besides, he very well knows, that his brother is as much baptized now as he was when first received into communion; and the whole that is laid to his charge relates to baptism: and to "PULL *him into the water*" will never do, whatever a *witty* and *polite* opponent may have said to the contrary.[11] Besides, as MR. BUNYAN observes, "the law is not made for a righteous man, neither to debar him from communion, nor to cast him out, if he were in."[12] So very pliable, so superlatively complai-

---

[11] Dr. MAYO, in his True Scripture Doctrine of Baptism, page 33.
[12] BUNYAN's *Works*, Vol. 1. page 134.

sant, is free communion, that it cannot bear the thought of refusing fellowship at the Lord's table to any believer, even though he consider himself as unbaptized: far less can it endure the thought of giving any one much disturbance, who has a place at the Lord's table; even though he stand convicted in the eyes of God and man, in the court of his own conscience and before the church to which he belongs, of being unbaptized, and of living in the total neglect of that divine institution.

Nor would the *sacred supper* be long practised in the church of God, or be esteemed a branch of divine worship, were the same principle applied to it and suffered to operate without restraint. Suppose, for instance, that a weak but well meaning man, is a candidate for fellowship, with a church that practises free communion; that he gives the community full satisfaction, as to his being a partaker of divine grace, and has been baptized in infancy; but, at the same time, frankly declares, "I see no propriety, nor any utility, in *receiving bread and wine,* under the notion of its being an appointment of Jesus Christ. I consider the Lord's supper as a temporary institution; intended for the Christian church in the apostolic age, as a happy mean of attaching such persons to her worship and interests, as were newly converted from the antiquated ceremonies of Judiasm, or the detestable superstitions of Paganism; and that the command to observe it, ceased long since to be obligatory. Admitting, however, that I am under a mistake in this particular; yet, as I have a natural aversion to wine,[13] and as the bread and wine are *mere emblems* of the body and blood of Christ, and the reception of them an *external ceremony; I* think it is quite sufficient for me, if admitted into your fellowship, to *behold* the bread as broken, and the wine as poured out: which may, perhaps, if there be any thing useful in those outward signs, assist my meditations on the sufferings and death of our

---

[13] BELLARMINE gives it as one reason for with-holding the cup from the laity, that *Multi abhorrent da'vine.* Apud AMESIUM. *Bell. Enervat.* Tom. III. pag. 172.

crucified Lord. But though I cannot partake with you of bread and wine, in your monthly communion; yet I should hope for advantage, great advantage, by having fellowship with you in every other public act of devotion; in the expressions of mutual, brotherly love; and in the exercise of holy discipline, according to the laws of Christ. Nor need I inform you, that it is the devotion of the *heart,* real *affection* one for another as brethren, and *a strict regard* to the moral conduct of all the members of a religious community, that are the capital things in a Christian church. And should you, for a moment, hesitate on the propriety of granting my sincere request; I would beg leave to remind you, that as being, on your principles, unbaptized, is no bar to my having fellowship with you; so your well known candour must plead in my favour with equal force, though, at present, I cannot conscientiously partake with you at the Lord's table. For what is there—I appeal to that catholic spirit, for which you are so remarkable—what is there essential to a church of Christ, in *a participation* of bread and wine, any more than in *immersion* in water? for upon your own principles, the holy supper may as well be celebrated without the *former,* as baptism can be administered without the *latter.* Or, what authority is needful for you to dispense with the Lord's supper, which is not included in that warrant by which you dispense with baptism?"

Now, in such a case, what must be done? Here is a person whom that very church considers, as a BELIEVER IN CHRIST and RECEIVED OF GOD. But this is her *grand criterion* of a qualification for church fellowship. So that if she violate, deliberately and openly violate, this *capital* rule of her conduct, she contradicts herself; she, according to her wonted application of the rule, disobeys God, and leaves free communion at the mercy of every opposer. She must, therefore, give him the right hand of fellowship; she cannot put a negative on his request, without exposing herself to those very censures which our brethren so freely pass upon us; not excepting that severest of all in which we are charged, with "NOT A LITTLE *contributing to the cause of*

An Apology for the Baptists

INFIDELITY." But this, even the *strict* Baptists will charitably suppose, she would not do on any account; and that she would be equally careful to stand clear of that keen rebuke; "Thou art inexcusable who judgeth. For wherein thou judgest another, thou condemnest thyself; for thou that judgest, doest the same things." I conclude, then, though such a proceeding would be quite novel, absolutely unexampled in the churches of Christ, and would, probably, both astonish and offend her sister communities, she must receive him. But if it be lawful in one instance, it must be so in a thousand; and, therefore, a church, might thus go on, till the Lord's supper were entirely rejected by all her members, and banished from the worship of God, as it is among the Quakers.

The church of England has justly incurred the censure of all Protestant Dissenters, for her arrogant claim of "power to *decree rites* or *ceremonies,*" in the worship of God, and of authority in controversies of faith;"[14] because such a claim infringes on the prerogative royal of Jesus Christ. But do not our brethren tacitly assume a similar power, when they presume to set aside an ordinance of Christ, or to reverse the order of divine institutions? it being demonstrable, that as great an authority is necessary to lay aside an old, established rite; or to invert the order and break the connection of several rites; as can be required to institute one that is entirely new. "For it is a maxim in law;" and holds good in divinity, "That it requires the same strength to *dissolve,* as to *create* an obligation."[15] —Such a practice, therefore, as that of our brethren, were it adopted by the Baptists in general, would render our separation from the Established Church very suspicious. It would seem like the fruit of obstinacy, rather than the effect of a tender conscience; like a determined opposition to the ecclesiastical hierarchy, more than a desire of purer worship and stricter discipline. For, while we omit a positive and plain

---

[14] ARTICLES *of the Church of England,* No. xx.
[15] BLACKSTONE's *Comment. on the Laws of England,* Vol. I. Book I. Chap. 2.

appointment of Jesus Christ, and connive at what we ourselves consider as a human invention; we have little reason to scruple the lawfulness of subscribing the Article to which I have just referred: and if we can do that, with a good conscience, we have not much reason to dissent, on account of any thing else that is required in order to ecclesiastical Conformity.[16] For if it be lawful to dispense with an appointment of God, out of regard to our *weaker brethren;* we cannot reasonably think it unlawful to practise the appointments of our National Church, out of regard to the *ruling powers; submission* to the latter, being no less plainly required, in scripture, than *condescension* to the former. And if we may safely connive at *one* human invention, so as to supersede and take place of a divine institution; why may not the Church of England make what appointments she pleases? A little reflection will convince us, that he whose authority is competent, to the setting aside, or altering, of *one* divine institution, has a power equal to his wishes—may ordain times, and forms, and rites of worship; may model the house of God according to his own pleasure. But can such an authority belong to any besides the GREAT SUPREME? No: to such an ordaining, or dispensing power, neither church nor synod, neither parliament nor conclave, neither king nor pope, has the least claim. For as the exertion of Omnipotence was equally necessary to the creation of a worm, as an angel; of an atom, as a world; so the interposition of divine authority is no less necessary to set aside, or to alter, *one* branch of instituted worship; than to add *a thousand* religious rites, or essentially to alter the whole Christian system.

Nor are those writers who have appeared in vindication of our National Establishment, ignorant of their advantage over such Protestant Dissenters as proceed on the principle here opposed. For thus they argue; "If, notwithstanding the evidence produced, that baptism *by immersion is* suitable, both to the institution of our Lord and his apostles; and was

---

[16] DISSENTING GENT. *Lett. to* Mr. WHITE, Lett. I. p. 2.

An Apology for the Baptists

by them ordained to represent our burial with Christ, and so our dying unto sin, and our conformity to his resurrection by newness of life; as the apostle doth clearly maintain the meaning of that rite: I say, if notwithstanding this, all our [Pædobaptist] Dissenters do agree to *sprinkle* the baptized infant; why may they not as well submit to the significant ceremonies imposed by our church? For since it is as lawful to *add* unto Christ's institutions a significant ceremony, as to *diminish* a significant ceremony which he or his apostles instituted, and use another in its stead, which they never did institute; what reason can they have to do the *latter,* and yet refuse submission to the *former?* And why should not the *peace* and *union* of the church be as prevailing with them to perform the one, as is their *mercy* to the infant's body to neglect the other?— "[17] I leave the intelligent reader to apply this reasoning to the case before us, and shall only observe; That if this learned writer had been addressing those Dissenters who practise free communion, his argument would have had superior force. Because our Dissenting Pædobaptist brethren believe that infant sprinkling is *real* baptism, and practise it as having the stamp of divine authority; whereas those Dissenters with whom I am now concerned, believe no such thing. They consider it as a human invention; they speak of it as a human invention; and yet receive Pædobaptists into their churches, as if they were rightly and truly baptized, according to the command of Christ. Now, as Mr. THOMAS BRADBURY observes, "There is a great difference between *mistaking* the divine rule, and totally *laying it aside.* The reason, adds, he, why we do not act as some other Christians [*i.e.* the Baptists] do, is, because we think these demands [relating to a profession of faith and immersion, as necessary to baptism] are not made in scripture."[18]

As the sovereign authority and universal dominion of God, over his rational creatures; as his absolute right, not only to

---

[17] Dr. WHITBY's Protestant Reconciler, p. 289.
[18] *Duty and Doct. of Bap.* p. 25, 26.

worship, but also to be worshipped in his *own way;* are more strongly asserted and brightly displayed in his positive institutions, than in any other branches of his worship; so, it is manifest, that we cannot disobey his revealed will concerning them, without impeaching his wisdom and opposing his sovereignty. Because a special interposition of divine authority, and an express revelation of the divine will, constitute the basis, the only basis, on which such institutions rest, in regard to their mode and subject, their order and connection one with another. Surely, then, such of our brethren who admit, as a divine institution, what they verily believe is a human invention, cannot but act an unjustifiable part. For, on their own principles, infinite wisdom chose and absolute sovereignty ordained professing believers as the subjects, and immersion as the mode of baptism: and it appears, by their frequently baptizing persons who were sprinkled in their infancy, that they look upon such a subject and such a mode of administration, as essential to the ordinance. By their conduct, in many instances, it also appears they are no less persuaded, that unerring wisdom and supreme authority united in appointing baptism to be administered prior to the Lord's supper: for, where the views and the inclinations of the candidates for fellowship with them do not interfere, they always baptize, before they admit to the holy table. Thus, then, stands the case with our brethren, in regard to the positive appointments of heaven. They are verily persuaded that the wisdom and sovereignty of God united in ordaining, that immersion should be the mode of baptism, yet they connive at sprinkling; that professing believers should be the subjects, yet they admit of infants; that baptism should be administered to a believer, before he receive the Lord's supper, and yet they permit unbaptized persons to have communion with them in that sacred ordinance. A paradoxical conduct this, which nothing, in my opinion, short of a plenary dispensing power can possibly vindicate.[19]

---

[19] Some of my readers will be pleased, I doubt not, with the following thoughts of OROBIUS, a learned Jew, on the subject of positive

An Apology for the Baptists

Again: as the sovereign will of God is more concerned and manifested in positive ordinances than in any other branches of holy worship; so it is evident, from the history of the Jewish church, which is the history of Providence for near two thousand years; that the divine jealousy was never sooner inflamed, nor ever more awfully expressed, than when God's ancient people failed in their obedience to such commands, or deviated from the prescribed rule of such institutions. The destruction of Nadab and Abihu, by fire from heaven; the breach that was made upon Uzzah; the stigma fixed and the curse denounced on Jeroboam; together with the fall and ruin of all mankind, by our first father's disobedience to a positive command, are among the many authentic proofs of this assertion. —Nor need we wonder at the divine procedure, in severely punishing such offenders. For, knowingly to disobey the positive laws of JEHOVAH, is to impeach his wisdom, or his goodness, in such institutions; and impiously to deny his legislative authority and absolute dominion over his creatures. And though the methods of

---

institutions. The ritual law depends upon the judgment of the law giver, in most cases, or whenever, as is most often the case, no foundational principle may be discerned by natural reason: but the law does not on this account obtain a lower grade of perfection, reasoning that the infinite Wisdom and Goodness of the lawgiver has been spuriously subjoined: rather he ought to be held to be of another, more sublime, order: and if this is granted, because he is most good, and because the wise God does not prescribe empty and useless laws to man: by how ever much their purpose has been concealed from us, by so much more it pertains to the secret of his divine Wisdom—so it behooves us to believe; this can not be fathomed by us, whether inquisitively or by means of philosophy, but rather it must be submitted obediently to His power, by which we might prove our love and the reverence due to the highest Creator: all things which he sets forth for our observation are worthy of His infinite wisdom, and surely they are good, and most perfect so we believe with our whole heart: be it that He can, if he wishes, impart these things, or on another occasion, keep them hidden: and this is the mark of a more distinguished obedience, that is, to observe these things, rather than the things which we discover by our reason to have been ordered by God: and if men are able to know these things, although God has not bidden it, and are able to observe them, it shall be the case that most often they shall have been done without any regard to Him." Apud STAPFEXUM, Institut. Theolog. Polm. Tom. III. Chap. XI. § 238.

Providence, under the gospel œconomy, are apparently much more mild and gentle, in regard to offenders in similar cases; yet our obligations to a conscientious and punctual obedience are not in the least relaxed. For that divine declaration, occasioned by the dreadful catastrophe of Aaron's disobedient sons, is an eternal truth, and binding on all generations; "I WILL BE SANCTIFIED IN THEM THAT COME NIGH ME."[20] When God speaks, we should be *all attention;* and when he commands, we should be *all submission.* The clearer light which God has afforded, and the richer grace which Christ has manifested, under the present dispensation; are so far from *lessening,* that they evidently *increase* our obligations to perform every divine command relating to Christian worship. For, certainly, it must be allowed, that they on whom greater favours are bestowed and higher honours conferred, are so much the more obliged to revere, love, and obey their divine Benefactor. And, as a certain author justly observes, "To take advantage of dark surmises, or doubtful reasoning, to elude obligations of any kind; is always looked upon as an indication of a dishonest heart."[21] Accursed, then, is the principle, and rebellious is the conduct of those professors, who think themselves warranted, by the grace of the gospel, to trifle with God's positive appointments, any more than the priests or the people were of old. For whether JEHOVAH lay his commands on Gabriel in glory, or on Adam in paradise; whether he enjoin the performance of any thing on Patriarchs, or Jews, or Christians, they are all and equally bound to obey, or else his commands must stand for nothing. Neither diversity of oeconomy, nor difference of state, makes any alteration in this respect: for we must be absolutely independent of God, before our obligations to obey him can be dissolved. But as the former is impossible, so is the latter.[22]

When I consider myself as contending with PACIFICUS, I

---

[20] See Levit, x. 1, 2, 3.
[21] Dr. OSWALD's *Appeal to Common Sense, p.* 21.
[22] *WITSII Miscel. Sac.* Tom, L Lib. II. Dissert. II § 3.

cannot but esteem it a happiness to find, that my reasoning, in the last paragraph, is very strongly supported by the following quotation; which is taken from a little publication that received something more than a bare *imprimatur,* from Mr. JOHN RYLAND. And as PACIFICUS pays an uncommon regard to Mr. RYLAND'S judgment, in matters of this kind; I shall not be thought assuming, if I summons his attention to what the latter avows, as expressing his own opinion. The passage to which I refer, is this: "The ordinances of the gospel are established by the authority of Christ, as king and supreme law-giver in his church; they are particularly enforced by his own example, and his will expressly declared: and as they have no dependance on any circumstances, which are liable to vary in different countries or distant periods of time, it necessarily follows that the primitive model of administration *should be strictly and conscientiously adhered to.* No pretence to greater propriety, nor any plea of inconveniency, can justify our *boldly opposing the authority of* GOD *by the alteration of his law,* and substituting a human ordinance instead of a divine. In a former dispensation in which the ritual was numerous and burdensome, the great JEHOVAH was particularly jealous of his honour as *Supreme Lawgiver,* and looked upon the *least innovation as* A DIRECT OPPOSITION OF HIS AUTHORITY. Moses, we are informed, was *admonished of God to make all things according to the pattern shewed him in the mount.* And those unfortunate youths who presumed to alter the form of his religion, and worshipped him in a way he had not commanded, fell under the severest marks of his displeasure; which shews that he looked upon the least innovation in the *ceremonial part* of his precepts, as an *impious* and *daring opposition and contempt* of his authority, and as deserving of peculiar and distinguished vengeance, as a direct and open violation of the moral law. And as the great KING of the universe required such strictness and punctuality, and insisted on such scrupulous exactness in the performance of the minutest rite belonging to the *legal* dispensation; it would be extremely difficult to assign a reason why he should be more *lax* and *careless,* and allow *a greater scope* to human discretion under the *Christian* [œconomy]. The *greater light* which shines in our religion, the *small number* and *simplicity of* its ceremonials, and the *end* and *design* of those institutions being more clearly revealed; are reasons which *strongly indicate the contrary.* And if it be further observed, that the religion of JESUS is particularly calculated to *set aside worldly wisdom and mortify the pride of man;* it cannot, without great absurdity, be supposed, that the sublime Author of it *will dispense with the performance of his positive laws, or admit of the least variation,* to honour that wisdom, or indulge that pride which the whole scope of his gospel hath a manifest tendency to abase. Surely then it behoves Christians, in an affair of such consequence, to be circumspect and wary; it will certainly be well for them, if they can give a good account of their practice, and a satisfactory answer to that important question, *Who hath required this at your hand?*"[23] —Had MR. RYLAND only *recommended* that little piece to the public, which contains this excellent passage, he would certainly have deserved my sincerest thanks. For the quotation produced may be justly considered as *a compendious answer* to all that PACIFICUS has wrote, and to all that he can write, in defence of free communion, so long as he professes himself a Baptist. Whether he will make a reply to the animadversions of *my* feeble pen, I cannot pretend to say; but I think he will hardly have courage, in any future publication on the subject before us, openly to confront and attack his *dearest* and *most intimate* friend, Mr. RYLAND.

Though the Lord's supper is a positive institution of Jesus Christ, and though we cannot know any thing at all about it, but what we learn from the New Testament; yet our brethren make, not the word of revelation, but the measure of light and the dispositions of a candidate for fellowship, the rule of admission to it. —This appears from hence. A person applies to one of their churches for communion in the ordinances of God's house; the pastor of which community, and a great

---

[23] *Six Views of Believ. Bap.* p. 17, 14, 19, 20.

An Apology for the Baptists

majority of its members, are Baptists. He gives reason of the hope that is in him, to general satisfaction. His moral conduct is good, and his character amiable. The pastor in the name of the church, desires to know, what are his views of *baptism.* He declares himself a Pædobaptist; says he was baptized in his infancy, and is quite satisfied with it. Now, neither the pastor, nor the generality of his people, can look upon this as baptism; but consider it as an invention of men, and a corruption in the worship of God. Consequently, they would be glad if his views, in that respect, were otherwise. They agree, however, to receive him into communion. And why? Because they believe that Christ commanded, or that the scriptures warrant, *infant sprinkling?* No such thing. Because the New Testament plainly informs them, that *unbaptized converts* were admitted to the Lord's table in the apostolic churches? Not in the least. Because Jesus Christ has expressly granted them *a dispensing power,* in regard to baptism? They disclaim any such grant.[24] What, then, is the ground on which they proceed? Why, truly, the candidate *believes, is fully persuaded,* that infant sprinkling is real baptism; and has been informed, that he was actually sprinkled in the first stage of his life. On this foundation they admit him to the Lord's table: and, which is very remarkable, they receive him with a cordial good will, to have him baptized afterwards, if ever he discover an inclination towards it. Their charity forbids them treating a Christian as *unbaptized,* if he do but *heartily believe* himself to be baptized. As if that could not be wrong, which a sincere disciple of Christ firmly concludes to be right! Or, as if we were bound, in certain cases, practically to allow that to be right, which we are fully persuaded is really wrong! —But

---

[24] The church of Rome frankly acknowledges, by her delegates assembled in the Council of Trent, that our sovereign Lord, when he instituted the holy supper, administered it in both kinds, and that it was so administered for some time; she, however, expressly claims an authority to dispense with that order. Now, though I would by no means insinuate, that our brethren are equally culpable with that mother of abominations; yet it may admit of a query, whether, in this particular, she be not more *consistent with herself,* than they? *Concil. Trident. Sess. XXI.* Cap. I, II, III.

might not the pastor of such a church, on the same principle and with equal countenance from the scripture, *baptize a* person desirous of it, without a profession of faith, and without any evidence that he is a believer in Jesus Christ? For, as PACIFICUS and CANDIDUS argue, in regard to baptism, Who is to be the judge of what is, or is not *faith?* Most certainly *every man for himself,* and not one for another; else we destroy the "right of private judgment, and go about to establish a Popish infallibility against the liberty of the gospel. I have no business with any man's conscience but my own, unless in endeavouring, in a proper manner, better to instruct it where it appears to be wrong. If my Pædobaptist brother is satisfied in his *own mind* that he is rightly baptized [or truly converted] he is so to himself.'— What is there in a false persuasion, relating to baptism, that merits the regard of a *church;* any more than in a deception about faith and conversion, to deserve the connivance of a *minister?* for the self-deception is supposed to be as *real* in the one case, as in the other; though the state of the two candidates, and the danger attending their respective mistakes, are undoubtedly very different. If, notwithstanding, our sovereign Lord has not virtually forbidden us to baptize any without a profession of faith, what right have we so to limit the administration of that ordinance? And if our divine Lawgiver has tacitly prohibited unbaptized believers approaching his table, by what authority do we admit them? Now I appeal to the reader, I appeal to Christians in general, whether there be not as much evidence in the New Testament, that baptism was administered by the apostles to such whom they did not consider *as believers* in Jesus Christ; as there is to conclude, that they received any to communion, before they considered them *as baptized* believers. It is not the measure of a believer's knowledge, nor the evidence of his intregrity; nor is it the charitable opinion we form about his acceptance with God, that is the rule of his admission to the sacred supper; but the *precepts* of Jesus Christ, and the *practice* of the apostolic churches. To depart from this only rule of our conduct, through ignorance, is a culpable error; and knowingly to deviate from it, is nothing short of rebellion against the sovereign majesty of Zion's King.

To dispense with the positive appointments of Jesus Christ, or to reverse the order of their administration, in condescension to weak believers and with a view to the glory of God, cannot be right. For, as an eminent author observes, "They must be evasions past understanding, that can hold water against a divine order—God never gave power to any man, to change his ordinances, or to dispense with them—God is a jealous God, and careful of his sovereignty! Tis not for any inferior person to alter the stamp and impression the prince commands. None can coin ordinances but Christ; and, till he call them in, they ought to be current among us."[25] — To which I may add the testimony of another learned writer, who says, when speaking of baptism; "As the salvation of men ought to be dear unto us; so the glory of God, which consisteth in that *his orders be kept,* ought to be *much more dear.*"[26] —Yet here, I humbly conceive, our brethren are faulty. For what is *dispensing* with a positive appointment, but laying it aside, or conniving at a neglect of it, on such occasions in which it was commanded to be administered? Now, on their Antipædobaptist principles, they admit unbaptized persons to the Lord's table; many of whom are never baptized. In regard to such, therefore, they lay entirely aside, they annul the ordinance. That they *reverse the order* of two positive institutions, is equally clear; numbers of those whom they admit to the Lord's table having communion with them in that ordinance for many years, before they are baptized. And that this very singular conduct proceeds from a regard to the edification of sincere, but less informed believers, and in hopes that God will be glorified by it; they often assert. Dispense with a divine institution, for the edification of weak believers! Invert the order of God's appointments and break his positive laws, with a view to his glory! Theological paradoxes these, which seem to border on that hateful,

---

[25] CHARNOCK's *Works,* Vol. II, p. 763, 773, 774, Edit. †
[26] CARTWRIGHT, in WALL's *Hist. Inf. Bap.* Part I. Chap. 13.

Antinomian maxim; "Let us do evil that good may come." A position, which the pen of inspiration execrates; which every virtuous mind abhors. —But that no pretence of doing honour to God, not any plea of being useful to men, can possibly deserve the least regard, if the measures which must be pursued to obtain the end interfere with the divine revealed will, we learn from various facts recorded in the Bible. Uzzah, for instance, when he put forth his hand to support the tottering ark, thought, no doubt, he was doing honour to him who dwelt between the Cherubim over the mercy-seat; and, at the same time, as that sacred coffer was of the last importance in the ancient sanctuary, he shewed an equal regard to the edification of his fellow worshippers, by endeavouring to preserve it from injury. But, notwithstanding this fair pretext; nay, though the man after God's own heart saw little amiss in his conduct; (perhaps, thought he deserved praise) as the ark, with all that pertained to it, and its whole management, were of *positive* appointment; he, whose name is JEALOUS, was greatly offended. The sincere, the well meaning man, having no command, nor any example for what he did; fell under JEHOVAH's anger and lost his life, as the reward of his officiousness. And as the Holy Ghost has recorded the fact so circumstantially,[27] we have reason to consider it as a warning to all, of the danger there is in tampering with *positive* ordinances; and as a standing evidence, that God will have his cause supported and his appointments administered, IN HIS OWN WAY. —The case of Saul, and the language of Samuel to that disobedient monarch, inculcate the same truth. "The people, said Saul to the venerable prophet, took of the spoil, sheep and oxen—to *sacrifice unto the Lord thy God* in Gilgal. And Samuel said, Hath the Lord as great delight in burnt-offerings and sacrifices, as *in obeying the voice* of the Lord? Behold, *to obey is better* than sacrifice, and *to hearken* than the fat of rams. For rebellion is as the sin of witchcraft, and stubbornness is

---

[27] 2 Sam. vi. 1-7.

as iniquity and idolatry."[28] Remarkable words! The king of Israel, we find, pleaded a regard to the worship and the honour of God. The cattle were spared, that JEHOVAH's altar might be furnished with plenty of the finest sacrifices. But Samuel soon overruled this fair pretence. He quickly informed the infatuated prince, that obedience to divine appointments, especially in such duties as depend entirely on an *express* command (as the utter destruction of Amalek did, and as communion at the Lord's table now does) is better in the sight of God, than hecatombs of bleeding sacrifices, or clouds of smoking incense: and, consequently, better than a misapplied tenderness to any of our fellow creatures, or a misguided zeal to promote their peace and edification. At the same time the prophet assures him, that when the Most High commands, nothing can excuse a non-performance: because disobedience to *a plain, positive, known* command, is justly classed with *idolatry* and *witchcraft*.

A very sensible writer, in the conclusion of a discourse upon this passage, observes; That we may learn from this text, what are the true characteristics of acceptable obedience. "It must be *implicit;* founded immediately on the authority of God. We must not take upon us to judge of the moment and importance of any part of his will, further than he hath made it known himself. It is a VERY DANGEROUS THING for us to make comparisons between one duty and another; especially with a view of *dispensing* with any of them, or *altering their order,* and substituting one in another's place.'—Another "character of true obedience is, that it be *self-denied* and *impartial;* that it be not directed or qualified by our present interest —It is too common, that our own interest both points out the object, and assigns the measure of our obedience; and in that case, it does not deserve the name of obedience to God at all. When the Christian is devoted to God, ready at his call, and equally disposed to any employment assigned him in providence, he then may be said indeed to do his will.'—It must "be *universal,* without any

---

[28] I Sam. xv. 21, 22, 23.

exception. Saul, and the children of Israel, had complied so far with the order given them, that the greatest part both of the people and substance of Amalek was destroyed; but he stopped short, and knowingly left unfinished what had been enjoined him by the same authority."[29]

When a Pædobaptist applies for communion with Baptists, he acts upon a persuasion that he has been rightly and truly baptized: for there is reason to believe, that the generality of our Pædobaptist brethren would start at the thought of partaking at the Lord's table, while they consider themselves as unbaptized. Consequently, when our opponents admit one of them to communion, they confirm him in what they consider as a false presumption, and practically approve of what, at other times, they boldly pronounce *a human invention, a tradition of men,* and *will-worship;* for such infant sprinkling must be, if not a divine appointment. Nor can they exculpate themselves, in this respect, unless they were *professedly* to receive him, *as unbaptized.* Because he *considers* himself as baptized; he *desires communion* as baptized; nor has he any idea of sitting down at the Lord's table, *as unbaptized;* well knowing, that such an attempt would be contrary to the apostolic pattern, and to the sense of the Christian church in general.

That circumcision was, by divine command, an indispensable qualification, in every male, for a participation of the Jewish passover, and communion in the sanctuary worship, is generally allowed. And though I am far from thinking that baptism came in the place of circumcision, as many of our Pædobaptist brethren suppose; yet that the former is equally necessary to communion at the Lord's table, under the Christian œconomy, as the latter was to every male, in order to partake of the paschal feast, and to unite in the tabernacle service, I am fully persuaded. Nor is my opinion singular. It has been the sense of the Christian church in every age; and, excepting those Baptists who plead for free communion, it is the voice of the Christian world in general at this day. —I do

---

[29] Dr. WITHERSPOON's *Practic. Disc.* Vol. I, p. 335, 336

not find that the necessity of circumcision, for the purpose just mentioned, was ever controverted, either by the ancient or modern Jews. We will suppose, however, for the sake of argument, that it was disputed in the Jewish church; and that, amidst a great variety of interesting intelligence, which the Rabbinical writers pretend to give, concerning ancient customs and ancient disputes, they are found to speak as follows: "In the days of our master, Moses, disputes arose about the nature and necessity of circumcision: that is, whether the ancient rite was to be performed on the *foreskin,* or on *a finger;* and, whether it was an indispensably requisite qualification, in every male, for a seat at the paschal feast and admission to the sanctuary worship. The generality of our fathers maintained, that no male, though a son of Abraham; that no Gentile, though he might acknowledge and serve Abraham's God; had any claim to communion in those joyful and solemn services, if he was not circumcised according to the divine command. Others contended, with no less assurance, that circumcision being only an *outward sign* of what is internal and spiritual; every male, whether a descendent from the loins of our father Abraham, or one of the Gentile race, who knew and feared the God of Israel, had an undeniable claim to fellowship, though it were not the foreskin of his flesh, but a finger that was circumcised. The latter asserted, with great confidence, that the holy blessed God having accepted such; as plainly appeared by their having the internal and spiritual circumcision; it would be *absurd* and *uncharitable* to refuse them communion. And, when disputing with their opponents, they would with an air of superior confidence demand; Will *you* reject from fellowship those whom GOD has received! —Absolutely reject those who have *the thing signified,* barely because, in your opinion, they want the *external* sign! —Those who possess the *substance,* perhaps, to a much greater degree than yourselves, merely because they want the *shadow!* What, will you refuse communion to a brother Israelite, or a pious Gentile, in the *tabernacle* here below, with whom you hope to enjoy everlasting fellowship in the *temple* above! Strange attachment to the manner of performing an external rite!—

Besides, great allowances must be made for the prejudices of education. These our brethren whom you reject, as if they were Heathens, as if they were absolutely unclean; have been educated in the strongest prejudices against what we think the true circumcision. They have been taught from their earliest infancy, that though our fathers, for a few centuries after the rite was established, generally circumcised the foreskin; yet that the part on which the ceremony was first performed, is by no means *essential* to the ordinance. And, therefore, as various inconveniences were found to attend the mode of administration then generally practised; instead of cutting off the *praeputium,* many began to circumcise *a finger;* which has been the custom in some of our tribes ever since, and which, they strenuously plead, is not forbidden by any divine revelation. This, we readily acknowledge, is a mistake; nor dare we, on any account, imitate their proceedings in that respect: because, with us, there is no doubt, that the God of our fathers ordained it otherwise. But yet, as all have not the same opportunities of information, nor an equal measure of light; and as our brethren are verily persuaded that they have been circumcised according to the divine command; (for if they were not, they would readily comply with our mode of proceeding) it is our indispensable duty to receive them in love, and not harrass their minds with "doubtful disputations" about a matter that is not essential. For we all worship the *same God;* and so far as his *moral* worship is concerned, in the *same way;* though we happen to differ about an external rite, that is by no means essential, either to spiritual worship here, or to the salvation of our souls hereafter. Besides, though it be admitted that the divinely appointed mode of administering the sacred rite is of *some* importance; yet it must be admitted, that the edification of such as truly fear God, is of *infinitely greater importance.* But, if you exclude them from the solemn sanctuary worship, you debar them from a capital mean of their spiritual benefit. You should also consider, who is to be the judge of what is, or is not, the true circumcision. Every man, most certainly, must judge for himself, and not one for another; else you destroy the right of private judgment; you invade the sacred prerogative of conscience; and tacitly advance a claim to infallibility. If your brethren, who circumcise a finger instead of the part appointed, be satisfied in their *own minds,* they are circumcised *to themselves;* and while the answer of a good conscience attends it, God will and does own them in it, to all the ends designed by it; so that while they consider it as laying them under the same obligations to holiness of heart and life, as we consider our circumcision to do us, why should you not have fellowship with them? —Nor are you sufficiently aware, how *much you injure* the cause of real religion, and *promote* the baneful interests of infidelity, by being so strict and rigid. Were you to be more candid and charitable, in regard to this matter, it might be expected that numbers of our brethren, who, it must be allowed, administer this rite in a very improper manner; would cordially unite with us, and, in time, utterly renounce their mistake. We should also have reason to hope, that many of our Gentile neighbours, who *detest circumcision,* as performed by us, might become proselytes to the Jewish religion, and worship the most high God in fellowship with us. But so long as you insist, not only on the rite itself, (for that we ourselves are not willing to give up entirely) but on that *mode* of administration which is so obnoxious to them, as indispensably necessary to communion with you; it will be, not only a *wall of partition* between us and them, but *a bone of contention* among the chosen tribes themselves. Consequently, it must impede, greatly impede, the exercise of that love to God and that affection for man, which are of much greater importance than the most accurate performance of a merely external rite.'

Now supposing our brethren in the course of their reading to meet with such an account, what would they think of it? What would they say? They would, undoubtedly, suspect the truth of the whole. They would consider it as a Rabbinical fable. But how would their indignation rise, were the fabulous narrator to proceed and assert; "That Moses and Joshua, warmly espousing this latter opinion, added much to its credit!" This, they would say, is absolutely incredible, and a vile aspersion on the characters of those illustrious saints. Had Nadab and Abihu been mentioned as the abettors of this unscriptural practice, there would have been less reason to deny the truth of the whole relation; because they were guilty of innovating in the worship of God, and were awfully punished for it. But thus to represent the most pious, exemplary, and excellent men in all the Israelitish camp, is beyond the bounds, not only of credibility, but also of decency. Reflections of this kind, I am persuaded, they would readily make, were they to find such a narration in the Talmud, or in any Rabbinical author. —And now give me leave again to remind them; That, according to the judgement of the Christian world in general, circumcision was not more necessary for all the males, who desired communion at the paschal supper and in the solemn services of the tabernacle, than baptism is to fellowship in the Christian church and a seat at the Lord's table—That there is, on their own principles, a wider and a more material difference between baptism, as now administered to infants, and baptism, as appointed by Jesus Christ; than there would have been, between cutting off the foreskin, and circumcising a finger: because the latter would have been *circumcision,* and the circumcision of *a proper subject* also, though not of the part required; but *sprinkling,* whether infants or adults, is no more *baptism,* in their account, than it is *immersion* — And that, had any members of the ancient synagogue introduced, or admitted, such an alteration as that supposed; they might have defended it on the same general grounds, and with much greater plausibility, in several respects at least, than our brethren can the practice of free communion. For I appeal to my reader, whether the Pentateuch of Moses and the scriptures of the prophets do not say as much of the one, as the evangelical history and the writings of the apostles do of the other?

Paul, when meeting with certain disciples at Ephesus, desired to know, whether they had received the Holy Ghost since they believed. To whom they answered, "We have not so much as heard whether there be any Holy Ghost." On which the apostle put the following question: "Unto what then were ye *baptized?*" And they said, "Unto John's baptism." From which it plainly appears, that as these persons professed to be disciples of Jesus Christ, Paul *took it for granted* they had been baptized. For his query is not, Have you been *baptized?* But, *"Unto,"* or into, *what* then were ye baptized?" He inferred their baptism from their profession: and he had reason so to do. For he well knew, that the first administrator of the ordinance required a submission to it, of all that brought "forth fruits meet for repentance;" that the apostolic ministry demanded the same act of obedience, from all that believed in Jesus Christ; and that the administration of baptism is a part of the ministerial office, being strictly connected with teaching the disciples of Christ, "to observe all things which he has commanded." And, as an author before quoted, justly remarks: "We find that the preachers of the gospel always did it, and the people who gladly received the word, desired it. How indifferent soever it appears to some in our days, yet the grace of God *never failed* to stir up an early regard to it in times of old."[30] But though the great apostle, when meeting with those disciples at Ephesus, made *no doubt* of their having been baptized, even before they informed him of it; yet our brethren's conduct forbids us forming the same conclusion, with equal ease and certainty, concerning all that are in communion with them. Nay, PACIFICUS himself, for instance, does not consider *all* that belong to his community as *baptized* persons. So that were the apostle's query addressed to him, with a little alteration; *Into what* were the Pædobaptist members of your church baptized? His answer, as a Baptist, must be; Into—

---

[30] Mr. BRADBURY's *Duty and Doct. Bap.* p. 50.—In a preceding page of the same Treatise, he says; "I hear there are several who suppose that baptism is only the work of those that are grown up, and yet neglect it themselves. My brethren, whoever is in the right in *doctrine,* you are quite wrong in *practice.* Do not despise the advice of one who has more value for your happiness, than he has for his own opinion. I will give you it in the words of Ananias; *Why tarriest thou? Arise and be baptized, washing away thy sins, and calling on the name of the Lord.'* See, as above, p. 16.

NOTHING: for I do not consider them as baptized at all. — Paul, as before observed, when correcting some irregularities in the church at Corinth, says: "We have no such custom, neither the churches of God." From which we may safely conclude, that whatever is now practised in the worship of God, which has not a precedent in the conduct of the apostles and the primitive churches, is unwarrantable. And as our opponents believe that Paul knew of no such custom as infant sprinkling; as it also appears from his language to the disciples at Ephesus, that he knew of no such custom, among believers, as deferring a submission to baptism for months and years; so we have reason to infer, that he was equally ignorant of any such custom, as admitting unbaptized believers to the Lord's table. Nay, our brethren do not pretend that he knew of any such thing. But, however, it was in the apostolic age, which is now hoary with great antiquity, that bold perverter of gospel truth, SOCINUS, introduced the custom of receiving unbaptized persons to communion; many of his pupils adopted it; and our brethren continue it: which reminds us of the old saying, *The times are changed, and we are changed in them.*

Once more: Either Jesus Christ has informed us in the New Testament what baptism *is,* and what is *requisite to communion* at his table, or he has not. If the *former,* we cannot admit any thing *as* baptism, which we believe is not so; nor receive any to communion, but those whom we consider as qualified according to his directions, without violating our allegiance to him as the King Messiah, and rebelling against his government. If the *latter,* there is no judge in Israel, and every one may do that which is right in his own eyes, in regard to these institutions. Yes, if our Lord instituted baptism, and left it undetermined *how* and to *whom* it should be administered; if he appointed the sacred supper, without *characterizing* those who are to partake of it; his ministering servants have a discretional power to administer them how and to whom they please. And if so, our brethren may sprinkle or immerse, infants or adults, just as their own conveniency and the dispositions of their people require. Nay, they may proceed a step further, and admit the infant offspring of their Pædobaptist friends to the Lord's table; which was the general custom for several ages, in the apostate state of the Christian church, and, as a learned author informs us, is yet the practice of "very near *half* the Christians in the world.[31] Then their communion would be *free indeed;* entirely free from the shackles of divine commands, and from the untoward influence of apostolic precedent.

---

[31] Dr. WALL's *His. Infant Bap.* Part II. Chap. IX.

SECTION IV.

Several Passages of Scripture considered, which our Brethren produce in favour of their Sentiments.

The cause which our brethren undertake to defend, is denominated by them, FREE COMMUNION. That communion, then, for which they plead is *free*. But here I beg leave to ask, From *what?* The restraints of *men?* that is laudable freedom. From the laws of *Heaven?* that were a licentious liberty. Absurd, in theory; impossible, in fact. It never was, it never can be the case, that God should institute a positive ordinance of divine worship, as the Lord's supper undoubtedly is; and leave it entirely to the discretion of men, to whom it should be administered. Free—for *whom?* For every one that will? This they do not pretend. For all who imagine themselves believers and qualified for it? This they dare not assert. For, withstanding all their candour and all their Catholicism, they do not consider every one that thinks himself a believer and desires communion, as fit for it. Hence it is, they ask a reason of the candidate's hope, and take the liberty of judging for themselves, what his hope and the ground of it are. They think it their duty to inquire, in what light he views himself, and what he believes concerning the Son of God. And if, in their judgment, he be not converted to Jesus Christ, they put a negative on his request; even though they feel an affection for him, as a moral, a sincere, a well meaning man. Here, then, is another and a great limitation; a boundary which it would not be lawful to set, if a positive institution were not concerned, and if such limitation were not fixed by the divine Institutor. By parity of reason, therefore, if our Lord has given any other direction, relating to the same ordinance, it should be regarded with equal reverence and equal punctuality.

What, then, is the *freedom* for which they plead? Why, that Baptist churches should admit Pædobaptists into communion with them. In other words, That they should admit believers to the Lord's table, whom they consider as unbaptized. A very extraordinary position this! Such, however, is *free communion:* in defense of which, several pamphlets have, of late, been published. And who can tell, but some of our brethren may so improve on the doctrine of liberty, in regard to divine institutions of a positive nature, as to favour us, ere long, with a PLEA FOR FREE BAPTISM? —With a dissertation, intended to prove the lawfulness, and, in some cases, the necessity, of administering baptism to such whom we consider as unbelievers? especially, if the candidates for that ordinance be firmly persuaded in their own minds, that they are believers in Jesus Christ. At the same time declaring, that it will be at the peril of greatly dishonouring real religion, "AND NOT A LITTLE CONTRIBUTING TO THE CAUSE OF INFIDELITY," if we refuse. —But let us now briefly consider what they say, in defense of their hypothesis. They argue, from *several passages* of scripture; from the *temper* required of real Christians, in their behaviour one towards another; and object against us our *own conduct,* in another respect.

The principal passages adduced from holy writ, and here to be considered, are the following: "Him that is weak in the faith receive ye, but not to doubtful disputations—for God hath received him—Receive ye one another as Christ also received us, to the glory of God—God, which knoweth the hearts, bare them witness, giving them the Holy Ghost, even as he did unto us: and put no difference between us and them, purifying their hearts by faith —I am made all things to all men, that I might by all means save some."[1] —On which passages we may observe in general; Whatever their

---

[1] Rom. xiv. 1, 3, and xv. 7. Acts xv. 8, 9, 1 Cor. ix. 19-23.

meaning may be, except our opponents can make it appear, that they contain the grant of *a dispensing power* to gospel ministers and churches; that is, unless these divine declarations authorize the ministers and churches of Christ, to set aside an ordinance of his, or to invert the order of its administration, as they may think proper; they are far from answering the exigencies of their case, or serving the purpose for which they are cited.

Again: The texts produced do not so much as *mention* communion at the Lord's table, nor appear to have the least reference to it. No; the Holy Ghost has other objects in view, in each of the contexts. And as these are the principal passages to which our brethren appeal in proof of their point, we may take it for granted, that better are not to be found; and, consequently, as a tacit acknowledgment, that positive proof is wanting. But if it be allowed, that there is no *positive* evidence in favour of their practice, it amounts to a concession that there is *no proof* at all. Because nothing of a positive and ritual nature can be proved a duty, or agreeable to the will of God, merely by our own reasonings; nor by arguments formed on moral precepts and general rules of conduct. For if once we admit any thing in the worship of God, as a duty, that is grounded, either on far-fetched inferences from particular declarations of scripture, in which the holy penmen do not appear to have had the least thought of the matter in question; or on our own ideas of expediency and usefulness, we shall not know where to stop. On this principle, a great number of ceremonies were brought into the church of Rome, and might be introduced by us, though not one of them could stand that divine query, "Who hath required this at your hand?" As it cannot be proved, by the deductions of reason, that it is the duty of any man to eat bread and to drink wine, as a branch of divine worship, but only from the testimony of God; so, what he has revealed in regard to that matter, is our only rule in all that relates to the Lord's supper.[2] Consequently, as these passages say

---

[2] *Plain Account of Bap. in a Course of Lett. to Bp.* HOADLY, page, 127,

nothing at all about baptism, nor about communion at the Lord's table, either *strict,* or *free;* they have little pertinency of application, or force of argument in them.

Our brethren maintain, when disputing with Pædobaptists, that the New Testament knows no more of infant *baptism,* than it does of infant *communion:* and that many of the arguments adduced in defence of the former, will equally apply to the latter.[3] Here they seem quite confident that they have truth and fact on their side. But might not Dr. PRIESTLEY, for instance, who maintains both, retort; "That sacred code of Christian worship to which you appeal, knows as much of our sentiments and practice as it does of yours? Produce your warrant from those heavenly institutes contained in the New Testament, for admitting a believer to the Lord's table, in a church of Christ, while that very church considers him as unbaptized; and you shall not wait long for equally authentic evidence, that infant baptism and infant communion have the sanction of divine authority. You frequently assert, that our arguments formed on the covenant made with Abraham; on the rite of circumcision; on the holiness attributed, by Paul, to the children of believers; and on several other passages of scripture, in defence of an infant's right to baptism, are inconclusive; not only because that sacred institution is not expressly mentioned in any of those places; but also because, in your opinion, nothing short of an express command, or a plain, apostolic example, can suffice to direct our practice, in the administration of ordinances that are of a positive kind. Yet, when pleading for free communion, you adopt this very method of arguing, and think it quite conclusive: otherwise you never would appeal with such confidence as many of you do, to the passages now

---

128.
[3] Dr. PRIESTLEY is also of the same opinion. For he says, "No objection can be made to this custom, [*i.e.* of giving the Lord's supper to infants] but what may, with *equal force,* be made to the custom of baptizing infants.' And he informs us, that "Infant communion is to this day the practice of the Greek churches, of the Russians, the Armenians, the Maronites, the Copts, the Assyrians, and probably all other oriental churches.' *Address to Protest. Dissent. on giving the Lord's Sup. to Children,* p. 28, 31.

produced."⁴—But let us take a more particular view of the passages now before us.

The converted Romans were commanded by Paul, to "receive them that were weak in faith, as God and Christ had received them." And we are plainly informed, that the persons intended were such, as had not a clear discernment of their Christian liberty, in regard to *the eating of meats* forbidden by the ceremonial law, and the *observation of days*, that was of old required by it. But what has this to do with *free communion?* Is there no way of "receiving him that is weak in faith," but by admitting him to the Lord's table? Must the exhortation to receive a Christian brother, be confined to that single instance of true benevolence? Or, is our so doing the capital idea and the primary sense of the precept, in any of Paul's writings? He says, in this very epistle, "I commend unto you Phoebe our sister, that *ye receive her* in the Lord." Was her admission to the holy table the principal thing that he desired of the believing Romans, on her account? No; he evidently had something else in view; something that would manifest their love to a disciple of Christ, much more than barely permitting her to have communion with them in the sacred supper. For he immediately adds; "And that *ye assist her* in whatsoever business she hath need of you."⁵ Or, did he solicit admission to the Lord's table, for himself and his fellow ministers, among the Corinthians, when he said; *"Receive us;* we have wronged no man; we have corrupted no man; we have defrauded no man?"⁶ Or, for Epaphroditus, when he thus expressed himself to the Phillippians; *"Receive him,*

---

⁴ In things of external appointment, says Dr. SAMUEL CLARKS, and *mere positive* institution, where we cannot, as in matters of *natural* and *moral* duty, argue concerning the natural reason and ground of the obligation, and the original necessity of the thing itself; we have nothing to do but to obey the positive command. God is infinitely better able than we, to judge of the *propriety* and *usefulness* of the things he institutes; and it becomes us to *obey* with humility and reverence. *Expos. of Church Catech.* p. 305, 306. Edit 2.
⁵ Rom. xvi. 1, 2.
⁶ 2 Cor. vii. 2.

therefore, in the Lord, with all gladness, and hold such in reputation?"[7] Or, for Onesimus, when he said to Philemon; "*Receive him,* that is, mine own bowels—*Receive him* as myself?"[8] Or, was communion at the Lord's table the principal thing which the apostle John had in his eye, when he said; "We therefore ought to *receive such,* that we might be fellow helpers to the truth?"[9] It is, I will venture to affirm, a much greater thing to receive either a weak or a strong believer, in the sense of these exhortations; than merely to grant him a place at the Lord's table. Why, then, should our brethren plead for it as they do, as if it were the grand criterion of our acknowledging Pædobaptists to be real converts, and of our love to them, as such?

Besides, the faith of a sincere believer may be as weak, and require as much forbearance, in regard to the holy supper, as in respect of baptism. A reformed and really converted Catholic may desire fellowship with us, who still retains the Popish error or communion in one kind only: but are we obliged by this apostolic precept, to mutilate the sacred ordinance in condescension to his weakness? —To embrace the weak, as well as the strong believer, in the arms of Christian affection, is a capital duty of the moral law. To bear with a brother's infirmities, and to "forbear one another in love," are certainly required by that command which says; "Thou shalt love thy neighbour as thyself;" and would have been our duty, if neither baptism, nor the Lord's supper, had ever existed. But are we to regulate our conduct, in the admission of persons to *a positive* institution; to one which depends entirely on the *sovereign pleasure* of God, by inferences drawn from the *general* and *natural* duties of the moral law? Were the precepts of that eternal law ever considered by the priests or the people of old, as the rule of administering positive institutions? Had they not another system of precepts, *express precepts,* intended for that purpose? and was not such a ritual absolutely necessary?

---

[7] Philip. ii. 29.
[8] Philem. 12, 17.
[9] 3 John 8.

Supposing, however, that there were no way of receiving one that is weak in faith, but by admitting him to the Lord's table, this text would be far from proving what our opponents desire; unless they could make it appear, that the persons of whom the apostle immediately speaks, were *not members* of the church of Rome, when he gave the advice. There being disputes among the believing Romans, about the eating of meats and the observation of days, affords no proof, nor any shadow of proof, that they had not communion together at the Lord's table. —But admitting that to be a fact, of which there is not the least evidence, the conclusion drawn from the passage would not be just, except it were also proved, that the "weak in faith" were *unbaptized;* or, at least, so considered by their stronger brethren; for *that is* the point in dispute between us. But that Paul considered the believing Romans to whom he wrote, as baptized Christians, is allowed by all, so far as I have observed, who have no hypothesis to serve, by admitting a contrary supposition.[10] For, as Dr. GOODWIN observes, "He argues from the known and generally received profession and practice of *all* Christians. *Know ye not that so many of us as were baptized;* That is, that whoever of us that profess baptisim into Christ, profess baptism into his death, as the thing intended by it. The *us,* there, is the generality of Christians, distinguished usually by that word from Heathens: as, Rom. xiv. 7. I Cor. viii. 6. *To us there is but one God,* &c. That is, we Christians profess all,

---

[10] The SOCINIANS, the QUAKERS, and Mr. BUNYAN agree, in referring us to Rom. vi. 3. I Cor. 14, 15, 16. and Gal. iii. 27, with a view to serve their several hypotheses, which all unite in greatly depreciating the ordinance of baptism. The words of Mr. BUNYAN, when speaking of the apostolic times, and mentioning these three passages, are as follows: "That all that were received into fellowship were even then baptized *first,* would strain a weak man's wit to prove it, if arguments were closely made upon these three texts of holy scriptures.'—And, a few pages after, when arguing from the *second* of these apostolic testimonies, he says; "By this negligent relating who were baptized by him [Paul,] he sheweth, that he made *no such matter* of baptism, as some in these days do; nay, that he made NO MATTER AT ALL thereof, with respect to church communion.' *Works, Vol. I.* p. 135, 144.

and generally so. And his scope being to shew, how sanctification flows from being in Christ; his argument is drawn from a general principle of the US of Christians—So that this expression, *as many of us,* imports not, as if some were, and some not, baptized; for then his argument of sanctification had not been binding to the generality of Christians, which, it is evident, it was in his intention: but it imports the contrary, that *as many as were Christians,* WERE ALL BAPTIZED, and were taught this to be the meaning of that great point and principle of religion, that as they were baptized into Christ thereby, so also into his death."[11]

"But God receives the weak in faith; and we are expressly commanded to receive one another, not to doubtful disputations, but as Christ hath received us to the glory of God should be." Granted: yet permit me to ask, Is the divine conduct, is the favour of God, or the kindness of Christ, in receiving sinners, the rule of our proceeding in the administration of positive institutions? Whom does God, whom does Christ receive? None but those that believe and profess faith in the Lord Messiah? Our brethren will not affirm it. For if divine compassion did not extend to the dead in sin; if the kindness of Christ did not relieve the enemies of God; none of our fallen race would ever be saved. But does it hence follow, that we must admit the unbelieving and the unconverted, either to baptism, or the holy table? Our gracious Lord freely accepts all that desire it and all that come; but are we bound, by his example, to receive every one that solicits communion with us? Our opponents dare not assert it. For though the Great Supreme is entirely at liberty to do as he pleases, to reject or accept whom he will; yet it is not so with his ministering servants and professing people, in regard to the sacred supper. No; it is their indispensable duty and their everlasting honour, to regard his revealed will and obey his righteous commands. The divine *precepts* contained in the Bible, not the divine *conduct* in the administration of a

---

[11] *Works,* Vol. IV. *On the Government of the Churches of Christ,* p. 30. Vid. HOORNBEEK. *Socin. Conf.* Tom. III. p. 431, 432.

sovereign Providence, are the only rule of our obedience in all things relating to positive institutions.

Besides, gospel churches are sometimes obliged, by the laws of Christ, to exclude from their communion those whom he has received; as appears from the case of the incestuous person in the church at Corinth. And have those churches that practice free communion never excluded any for scandalous backslidings; whom, notwithstanding, they could not but consider as received of Christ? What, do they never exclude any from fellowship with them, but such of whom they have no hope! I cannot suppose, nor will they affirm any such thing. But if there may be a just cause of *excluding* such from communion whom God has received, though at present in a state of backsliding; why may there not be a sufficient reason of *refusing* communion to some, whom we look upon as the objects of God's peculiar favour? Is there not as great a degree of disapprobation discovered in the *former* case, as there is in the *latter?* and is not the word of God our only rule in both cases? It is not every one, therefore, that is received of Jesus Christ who is entitled to communion at his table; but such, and only such, as revere his authority, submit to his ordinances, and obey the laws of his house.

And are our opponents verily persuaded that *baptism is* a matter of "doubtful disputation"? Why, then, do they not both sprinkle and immerse, infants and adults, that they may be sure, in some instances at least, of doing that which is right? Why so *positive,* on certain occasions, when they preach, or publish, upon the subject? That it has been, and is *disputed,* must be allowed: and so has almost every article of the Christian faith; especially such articles as appear to us the clearest and of the greatest importance. Witness those doctrines relating to the Trinity and the Deity of Christ; his vicarious atonement and original sin. These have been much oftener disputed, in ancient and modern times, than the mode and subject of baptism. —And has not almost every branch of Christian worship been disputed? The supper of our Lord has been much more frequently controverted, between Papists and Protestants, between Lutherans and Calvinists, than ever baptism was among any professors of Christianity. Yet who, among our brethren, will dare to assert, that no Catholic, who ever disputed for with-holding the cup from the people, was received by Jesus Christ? For that matter is not so *clear,* but real Christians *may possibly* differ in their judgment and practice concerning it. Nay, such doubts and difficulties are there attending the holy supper, that BELLARMINE assures us, we cannot certainly determine from the express words of scripture only, *what there was* in the cup, before our Lord blessed it; whether a little *wine,* or wine mixed *with water,* or *strong drink,* or *water only.*[12] And will PACIFICUS, or CANDIDUS, dare to assert, that the zealous Cardinal was absolutely rejected of God? No; they cannot do it, without violating the amiable import of their several names. —The Quakers also, have disputed the whole ordinance, and every pretence to it, as well as baptism, out of their assemblies. But is it lawful hence to conclude that they are all rejected of Jesus Christ? So true are those words of PACIFICUS and of CANDIDUS, his colleague: "The points in baptism [and the Lord's supper, about which we Papists and Lutherans, Quakers, Pædobaptists, and Antipædobaptists] differ; are not so *clearly stated* in the Bible (however clear to us) but that even sincere Christians *may* mistake them." We may, therfore, henceforth consider baptism and the Lord's supper, the only positive institutions in the Christian church, as justly reckoned among those things that are of "doubtful disputation:" but whether they are to have the *first* place among Paul's settling of accounts, I leave our brethren to determine. For to them the honour of classing a positive institution of Christ among things AMBIGUOUS, is undoubtedly due; since all besides themselves look upon it as *evident,* either, that baptism is an *indifferent* thing, as SOCINUS, and some of his followers;[13] or, that it should be

---

[12] Quid in calice fuerit ante consecrationem, an *vinum* parum, an winum *aqua mixtum,* an *sicera,* an *aqua sola,* ex Sola Scriptura expresse non habetur. Apud VOSS. *Theses Theolog. p. 486.*
[13] Baptismum aquaerem indifferentem effestatuinus. THEOPH.

entirely laid aside, as the Quakers; or, that it is *a term of communion,* which has ever been the opinion and practice of the Christian church in general. One step further, and it will be matter of doubtful disputation, whether both the positive appointments of our divine Lord should not be quite discarded. For, that baptism ought to be administered prior to the sacred supper, is as clearly revealed, as that either of them was intended for the use of believers in all succeeding ages.

Our honest friend, BARCLAY, when taking notice of those disputes which have been about the sacred supper, says; "The ground and matter of their contest lies in things extrinsic from, and unnecessary to, the main matter. And this has been often the policy of Satan, to busy people and amuse them with *outward signs, shadows,* and *forms;* making them contend about it [them]; while, in the mean time, the *substance* is neglected—for there have been more animosities and heats about this *one particular,* and more bloodshed and contention, than about *any other.* And, surely, they are little acquainted with the state of Protestant affairs, who know not, that their contentions about this have been more hurtful to the Reformation, than all the opposition they met with from their common adversaries."[14] He advises, therefore, to give up the ordinance for the sake of peace, and as the only effectual way of securing tranquility in the church of God. —So the Socinians maintain, that we may either administer or dispense with baptism, as occasion requires. For, says VOLKELIUS, "As all other indifferent things may be either used or omitted, as charity shall direct; even so *baptism,* if the honour of God and the love of our neighbour demand it, seems at sometimes absolutely necessary to be administered, in order to avoid giving offence."[15]

NICHOLAID. *De Eccles.* p. 22. Apud HOORNE. *Socin. Conf.* Tom. III. p. 250.
[14] BARCLAY's *Apology,* p. 455, 456.
[15] Ut omnia alia adiaphora-pro eo ac charitas praefscribit, jam ufurpari, jam omitti poffunt: ita et baptismus iste, divinergloriae ratione, et proximi amore postulante, ut nimirum scandalum vitetur, adhibendus interdum

And as the Socinian pleads for the administration of baptism, on some occasions; so Mr. BUNYAN strongly asserts the necessity of its omission, on others. These are his words: "If water baptism, as the circumstances with which the churches were pestered of old, trouble the peace, wound the consciences of the godly, dismember and break their fellowships, it is, although an ORDINANCE, for the present, to be PRUDENTLY SHUNNED."[16] —How slight the barrier, how thin the partition, between free communion and Katabaptism! Thus baptism is treated, not as *a branch of divine worship,* but as *a tool of human convenience;* not as *an ordinance of* GOD and a mean of his glory, but as *a happy expedient* in the hands of men, to secure that applause of their fellow mortals;—that applause which is considered as due to persons of a condescending, candid, catholic spirit. If the omission of it would give offence, let it by all means be administered: and if the use of it would be attended with the same inconvenience, lay it aside and say not a word about it. Such is the advice of VOLKELIUS and BUNYAN.

The reader, I take it for granted, can hardly forbear observing, what an admirable method is here proposed by this triumverate, VOLKELIUS, BARCLAY, and BUNYAN, in order to promote and secure peace among Christian brethren. A method, it must be confessed, that is at once very comprehensive, quite expeditious, and extremely easy. *So comprehensive,* that it will apply to every case: *so expeditious,* that any controversy may, by the happy expedient, be finished in a trice: and so *easy,* that every one may have the benefit of it. Were it universally known and universally pursued, there would soon be no disputes at all, either about truth or duty. For the whole process consists in this; If divulging a truth believed, or practising a duty required, should at any time give offence, or be likely so to do; keep the former to yourself, let the latter alone, and all shall be well. But how much more agreeable to scripture, is the following maxim of a celebrated author; "The appointment of God, is

---

plane videtur. Apud HOORNE, ubi supra, p. 266.
[16] *Works, Vol.* I p. 136.

the *highest law,* the SUPREME NECESSITY; which we ought rather to obey, than indulge popular ignorance and weakness."[17] —From the manner of reasoning sometimes used by our opponents, and by those three authors to whom I have just referred; one would imagine, that Socinians, Quakers, and those Baptists who plead for free communion, were almost the only persons in the Christian world, that exercise a proper degree of candour towards professors of other denominations, or have a due regard for peace among the people of God: but whether this be a fact the reader will judge.

But is it possible for our opponents to imagine, that Paul intended to place *baptism* on the same footing with certain *meats* and *days;* the former of which were forbidden, the latter enjoined, by the God of Israel, under the Jewish œconomy? What, baptism become an article of "doubtful disputation" in so early a day! If, on the other hand, that inspired writer had so *thought* of baptism when he mentioned "doubtful disputations;" if what he there says about matters then in dispute, regard things that belonged to an *antiquated ritual;* what authority have our brethren to put baptism on a level with them? Or where is the force of their argument from the passage?

"Receive ye one another, as Christ also hath received us." These words have been understood in a larger sense than that for which our brethren plead. For some Pædobaptists have concluded from hence, that it is the indispensable duty of a particular church to allow communion to *all* that desire it: taking it for granted, no doubt, that none would request the privilege but those who were baptized. This, the reader will certainly think, is FREE communion. And, indeed, if this text warrant our brethren's practice, I see but little objection against its being understood in such a latitude of signification. But, in opposition to such a sense of the

---

[17] Dei ordinatio nobis summa lex, suprema necessitas, cui potius parendum, quam populari ignorantiae et infirmitati indulgendum. TURRETTINI *Inst. Theolog.* Tom. III. Loc. XIX. Quaest. XIV. § 14.

passage, a Pædobaptist writer observes; "This inference is glaringly forced and wide, discovering their ignorance of the true meaning and design of the text who make it. The apostle is not here speaking of ADMISSION TO CHURCH-MEMBERSHIP at all;—nor does he consider those to whom he writes in the precise light of members of the church universal; but as members of *a particular* church, or body; among whom there was some difference of opinion about meats, &c. which was like to break their communion together, as is plain from the preceding chapter. The apostle sets himself to prevent this, and to accomplish a reconciliation. And, after a number of healing things, he concludes with these words, *Receive ye one another.* That is, ye who are saints at Rome, who have agreed to walk together in the commandments and ordinances of the Lord Jesus; ye who are professedly united in church-communion, receive ye one another in love, as becometh saints, united in one body for mutual benefit. Bear ye one another's burdens: watch over and admonish one another in love, notwithstanding of some difference in sentiment among you: as to the eating certain meats and regarding certain days, let not that difference make any breach in your communion together as a church of Christ. But let the strong bear with those that are weak, and the weak not be offended with the liberty of the strong. Judge not one another uncharitably, but let brotherly love continue. —This is precisely the apostle's meaning; as will appear to those who look impartially into the connection of his argument; and by no means serves the purpose for which the objectors bring it."[18]

And supposing our brethren to argue from this passage only by way of *analogy,* their inference is equally weak, and their conclusion palpably forced: there being a great, an essential difference, between eating or not eating of certain meats, in the apostolic times; and our being baptized or not baptized, prior to communion at the Lord's table. For though, while the

---

[18] SMITH's *Compend, Account of the Form and Order of the Church,* p. 109, 110.

ceremonial law was in force; the Jews were obliged to abstain from prohibited meats; yet our opponents will not affirm, that their observance of a negative precept was intended by the Eternal Sovereign, to answer similar purposes with the ordinance of baptism, as appointed by Jesus Christ. The *latter is* a solemn institution of divine worship: but can this be asserted of the *former?* Baptism was instituted prior to the sacred supper; was commanded to be administered to professing believers, before they approached the holy table; and, in the apostolic age, for aught appears to the contrary, was constantly administered to believers previous to their having communion in the Christian church. But can similar things be affirmed concerning that abstinence from certain meats, which were forbidden under the Jewish œconomy?

To conclude my remarks on the text before us, and to illustrate the passage. CANDIDUS, we will suppose, is the pastor of a Baptist church, and that a dispute arises among his people, about the lawfulness of *eating blood,* or any thing *strangled.* The controversy rises high, and is carried on with too much heat of temper. Each party is blamed by the other; the one, as judaizing; the other, as violating a plain apostolic precept. —A report of this comes to IRENAEUS. Concerned and grieved at such contentions and such a breach of brotherly love, in a once flourishing and happy church, he writes them a friendly letter; in which he bewails their hurtful contests, gives them his best advice, and, among other things, he says: "Him that is weak in the faith, receive ye, but not to doubtful disputations. For one believeth that he may eat all things: another who is weak, eateth herbs. Let not him that eateth, despise him that eateth not: and let not him which eateth not, judge him that eateth; for God hath received him. Wherefore receive ye one another, as Christ also received us to the glory of God."—In a while after, this healing epistle is published, and read by many. In the perusal of which, some suspect, and others conclude, that the persons exhorted to mutual forbearance, had *not communion* one with another, under the pastoral care of CANDIDUS; and that they who are stiled, "weak in faith," had never been *baptized.* Nay, some assert, that the mere *want of baptism,* in the opinion of IRENAEUS ought never to be objected against any that are candidates for communion at the Lord's table; nor ever be made a bar to fellowship in a church of Christ. Yet Irenaeus was never known, in any instance, to give the least cause for such a suspicion—The application is easy: I shall, therefore, only ask, Whether, in the supposed case, such inferences would be genuine and just, or forced and unnatural? And, whether they who drew them might not be suspected of being, either very fanciful and weak, or as acting under the power of some prejudice? The reader will pardon my prolixity on this passage when he considers that our opponents lay a very great stress upon it.

By the text produced from the Acts of the apostles we learn, that "God is not respecter of persons;" that he, as an absolute sovereign, bestows his favours on Jews and Gentiles without any difference. But will our brethren infer from hence, that they whose honour and happiness it is to be his obedient servants, are entirely at liberty to receive to communion at the Lord's table all that believe, without any difference? Can they justly conclude, that because JEHOVAH dispenses his blessings as *he* pleases, they may administer, or omit, his positive institutions as *they* please?

Once more: They produce, as much in their favour, the declarations of Paul to the church at Corinth,[19] relating to his own conduct. And what do we learn in general from this passage, but that he, out of his great concern for the good of mankind, and his abundant zeal for the glory of God, was willing to do, or forbear, any thing that was lawful, in order to gain an impartial hearing from both Jews and Gentiles wherever he came? I said, any thing *that was lawful:* the rule of which is the divine precept, or some example warranted by divine authority. Nor can we view these words in a more extensive sense, without implicitly charging the great apostle with *temporizing,* and highly impeaching his exalted character. —But what has this text, any more than the

---

[19] I Cor. ix. 19-23.

An Apology for the Baptists

former, to do with the administration, or laying aside, of positive institutions? It was the duty of Aaron, as well as of Paul, and of us, to seek the happiness of all his fellow creatures and the honour of God, to the utmost of his ability. But was this general obligation the rule of his performing the solemn sanctuary services on the great day of atonement? Could he conclude from hence, that if the dispositions of the people required it, he was at liberty to *omit* any of the sacred rites, or to *transpose* the order in which JEHOVAH commanded they should be performed? —If, however, any of our opponents can make it appear, that this passage really has a relation to the positive appointments of Christ; it must be considered as the MAGNA CHARTA of a dispensing, priestly power, in regard to those institutions. And, consequently, if our brethren can make out their claim to the honour, free communion will be established with a witness. In such a case it might be expected, that the next advocate for it, when citing the passage, would comment upon it, and address us in the following manner: "This text is full to my purpose. It contains all I could wish, when contending with my stricter brethren. For hence it is plain, that I am at liberty, perfectly at liberty, to omit, or administer, the ordinance of baptism, just as the dispositions and choice of my hearers may render it convenient. Yes, ye STRICT BAPTISTS! this admirable text authorizes me, in condescension to the weakness of my sincere hearers, not only to receive Pædobaptists into communion; for that is a mere trifle, with such a patent of church power in my hand; but also Semi-Quakers, who reject baptism; and converted Catholics, who mutilate the sacred supper; yea, to baptize the infant offspring of any who shall desire it. By doing of which, I hope to obtain the favour of many respectable Pædobaptists, who have been extremely offended by that rigid and forbidding conduct, for which you are so notorious. Yes, and by dispensing with baptism, in some instances, I doubt not but I shall convince many of the utility and necessity of it; which you know, would be an admirable method of producing conviction, and bring great honour to my cause. This text—what shall I say? this wonderfully comprehensive passage, gives me a discretionary power to do *just as I please* in the house of God, in regard to baptism and communion.'

Section V.

The Temper required of Christians one towards another, not contrary to our Practice —Our Conduct freed from the Charge of Inconsistency —No Reason to exalt the Lord's Supper, in point of Importance, as greatly superior to the Ordinance of Baptism.

Nothing is more common with our opponents, when pleading for free communion, than to display the excellence of Christian charity; and to urge the propriety, the utility, the necessity of bearing with one another's mistakes, in matters that are *non-essential;* in which number they class the ordinance of baptism. From considerations of this kind, they infer the lawfulness of admitting Pædobaptists to communion with them. —*Not-fundamental—non-essential.* These negative epithets they frequently apply to *baptism.* And might they not be applied, with equal propriety, to the *Lord's Supper?* But in what respect is a submission to baptism non-essential? To our justifying righteousness, our acceptance with God, or an interest in the divine favour? So is the Lord's supper; and so is every branch of our obedience. For they will readily allow, that an interest in the divine favour, is not *obtained* by the miserable sinner, but *granted* by the Eternal Sovereign— That a justifying righteousness is not the *result* of human endeavours, but the *work* of our heavenly Substitute, and *a gift* of boundless grace—And that acceptance with the high and holy God, is not on conditions performed *by us,* but in consideration of the *vicarious obedience* and *propitiatory sufferings* of the great Immanuel. Nay, since our first father's apostasy, there never was an ordinance appointed of God, there never was a command given to man, that was intended to answer any such end.

Baptism is *not fundamental; is not essential.* True; if limited to the foregoing cases. But are we hence to infer, that it is not necessary on *other accounts* and in *other views?* If so, we may alter, or lay it aside, just as we please; and, on the same principle, we may dismiss, as *non-essential,* all order and every ordinance in the church of God.

Is not the institution of baptism a branch of divine worship? And is not the administration of it, prior to the Lord's supper, essential to that order in which Christ commanded his positive appointments to be regarded? Nay, PACIFICUS himself tacitly allows, that the practice of free communion is a breach of order in gospel churches. For, in answer to an objection of this kind, he says; "Though it be admitted that the order of the churches is of *great* importance, yet is must be admitted that the edification of Christians and their obedience to the acknowledged command of Christ to all his disciples, "Do this in remembrance of me," are points of *infinitely greater* importance; the least therefore ought to give way to the greatest."—The order of churches, then, is of *great* importance, PACIFICUS himself being judge; and CANDIDUS, his colleague, acknowledges, that it "is of *some* importance." Nor could they deny it, without impeaching the wisdom, or the goodness of Christ, as Lord over his own house; and opposing that injunction of the Holy Ghost, "Let all things be done decently and in order." And as the Divine Spirit requires the observation of order in the church of God, so Paul commends the Corinthians for "keeping the ordinances *as he delivered them;"* and expresses a holy joy, on "beholding the order" of that Christian church which was at Colosse. But that order which the great Lord of all appointed, and in the practice of which the good apostle sincerely rejoiced, our brethren, it seems, consider as *a mere trifle*—as comparatively *nothing.* For what is any thing that has only *a finite* importance attending it, when compared with that which is of *infinite* importance? On such a comparison, it sinks into littleness; it is lost in obscurity. Yet thus our opponents venture to state the comparative worth of church order, and the edification of individuals. —But give me leave here to inquire. Whether the primitive order of gospel churches can be detached from the legislative authority of Jesus Christ? And, whether the exercise of that authority can be considered as having no connection with his honour? To answer these questions in the negative, free communion itself can hardly demur. Consequently, a breach of that order which Christ appointed, as king in Zion, must be considered as an opposition to his crown and dignity; and *his honour* is of much greater importance than the edification of believers. For our Jesus and our Lawgiver is JEHOVAH; between whose *honour* and the *happiness* of sinful worms, there is, there can be no comparison. For the latter is only *a mean,* whereas the former is the *grand end,* not only of a church state, but of the whole œconomy of providence and grace. I may, therefore, venture to retort the argument; Though it be admitted, that the edification of Christians is of *great* importance; yet it must be allowed, that the honour of our divine Sovereign is of *infinitely greater* importance; and, consequently, the primitive order of gospel churches should be observed.

Again: Are not my readers a little surprised at the reasoning of our opponents which I have just produced? Are they not ready to say, with some of old, "May we know what this new doctrine is?" What, reverse the order of churches, appointed by God himself, with a view to edification! Dispense with a positive ordinance of heaven and break a divine command, under the fair pretence of promoting obedience to Christ! Our brethren, in pleading for free communion, bring "certain strange things to our ears; we would know, therefore, what these things mean," and how they may be supported. For if we are obliged, in some cases, to set aside an ordinance of divine worship, and to break *a positive* command, in order that certain individuals may perform *another positive* injunction of the great Legislator; the laws of Christ are not half so consistent as Paul's preaching; which "was not yea and nay," as those would be, if the argument here opposed were valid. —Nor have we, that I remember, any thing like a parallel case, either in the Old or the New Testament. We find, indeed, an instance, or two, of positive and typical rites giving way to natural necessities and moral obligations, when the performance of both was impracticable; as, when David ate of the shew bread, without incurring a divine censure: but we have no example of a positive ordinance being set aside, in favour of any one's *ignorance,* or *prejudice* against it, that he might be edified by submitting to *another positive* institution, of which he desired to partake. That maxim of our Lord, "I will have mercy and not sacrifice;" is, therefore, totally inapplicable in the present case.

Mr. BUNYAN, I know, strenuously pleads the neglect of circumcision by the Israelites in the wilderness, while they attended on other positive appointments of God, as arguing strongly for free communion: but he seems to have forgotten that the omission of which he speaks, is keenly censured by the Holy Ghost. The uncircumcised state of the people, whatever might be the occasion of it, is called, *a reproach,* "the reproach of Egypt;" which odium was rolled from them on the borders of Canaan, and the place in which they were circumcised was called by a new name, to perpetuate the memory of that event.[1] Now, as that neglect of the Israelites was *a breach* of the divine command, *a reproach* to their character as the sons of Abraham, and stands *condemned* by the Spirit of God; it cannot be pleaded in defence of a similar omission, with the least appearance of reason. And if so, I leave our brethren to judge whether it can be imitated "without injuring the honour of true religion, and promoting the cause of infidelity." —Nor is that other instance, which the same author produces, relating to the feast of passover, in the reign of Hezekiah, any more to his purpose. For though many of the people were not "cleansed according to the purification of the sanctuary;" though they did eat the passover otherwise than it was written, and were accepted of God; yet Hezekiah was so conscious of those irregularities, that he deprecated the divine anger, saying, "The good Lord

---

[1] Josh. v. 9.

pardon every one that prepareth his heart to seek God, the Lord God of his fathers, though he be not cleansed according to the purification of the sanctuary. And the Lord hearkened to Hezekiah, and *healed* the people."[2] With what shadow of reason, then, or of reverence for God's commands, can any one plead this instance in favour of free communion? What, shall *a deviation* from the divine rule, in the performance of sacred rites—a deviation that is acknowledged as *criminal* before the Lord, and for which *pardon is* requested, be adduced as a precedent for the conduct of Christians! What would our brethren, what would Mr. BUNYAN himself have thought of Hezekiah and his people, had they taken the liberty of repeating the disorderly conduct, whenever they celebrated the paschal anniversary? Taken the liberty of transgressing the divine rule, because Jehovah had *once* graciously pardoned their irregularities, and accepted their services, on a similar occasion? Would they not have been chargeable with bold presumption, and with doing evil that good might come? —But, I return to our *candid* and *peaceful* opponents.

Disturb and break the order of churches, an order established by Jesus Christ, with a view to edification! The reader will here observe, the *order* intended is that of administering baptism to believers, *before* they are admitted to the Lord's table. That infraction of order, therefore, for which they plead, is no other than *setting aside* an ordinance, allowed to be divine; and this to promote the edification of those concerned. Very extraordinary, I must confess. For professors in every age, have been more disposed to *increase* the number of religious rites, than to *lessen* it, with a view to edification. So the Jews of old frequently acted, and as frequently offended God. So the church of Rome has appointed many forms and rites of worship, with a view to the edification of her deluded votaries. The church of England also has retained the sign of the cross in baptism, and claims a power to decree rites and ceremonies in divine

---

[2] 2 Chron. xxx. 18, 19, 20.

worship whenever she pleases; and all, no doubt, with a view to *edification.* Yet I never heard that either of those establishments, arrogant as the former is, ever talked of *altering* the primitive order of the Christian church, or of *omitting* an ordinance, allowed to be divine, with a view to edification. Our brethren, however, plead for this; and, which is equally wonderful, they plead for it under the specious pretext, that *a command* of Christ may be performed. But is not baptism *a command,* an *acknowledged* command of Christ? And was it not graciously intended, as well as the holy supper, for the *edification* of Christians? Or, do our opponents imagine, that we may slight, with impunity, one command, provided we be but careful to observe another; even though the command neglected has a prior claim on our obedience? —In opposition to their novel way of proceeding, and their unprecedented manner of talking, I will present my reader with the sage maxim of a smart writer. "He [Christ] has not published his laws as men do theirs, with those imperfections, that they must be explained and mended."[3] To which I may add the following declarations of a learned pen: "We must serve God, not as we think fit, but as he hath appointed. God must be judge of his own honour—Nothing, then, is small, whereupon depends the sanctity of God's commandment and our obedience."[4] There is, however, little need of the maxims, or the declarations of men, while we have the decision of HIM who purchased the church with his own blood; of HIM who is to be our final judge. Now the language of that sublime Being is; "In *all things* that I have said unto you, *be circumspect*—Teaching them *to observe all things* whatsoever I have commanded you." And it is worthy of being remarked, that it stands recorded, to the honour of Moses, seven or eight times in one chapter, that "he did as the Lord commanded him."[5]

The question is not, whatever our opponents may think, Whether baptism is essential to *our salvation?* But, Whether

---

[3] Mr. BRADBURY's *Duty and Doct. Bap.* p. 24.
[4] PEMBLE's Introduct. to Worthy Receiv. the Lord's sup. p. 21, 31.
[5] See Exod. xl.

An Apology for the Baptists

God has not *commanded* it? Whether it is not a believer's *duty* to be found in it? And, Whether the pastor and members of a gospel church can justify themselves, in admitting persons to communion that have *never been baptized?* On the principle assumed by our opposers, a professor that has no inclination to obey the divine command, in any particular instance, may vindicate his refusal by saying; "The performance of it is not essential to my happiness; for a sinner may be saved without it." A mode of arguing this, that is big with rebellion against the dominion of God: a vile Antinomian principle, which, pursued in its consequences, is pregnant with ruin to immortal souls. What, shall we avoid nothing that God has forbidden, except we consider it as inconsistent with a state of salvation! Shall we do nothing that God has commanded, unless we look upon it as essentially necessary to our future felicity! Is this the way to manifest our faith in Jesus and love to God! —How much better is the reasoning of Mr. CHARNOCK, when he says; "*Deus voluit,* is a sufficient motive; and we cannot free ourselves from the censure of disobedience, if we observe not his commands in the same manner that he enjoins them; in their *circumstances,* as well as their substance—Who can, upon a better account, challenge an exemption from positive institutions than our Saviour, who had no need of them? Yet how observant was he of them, because they were established by divine authority! So that he calls his submitting to be baptized of John, *a fulfilling of righteousness*—Is it not a great ingratitude to God, to despise what he commands as a privilege? Were not the apostles men of an extraordinary measure of the Spirit, because of their extraordinary employments? And did they not exercise themselves in the institutions of Christ? How have many [meaning the Quakers] proceeded from the slighting of Christ's institutions, to the denying the authority of his word! A slighting Christ himself crucified at Jerusalem, to set up an imaginary Christ within them!"[6]

---

[6] *Works,* Vol. II. p. 766, 773, 775.

'But must we not exercise Christian charity, and bear with one another's infirmities? Should we not seek peace, and endeavour to promote harmony among the people of God?" Undoubtedly: yet give me leave to ask, Is there no way to exercise love and forbearance without practicing free communion? Cannot we promote peace and harmony without practially approving of infant sprinkling, as if it were a divine ordinance; while we are firmly persuaded that God never appointed it? Or, are we bound to admit as a fact, what we verily believe is a falsehood? The distinction between a Christian who holds what I consider as a practical error in the worship of God, and the mistake maintained, is wide and obvious. It is not an erroneous principle, or an irregular practice, that is the object of genuine charity. No; it is the *person* who maintains an error, not the *mistake* defended, that calls for my candour. The *former, I* am bound by the highest authority, to love as myself; the *latter, I* should ever consider as inimical to the honour of God, as unfriendly to my neighbour's happiness, and therefore discourage it, in the exercise of Christian tempers, through the whole of my conduct. —It is freely allowed, that a mistake which relates merely to the mode and subject of baptism, is comparatively small; but still, while I consider the aspersion of infants as a human invention in the solemn service of God, I am bound to enter my protest against it; and by a uniform practice to shew, that I am *a Baptist*—the same when a Pædobaptist brother desires communion with me, as when one of my own persuasion makes a similar request. Thus proving that I act, not under the impulse of passion, but on a dictate of judgment: and then the most violent Pædobaptist opponents will have no shadow of reason to impeach my integrity;—no pretence for surmising, that when I give the right hand of fellowship to such as have been immersed on a profession of faith, I act on *principles of conscience;* but when admitting such to communion, who have been only sprinkled in their infancy, on *motives of convenience.* For it is allowed by all the world, that consistency is the best evidence of sincerity.

I would also take the liberty here to observe, that some of

those churches in which free communion has been practiced, have not been the most remarkable for brotherly love, or Christian peace and harmony. Has the pastor of a church so constituted, being a Baptist, never found, that his Pædobaptist brethren have been a little offended, when he has ventured freely to speak his mind on the mode and subject of baptism? When Pædobaptist candidates for communion have been proposed to such a church, have those members who espoused the same sentiment never discovered a degree of pleasure, in the thought of having their number and influence increased in the community, that has excited the jealousy of their Baptist brethren? When, on the contrary, there has been a considerable addition to the number of Baptist members, has not an equal degree of pleasure in them, raised similar suspicions in the minds of their Pædobaptist brethren? And are not suspicions and jealousies of this kind, the natural effects of such a constitution? Must not a Baptist, as such, desire his own sentiment and practice to increase and prevail, while he considers them as agreeable to the will and command of his Lord? And must not a Pædobaptist, as such, sincerely wish that his opinion and practice may spread and prevail, so long as he considers infant sprinkling in the light of a divine appointment? To suppose a member of such a church, whether he be Baptist or Pædobaptist, to love God, and firmly believe his own sentiment concerning baptism to be a divine truth; and yet be indifferent whether that or its opposite prevail, involves a contradiction. For he who is indifferent to the performance of what he considers as a command of God, treats God himself with an equal degree of indifference: there being no possible way of expressing our affection for God, but by regarding his revealed will. "This is the love of God, that we keep his commandments." —Now, as our opponents must allow, that their communities are liable to all those other imperfections which are common to the real churches of Christ; so, I presume, the reader will hardly forbear concluding, that free communion exposes them to some *additional* disadvantages, which are peculiar to themselves.

Besides, though many of our Pædobaptist friends annex those pleasing epithets, *candid* and *catholic,* to the names of our opposers; I would not have them be too much elated with such ascriptions of honour. For, is it not a fact, that others who plead for infant baptism, and those not less wise and discerning, consider their conduct in a very different point of light? Do they not look upon it as savouring more of *carnal policy,* than of Christian charity; and as being much better calculated to express their *desire for popularity,* in adding to the number of their communicants, by opening a back door for the members of Pædobaptist churches to enter, than to promote the edification of saints, or maintain the purity of divine worship, considering their avowed sentiments in regard to baptism? —A Pædobaptist, when remonstrating against the conduct of some Independent churches, that received Baptists into communion with them, says; "Let men pretend what they can for such *a hotchpotch* communion in their churches, I stedfastly believe the event and issue of such practices will, sooner or later, convince all gainsayers, that it neither pleases Christ, nor is any way promotive of true peace or gospel holiness in the churches of God's people—I shall never be reconciled to that *charity,* which, in pretence of *peace* and *moderation,* opens the church's door to church-disjointing principles." And he entitles his performance, "*The sin and danger of admitting Anabaptists to continue in the Congregational churches, and* THE INCONSISTENCY OF SUCH A PRACTICE WITH THE PRINCIPLES OF BOTH."[7] —Thus, while our opponents gain the applause of some Pædobaptists, they incur the censure of others, who consider their conduct as inconsistent with Antipædobaptist principles. Just as those Dissenters who have occasionally conformed to the National Establishment, with a view to secular honours or temporal emoluments; and who, by so doing, have converted the sacred supper into a mere tool of ambition, or of avarice; while they have pleased some Conformists, have offended others. For though such Dissenters have pretended a concern for the public good, as

---

[7] In CROSBY'S *Hist. Bap.* Vol. III. p. 45, 46, 47.

🕮 An Apology for the Baptists 🕮

the ruling motive, and have shewn that they were far from being *bigots* to the principles of Nonconformity; yet members of the National church have not been wanting, who despised their *duplicity* of conduct; who have censured it as *a criminal neutrality* in religion, and as "halting between two opinions," to the great dishonour of both; who have repeatedly sounded that startling query in their ears, *For God, or for Baal?* and have pronounced them, *amphibious Christians.*[8]

Here one can hardly avoid observing, the very peculiar treatment with which the Baptists in general meet from their Pædobaptist brethren. Do we strictly abide by our own principles, admitting none to communion with us, but those whom we consider as *baptized* believers? We are censured by many of them, as uncharitably rigid, and are called, by one gentleman, WATERY BIGOTS. Do any of our denomination, under a plea of Catholicism, depart from their avowed sentiments, and connive at *infant sprinkling?* They are suspected, by others of the Pædobaptists, as a set of *temporizers. So* that, like those unhappy persons who fell into the hands of Procrustes, some of us are too short, and we must be *stretched;* others are too long, and they must be *lopped.* —But I return to my argument.

It should be observed, that forbearance and love, not less than resolution and zeal, must be directed in the whole extent of their exercise, by the word of God; else we may greatly offend and become partakers of other men's sins, by conniving when we ought to reprove. If the divine precepts, relating to love and forbearance, will apply to the case in hand; or so as to justify our connivance at an alteration, a corruption, or an omission of baptism; they will do the same in regard to the Lord's supper. And then we are bound to bear with sincere Papists, in their mutilation of the *latter;* and to exculpate our upright friends the Quakers, in their opposition to *both.* For it cannot be proved that baptism is less fundamental than the sacred supper. — "There is *a false,*

---

[8] See Mr. STUBB's *Serm.* entitled, *For God or for Baal?* Published, 1702.

ungodly charity," says a sensible Pædobaptist writer, a strange fire that proceeds not from the Lord; a charity that gives up the honour of religion, merely because we will not be at the pains to defend it—Vile principles can easily cover themselves with the names of temper, charity, moderation, and forbearance; but those glorious things are not to be confounded with lukewarmness, self-seeking, laziness, or ignorance—As there is a cloke of covetousness, so there is a cloke of fear and cowardice—You are never to make peace with men at the expense of any truth, that is revealed to you by the great God; because that is offering up his glory in sacrifice to your own—Do not dismember the Christian religion, but take it all together: charity was never designed to be the tool of unbelief. See how the Spirit has connected both our principles and duties. Follow *peace* with all men, and *holiness,* without which no man shall see the Lord."[9] — "I know not that man in England, says Dr. OWEN, who is willing to go farther in forbearance, love, and communion with all that fear God, and hold the foundation, than I am: but this is *never to be done* by a condescension from the exactness of the least *apex* of gospel truth."[10]

Another Pædobaptist author, when treating on charity and forbearance, expresses himself in the following language. "A considerable succedaneum for the Christian unity, is the *catholic charity;* which is like the charity commended by Paul, in only this one circumstance, that is "groweth exceedingly" —Among the stricter sort, it goes chiefly under the name of *forbearance.* We shall be much mistaken if we think that, by this soft and agreeable word, is chiefly meant the tenderness and compassion inculcated by the precepts of Jesus Christ and his apostles. It strictly means, an agreement to differ quietly about the doctrines and commandments of the gospel, without interruption of visible fellowship. They distinguish carefully between *fundamentals,* or things necessary to be believed and practiced; and

---

[9] Mr. BRADBURY's *Duty and Doct. of Bap.* p. 201, 213, 214.
[10] In Mr. BRADBURY, as before, p. 198.

circumstantials, or things that are indifferent. Now whatever foundation there may be for such a distinction in *human* systems of religion; it certainly looks very ill-becoming in the churches of Christ, to *question how far* HE *is to be believed and obeyed.* Our modern churches—have nearly agreed to hold all those things *indifferent,* which would be inconvenient and disreputable; and to have communion together, in observing somewhat like the customs of their forefathers.

Many of the plainest sayings of Jesus Christ and the apostles, are treated with high contempt, by the advocates of this forbearance. —The common people are persuaded to believe, that all the ancient institutions of Christianity were merely *local* and *temporary;* excepting such as the learned have agreed to be suitable to these times; or, which have been customarily observed by their predecessors. But it would well become the doctors in divinity to shew, by what authority any injunction of God can be revoked, besides *his own:* or, how any man's conscience can be lawfully released, by custom, example, or human authority, from observing such things as were instituted by the apostles of Christ, in his name. —This corrupt forbearance had no allowed place in the primitive churches. The apostle, in the epistle to the Ephesians, required of them, to adorn their "vocation with all lowliness and meekness, with long suffering, forbearing one another *in love."* But had they dispensed with the laws of Christ, for convenience and ease, it had been forbearing one another *in hatred.* For those laws were expressions of his love; the most fervent love that was ever shewn among men, directed by infallible wisdom. Whosoever, therefore, would obliterate them, or any how attempt to change them, must either suppose himself *wiser* than Jesus Christ, or *a greater friend* to mankind. He must be moved, either by an enormous *self-conceit;* or by the spirit of *malevolence.* —The more thinking part of religious men, observing what great mischiefs have arisen from contentions about truth—have found it most desirable to let truth alone; and to concern themselves chiefly about living profitably in civil society. To be of some religion is but decent; and the interests of human life require that it be popular and compliant. If men have different notions of Jesus Christ, his divinity, his sacrifice, his kingdom, and the customs of his religion, even from what the apostles seemed to have; charity [with many] demands that we think well of their religious characters, notwithstanding this. It is unbecoming the modesty of wise men to be confident on any side; and *contending earnestly* for opinions, injures the peace of the Christian church. Thus kind and humble is modern charity. —Instead of rejoicing in, or with the truth, it rejoiceth in contemplating the admirable piety that may be produced from so many different, yea, oppposite principles—It is very true, that the power of godliness has often suffered in a zealous contention about rites and ceremonies; but the contention has been chiefly about forms of human device. The Christians of old time were taught, not to *dispute* about the institutions of their LORD, but to *observe* them thankfully; and hereby they expressed their affection to him and to each other. If that affection be granted to be more important than the tokens of it, it would be unjust to infer that the latter have no obligation; which would imply, that Christ and the apostles *meant nothing* by their precepts. The Methodists have not, indeed, gone so far as their spiritual brethren [the Quakers] have done, in rejecting all external ceremonies; but they are taught to believe, that all concern about the ancient order and customs of the Christians is mere party-spirit, and injurious to the devout exercises of the heart. Thus the modern charity vaunts itself, in answering better purposes than could be accomplished by keeping the words of Christ. It produces *a more extensive* and *generous communion;* and animates the devotion of men, without perplexing them by uncertain doctrines, or rigorous self denial—Although it supposes some revelation from God, and some honour due to Jesus Christ; it claims a right to *dispense* with both; to choose what, in his doctrine and religion, is fit to be believed and observed."[11] —So, that illegitimate charity and false moderation, which incline professors to treat divine

---

[11] *Strictures upon Modern Simony*, p. 48-55.

institutions as articles of small importance; led that great man, MELANCTHON, to place the *doctrine of justification* by faith alone, the *number* of positive institutions in the Christian church, the *jurisdiction* claimed by the Pope, and several *superstitious rites* of the Romish religion, among things *indifferent,* when an imperial edict required compliance.[12] But, "as we must take heed that we do not add the fancies of men to our divine religion; so we should take equal care that we do not *curtail* the appointments of Christ,"[13] out of any pretence to candour, or peace, or the edification of our fellow Christians. The charity for which many professors plead, is of so lax a nature, and so far beside the rule, both in regard to doctrine and worship; as gives too much occasion to ask, with Joshua, "Are you for us, or for our *adversaries?"*

Once more: Remarkably strong, and not foreign to my purpose, are the words of Mr. JOHN WESLEY, which are quoted with approbation by Mr. ROWLAND HILL. "A catholic spirit is not speculative latitudinarianism. It is not an indifference to all opinions. This is the spawn of hell; not the offspring of heaven. This unsettledness of thought, this being driven to and fro, and tossed about with every wind of doctrine, is a great curse, not a blessing; an irreconcilable enemy, not a true Catholicism. A man of a true catholic spirit—does not halt between two opinions; nor vainly endeavour to blend them into one. Observe this, you that know not what spirit you are of: who call yourselves of a catholic spirit, only because you are of a muddy understanding; because your mind is all in a mist; because you are of no settled, consistent principles, but are for jumbling all opinions together. Be convinced that you have quite missed your way. You know not where you are. You think you are got into the very Spirit of Christ; when, in truth, you are nearer the spirit of Anti-Christ."[14]

---

[12] MOSHEIM's *Eccles. Hist.* Vol. IV. p. 37, 38.
[13] Dr. WATT's *Humb. Attempt* p. 62.
[14] In Mr. ROWLAND HILL's *full Answer to* Mr. J. WESLEY's *Remarks*, p.

Our brethren with an air of superior confidence often demand, "What have you to do with *another's baptism?*" This interrogatory I would answer by proposing another: What have I to do with another's *faith, experience,* or *practice?* In one view, nothing at all, if he do not injure my person, character, or property; for to his own master he stands or falls. In another, much; that is, if he desire communion with me at the Lord's table. In such a case, I may lawfully address him in the following manner: What think you of Christ? What know you of yourself? Of yourself, as a sinner: of Christ, as a saviour? Of Christ, as King in Zion; of yourself, as a subject of his benign government? Are you desirous to be found in his righteousness, and sincerely willing to obey his commands? Are you ready to bear his cross, and to follow the Lamb whithersoever he goes? —Receiving satisfaction to these most important queries, we will suppose the conversation thus to proceed: "What are the divine commands?" After believing, baptism is the *first,* the *very first* that requires a public act of obedience. —But I have been baptized." Perhaps not. Make it appear, however, and I shall say no more on that subject. — "I am really persuaded of it in my own mind. Were it otherwise, I should think it my duty, I should not hesitate a moment, to be immersed on a profession of faith." I commend your integrity: abide by the dictates of conscience. Yet care should be taken, that her language be an echo to the voice of divine revelation; else you may neglect your duty and slight your privileges, offend God and injure your soul, even while you obey her commands. — "But I am persuaded Christ has accepted me, and that it is my duty to receive the holy supper." That Christ has received you, I have a pleasing persuasion; and so I conclude, in a judgment of charity, concerning all whom I baptize: but that it is the *immediate* duty of any unbaptized believer to approach the Lord's table, may, admit of a query: nay, the general practice of the Christian church in every age, has been quite in the negative. For a learned writer assures us, that "among *all the absurdities* that ever were held, none

40, 41.

ever maintained *that,* that any person should partake of the communion before he was baptized." Was it, think you, the duty of an ancient Israelite to worship at the sanctuary, or to partake of the paschal feast, before he was circumcised? Or, was it the duty of the Jewish priest to burn incense in the holy place, before they offered the morning or the evening sacrifice? The appointments of God must be administered in his own way, and in that order which he has fixed. For, to borrow an illustration from a well known author, "Suppose a master commands his servant to sow his ground; doth this give a right to him to go *immediately* and cast in the seed, before that ever he break the ground with the plough, and make it fit for the receiving the seed? Should he go thus to work, he were a disobedient servant. Neither could it excuse, that he had his master's immediate command to sow his ground. Even so in the present case"[15] —Christ commands believers to remember him at his own table. But were those believers to whom he first gave the command *unbaptized?* Or, can we infer, because it is the duty of all baptized believers to celebrate the Lord's supper, that it is the *immediate* duty of one that is not baptized, so to do? — "Could you produce an instance from the records of the New Testament, of any believer being refused communion, merely because he scrupled the propriety of being immersed on a profession of faith, it would warrant your present denial. But, whenever you shall make it appear, that a truly converted person, and one who was considered as such, desired fellowship with a church of Christ in the apostolic age; I will engage to prove that he was received, whatever might be his views relating to the mode and subject of baptism." And when you shall adduce an instance of any real convert, in those primitive times, conscientiously scrupling the use of the wine at the Lord's table; I will enter under the same obligation to prove, that the sacred supper was administered to him in his own way. — "Will you, then, dare to reject those whom Christ accepts!" Reject, from what? My

---

[15] Mr. THOMAS BOSTON'S *Works,* p. 386.

esteem and affection? Far be it! Under a persuasion that Christ has received you, I love and honour you as a Christian brother. His image appearing in your temper and conduct commands my regard. — "With what consistency, then, can you refuse me communion? If Christ has accepted me, if Christ Himself has communion with one why may not you?" Communion with you in the knowledge and comfort of the truth I have; and this would be both my honour and happiness, were you a converted Jew. Communion with you I also have in affection; but fellowship at the Lord's table is a distinct act, a very different thing; and is to be regulated entirely by the revealed will of Him that appointed it. Communion at the holy supper would never have been either the duty or privilege of any man, if Christ had not commanded it, any more than it is now my duty to celebrate the ancient passover. But that eternal law which requires me "to love my neighbour as myself," would have obliged me to love you, both as a man and a Christian, if baptism and the Lord's supper had never been ordained. "After all, your professions of affection for me as a believer in Jesus Christ, and your refusing to have communion with me at the holy table, carry the appearance of a strong inconsistency." Admitting they do, the inconsistency is not peculiar to me, nor to those of my persuasion; because I act on a principle received in common by the whole Christian church. There is no denomination of Christians, except those who plead for free communion, that would admit you to the Lord's table, if they did not think you had been baptized. This, therefore, is the principle on which I refuse to have communion with you: I consider you as unbaptized. Suppose a Jew, a Turk, or a Pagan, to be enlightened by divine grace, to have received the truth as it is in Jesus, to love God and desire communion with his people before he is baptized; would you think it right, could your own conscience admit it, as consistent with the revealed will of Christ and the practice of his apostles, that such a request should be granted by any gospel church? In a case of this kind, I presume,—and there have been millions of Jews and Heathens converted, since the Christian era commenced, —in such a case you would easily discern a consistency, between loving him as a believer, and refusing to have communion with him till he was baptized. Nay, I cannot help thinking, but you would be startled at the report of any religious community admitting such an one to the Lord's table; because it would strike you as a notorious departure from the divine rule of proceeding; from the laws and statutes of Heaven, in that case made and provided. Besides, you have already acknowledged, that if you did not consider yourself as baptized; if you thought immersion on a profession of faith essential to baptism, which you very well know is *my* sentiment; you should think it your duty to submit, you would not hesitate a moment. So that, were I to encourage your immediate approach to the sacred supper, I should stand condemned on your own principles. This, therefore, is the only question between us, *What is baptism?* For you dare not assert, you cannot suppose, that an unbaptized believer, descended from Christian parents, has any pre-eminence, in point of claim to communion, above a truly converted Jew: and you must allow that I have an equal right with you, or any other man, to judge for myself what is essential to baptism. You verily believe that you have been baptized; I am equally confident, from your own account of the matter, that you have not. Your conscience opposes the thought of being immersed on a profession of faith, because, in your opinion, it would be rebaptization; mine cannot encourage your approach to the Lord's table, because I consider infant baptism as invalid. — "I perceive, than, that you look upon me as an unbaptized Heathen: for you cannot imagine that I am, or ever was, a Turk or a Jew." Quite a mistake. I consider you as a real convert, and love you as a Christian brother. Were you persuaded that a son of Abraham after the flesh, or a dupe to Mahomet's imposture, or an uncultivated Hottentot, had received the truth and was converted to the Lord Redeemer; would you still call him, without limitation, a *Jew, a Turk,* or *a Heathen?* No, candour and common sense would forbid the thought. You would rather say, He is a believer in God's Messiah, and a lover of Jesus Christ; he feels the power of gospel truth on his heart, and his moral conduct is comely; but, as yet, he is unbaptized. I should rejoice to see him convinced of the importance of that institution, of the connection it has with other appointments of Christ, and behold him submit to it. Then, were I in communion, I should freely give him the right hand of fellowship, and break bread with him at the Lord's table. Till then, however, though I think it the duty of every Christian to love him for the truth's sake, I consider it as no breach of charity, in any community, not to admit him to the Lord's table. —Now I appeal to the reader, I appeal to our brethren themselves, Whether, on our AntiPædobaptist principles, we are not obliged to consider a truly converted but unbaptized Mussulman, and a converted Englishman, who has had no other than Pædobaptism, as on a level, in point of claim to communion with us? For God is no respecter of persons. It is no matter where a man was born, or how he was educated; whether he drew his first breath at Constantinople, or Peking, or London; whether his parents taught him to revere the Koran of MAHOMET, the Institutes of CONFUCIUS, or the well attested Revelation of God; if he be really born of the Spirit, he has an equal claim to all the privileges of a gospel church, with a true convert descended from Christian ancestors. And if so, while our brethren abide by their present hypothesis, they could not refuse the sacred supper to the one, any more than the other, without the most palpable inconsistency; though, by admitting the *former* to that divine appointment, they would surprise and offend all that heard of it.

Our opponents further suggest, nay, they seem quite confident, "That the Christian Jews in the primitive church, might, on our principles, have refused communion to the believing Gentiles, because they were not circumcised; and that the converted Gentiles might have denied fellowship to the believing Jews, for the opposite reason." But here our brethren take for granted, what we cannot by any means allow. For this way of talking supposes, that a submission to baptism is no more demanded of believers now, than circumcision was of Gentile converts in the apostolic age; and that we who plead for baptism, as a term of communion, have no more authority so to do, than Judaizing Christians then had for maintaining the necessity of circumcision. Now such extraordinary positions as these should not have been assumed *Gratis*, but *proved, soundly proved;* which, had our opposers well and truly peformed, would have made me and many of their stricter brethren, thorough proselytes to free communion. Nay, we should, probably, before now, have been in a hopeful way of getting entirely rid of that ordinance, about the order and importance of which we now contend. For neither PACIFICUS, nor CANDIDUS, will dare to assert, that our ascended Lord requires *any* of his disciples to be circumcised, either before or after the admission to the holy table: consequently, if their arguing from circumcision to baptism be conclusive, we may absolutely omit the latter, as converts of old the former, without fear of the least offence, or of any divine resentment.

And must we, indeed, consider the administration and the neglect of baptism, as on a perfect level with being circumcised or uncircumcised, in the apostolic times! Must an ordinance of the New Testament, submission to which our Lord requires of all his disciples, be placed on the same footing with an obsolete rite of the Jewish church! How kind it is of our brethren who possess this knowledge, and are so well acquainted with Christian liberty, relating to baptism, that they are willing to inform us of its true extent! For, as SOCINUS long ago observed, "Ignorance of it is the cause of *many evils.*"[16] I may, however, venture an appeal to the intelligent reader, Whether this way of arguing does not much better become the pen of SOCINUS, of VOLKELIUS, or of a QUAKER; than that of PACIFICUS, of CANDIDUS, or of any BAPTIST? Because, as HOORNBEEK remarks, in answer to the Socinians; "It is very absurd to explain the

---

[16] *Quyi* scientiam habet, ut inquit Paulus, apud fe habeat, coram Deo; non quin eam scientiam alios etiam docere posit, ut ipse Paulus saciebat, praefertim ubi ignorantia multorum malorum est causa; ut certe hoc tempore est ignoratio Christianae libertatis, in aqua baptismo suscipiendo. *SOCINUS de Baptismo*, Cap. XVII, apud HOORNE, *Secin. Conf. Tom. III.* p. 435, 436.

design, the command, and the obligation of baptism, by the abrogation and abuse of circumcision."[17] As our brethren detest the Socinian system in general, I cannot but wonder that they should so often use weapons, in defence of their novel sentiment, that were forged by SOCINUS, or some of his pupils, for a similar purpose. I could wish, therefore, that some such person as Mr. RYLAND, who is well known to have an utter aversion to the capital tenets of that pretended reformer of the Reformed church in Poland, would seriously take PACIFICUS to task, for paying so much honour to a depraver of divine truth and a mutilator of God's worship. For who knows but it might have a happy effect, and cause him to retract his *Modest* Plea?—Before I proceed to another objection, it may not be amiss to observe, What *a variety* of laudable and kindred purposes this argument is adapted to serve, according to its various application by different persons. In the hands of our *opponents,* it effectually proves the necessity of admitting infant sprinkling, in some cases, as a proper *succedaneum* for what they consider as real baptism. From the pen of SOCINUS, it evinces beyond a doubt, that baptism is an *indifferent thing.* And in the mouth of BARCLAY, it will equally well demonstrate, that baptism should be *entirely laid aside.* Well, then, might our CANDID and PEACEFUL opposers congratulate themselves on the safety of their cause, it being defended by such a *three edged* sword as this! And well might they unite, as one man, in saying; "If, therefore, this were the *only* thing that could be urged in favour of the latitude of communion I plead for, I should think it would be sufficient; at least sufficient to excuse our conduct, and stop the mouth of censure.'

But, notwithstanding all I have said, we stand charged by our brethren with *a notorious inconsistency* in our own conduct; because we occasionally admit, with pleasure,

---

[17] After giving various pertinent reasons against this old Socinian argument for free communion, he adds; Ut ex illis omnibus satis sit manifestum, absurdistime rationem, praeceptum, auctorita emque baptismi explicari, ex circumcisionis obrogatione et abusu. Ubi supra, p. 256.

An Apology for the Baptists

Pædobaptist ministers into our pulpits, to whom we should refuse communion at the Lord's table. This objection has been much insisted upon of late, and is sometimes urged against us by way of query, to the following effect. "Is not as much required in order to an *office* in the church, as to *private membership? Is* it not as inconsistent to receive a Pædobaptist, as *a minister,* and admit him into the *pulpit,* as to admit him into the *church* and to the *Lord's table?* Where have you either precept, or example, for receiving them as *ministers,* any more than for receiving them *as members?*'— These queries being considered, by many of our opponents, as quite unanswerable, I shall take the more notice of them.

The first thing then, that demands regard, is the state of the question which is now before us. For it is not, as these queries suggest, Whether as much be not required in order to an *office* in the church, as to *private communion?* This we readily allow; this we never denied. For what congregation of strict Baptists would think they acted consistently in making choice of a Pædobaptist for their pastor, or to officiate as a deacon? Besides, will not our brethren acknowledge, that in every orderly society, and more especially in a church of Christ, a person must be a member before he can be an officer in it? *This* is the point in dispute, at least it is this about which I contend; Whether baptism be equally necessary to the *occasional exercise* of ministerial gifts, as it is to *communion* at the Lord's table? and, Whether the scripture favour the one as much as the other? Such being the true state of the question, I now beg leave to ask; Supposing our brethren to prove the affirmative beyond a doubt, what is the consequence, and how are we affected by it? Is it, that we are found guilty of a direct violation of some divine command, that *requires us* to receive Pædobaptists into our communion? No such thing is pretended. Is it, that we oppose some plain apostolic, *precedent?* neither is this laid to our charge. For they do not believe there were any Pædobaptists in the apostolic times; and, consequently, they cannot suppose that the New Testament contains an example of such being received into communion. What, then, is the conclusion they would infer? It must, surely, be something formidable to every strict Baptist; otherwise it is hardly supposable that so much weight should be laid upon this objection. The consequence, however, is only this; The premises proved, *the strict Baptists have no reason to censure their brethren of a looser cast, because they themselves are equally culpable, though in a different respect.* Or, in other words, *The strict Baptists, like some other folks, are not quite infallible; do actually err; and, by reason of a mistake, impertinently blame the conduct of their more free, and open, and generous brethren, when they ought rather to examine and reform their own.* —But this inference can be of little service to the cause of free communion, except it be good logic and sound divinity, to attempt a justification of my own faults, by proving that he who accuses me is equally guilty: or to congratulate myself as an innocent man, because my neighbour cannot with a good grace reprove me. Our opponents, I persuade myself, will not be greatly offended with us, if this argument, *Herculean* as it seems to them; should not make us complete converts to free communion. So soon, however, as our brethren shall make it appear, that they have as good a warrant for receiving Pædobaptist believers into stated communion, as I have to admit a Pædobaptist minister occasionally into my pulpit; I will either *encourage* the former, or *entirely refuse* the latter.

But if these queries prove any thing, they prove too much; more at least, than the querists intend. For, according to the argument contained in them, it is equally unwarrantable for us to *hear a* Pædobaptist minister preach or to *unite with him* in public prayer; as it is for them to receive him into communion. For instance: do they demand, "Where have you either precept, or example, for admitting Pædobaptist ministers into your pulpits, any more than for receiving them as members? I retort, on their Baptist principles; Where have you either precept or example, in the New Testament, for *hearing* Pædobaptist ministers preach; or for *uniting with them* in public prayer, any more than for receiving them as members? And, to shew the futility of this argument, I again demand; If, in *hearing such* ministers preach, or by *uniting with them* in public prayer (which are undoubtedly branches of the *moral* worship of God, nor peculiar to any dispensation of religion) we act without any express command or plain example in the New Testament; with what propriety can we blame our brethren for admitting Pædobaptists to the Lord's supper (which is *a positive* institution; a part of divine worship that depends entirely on *a revelation* of the sovereign will of God) though they have neither precept nor precedent for so doing? Queries of this kind might be multiplied, but these may suffice.

But is there *no* difference between the two cases? *No* difference between occasionally admitting Pædobaptist ministers into our pulpits, and receiving them, or others of the same persuasion, into our communion? I can scarcely imagine that our brethren themselves will here answer in the negative; but that this difference may plainly appear, let the following things be observed. —Public preaching is not confined to persons in a *church state,* nor ever was; but the Lord's supper is a church ordinance, nor ought ever to be administered but to a particular church, *as such*. Now it is of a particular church, and of a positive ordinance peculiar to it, concerning which is all our dispute. —There is not that strict mutual relation between bare hearers of the word and their preachers, as there is between the members of a church and her pastor, or between the members themselves. And as, according to the appointment of God, persons must *believe* the gospel before they have any thing to do with positive institutions; so, in the ordinary course of Providence, they must *hear* the gospel in order to their believing. The Corinthians *heard* before they *believed;* they believed before they were *baptized;* and, no doubt, they were baptized before they received the *sacred supper*.[18] —When our opponents receive Pædobaptists into their fellowship, they practically allow what they themselves consider as a human invention, to supersede a positive, divine institution; and that with a

---

[18] Acts. xviii. 8.

view to their attending on another positive appointment of Jesus Christ. Not so, when we admit ministers of that persuasion into our pulpits. In this case there is no divine institution superseded; no human invention, in the worship of God, encouraged: nor is it done with a view to introduce them to any positive appointment of our sovereign Lord. — Again: When we admit Pædobaptist ministers into our pulpits, it is in expectation that they will preach the gospel; that very gospel which we believe and love, and about which there is no difference between them and us. But when they receive Pædobaptists into communion, they openly connive at what they consider as an error; an error both in judgment and practice; an error of that kind which the scripture calls, "will worship, and the traditions of men." There is, undoubtedly, a material difference, between hearing a minister who, in our judgment, is ignorant of the only true baptism, discourse on those doctrines he experimentally knows, and countenancing an invention of men. In the former case we shew an esteem for his personal talents, we honour his ministerial gifts, and manifest our love to the truth; in the latter, we set aside a divinely appointed prerequisite for communion at the Lord's table.

It has been already observed, as a fact, that persons have been called by grace, who were not baptized in their infancy; and, considering baptism as a temporary institution, have conscientiously refused a submission to that ordinance when converted, who yet desired communion in the holy supper. We will now suppose a community of such; and that they call to the ministry one of their number, who is allowed by all competent judges, to possess great ministerial gifts, and to be a very useful preacher:—Or we may suppose a reformed Catholic, equally the subject of divine grace, and endued with equal abilities for public service; yet conscientiously retaining the Popish error of communion in one kind only. Now, on either of these suppositions, I demand of our brethren, whether they would receive such an one into communion with the same readiness that they would admit him into their pulpits? If they answer in the negative, then, by their own confession, there is not so close a connection between admitting a person to preach amongst us, and receiving him into communion, as they pretend. And we may venture to retort upon them; Shall an excellent, laborious, and useful minister of Christ *work* for you, and shall he not be allowed to *eat* with you! What, shall he break the bread of life *to you,* and must he not be suffered to break bread at the Lord's table *with you!* —Again: We will suppose a good man and a useful preacher to be fully persuaded, with the Hydroparastates in the second century, that *water* should always be used at the Lord's table, instead of wine;[19] and that, on a principle of conscience, he absolutely refuses the latter:—Or, that it is more significant and more agreeable to *dip* the bread in the wine, and receive them both at once; as practised by some in the fourth century, and more frequently afterwards.[20] Or, that he conscientiously approves the custom of the Greeks, who mix *boiling water* with the wine, crumble the bread into it, and, taking it out with a spoon, receive the elements both together.[21] Now though, I confess, they could not refuse him a place among them at the Lord's table, to partake of the holy supper in his *own* way, without violating that grand rule of their conduct, "GOD HAS RECEIVED HIM;" and though PACIFICUS and CANDIDUS could not reject him, without contradicting the *titles* of their Plea for free communion; yet, I presume, the generality of our opponents would hardly allow of such a peculiar mode of proceeding, in any of their churches. No; they would be ready to say of such a candidate for fellowship; he ought to regard

---

[19] *VOSSII Thef. Theolog.* p. 487. Edit. Oxon. 1613. *SUICERI Thesaur. Eccles.* sub voce Cf. Holy Communion. MOSHEIM's *Eccles. Hist.* Vol. I. p. 180. 8vo. Edit.

[20] VOSSIUS, ubi supra, p. 522-525. SUICERUS, Id. ibid. EUSER. *Eccles. Hist.* L. VI. C. 44.

[21] *WITSII Œconom. Faed.* L. IV. C. XVII. § 10, 25. To what lengths of superstition and absurdity may persons professing the Christian religion run, when they leave the divine rule of proceeding! No branches of Jehovah's worship require a more punctual regard to the sacred rule, than those which are of *a positive* kind; yet none have been so mutilated, metamorphosed, and abused, as they have been, by the perverse inventions and bold impieties of men.

the example of Christ, who used *wine:* Or, he ought to obey the divine command, which requires that we should *drink* the wine. Yet they might not think it proper to refuse him the occasional use of a pulpit, and might hear him preach the truth, received in common, with pleasure.

Though, as Anti-Pædobaptists, it cannot be expected, that we should produce instances out of the New Testament of Pædobaptist ministers being encouraged in a similar way; because we are firmly persuaded there were none such, till after the sacred canon was completed: yet we find, in that inspired volume, a sufficient warrant for uniting with those that believe, in affection and walk, so far as agreed; notwithstanding their ignorance of some part of the counsel of God, to which a conscientious obedience is indispensably required, from all those by whom it is known.[22] Yes, the New Testament not only *permits,* as lawful, but *enjoins* as an indispensable duty, that we should love them that love the Lord; and that we should manifest this holy affection in every way, that is not inconsistent with a revelation of the divine will in some other respect. So it was under the ancient Jewish œconomy, and so it is now. To admit, therefore, a minister to preach among us, with whom we should have no objection to commune, could we allow the validity of infant baptism; as it is a token of our affection for a servant of Christ, of our love to the truth he preaches, and is not contrary to any part of divine revelation, must be lawful: or if not, it lies upon our brethren to prove it; because they cannot deny that the word of God requires us to love him, and to manifest our affection for him. But as to communion at the holy table, Christians in general have had no more doubt, whether baptism should *precede* it, according to a special revelation of the divine will; than whether baptism itself be a part of the counsel of God. —When we ask a Pædobaptist minister to preach in any of our churches, we act on the same general principle, as when we request him to pray with any of us in a private family. And as no one considers *this* as an

---

[22] Philip. iii. 15, 16.

act of church communion, but as a testimony of our affection for him, so we consider *that;* and it is viewed by the public, as a branch of that general intercourse which it is not only lawful, but commendable and profitable to have, with all that preach the gospel.

I take it for granted, that circumcision was absolutely necessary for every male, in order to communion at the paschal supper, and in the solemn worship of the sanctuary. And if so, had the most renouned Antediluvians that ever lived, or the most illustrious Gentiles that ever appeared in the world, been cotemporary with Moses and sojourners in the same wilderness, they could not have been admitted to communion in the Israelitish church, without submitting to circumcision. Enoch, though as a saint he walked with God; though as a prophet he foretold the coming of Christ to judgment—Noah, though an heir of the righteousness of faith, a preacher of that righteousness, and one of Ezekiel's worthies[23] — Melchisedeck, though a king, and a priest of the most high God; superior to Abraham, and the greatest personal type of the Lord Messiah that ever was among men—And Job, though for piety there was none like him upon earth, Jehovah himself being judge, and one of the prophet's illustrious triumvirate[24] —These, I say, notwithstanding all their piety and holiness; notwithstanding all their shining excellencies, exalted characters, and useful services; could not, as uncircumcised, have been admitted to communion with the chosen tribes at the tabernacle of the God of Israel, without a violation of the divine command. This, I persuade myself, our opponents must allow: this, I think, they dare not deny. Yet if Enoch, for instance, had been in the camp of Israel when Korah and his company mutinied, and had been disposed to give the rebels a lecture on the second coming of Christ; I cannot suppose that his offered service would have been rejected by Moses or Joshua, merely because he was not circumcised. Or, if Noah had been present at the erection of

---

[23] Chap. xiv. 14, 16, 18, 20.
[24] Ezek. as before.

the tabernacle, and inclined to give the people a sermon on the future incarnation of the Son of God, and the righteousness of faith; to which most important objects that sacred structure, with its costly utensils and solemn services, had a typical regard; I cannot but think they would have given him a hearing. Nay, I appeal to our opponents themselves, whether they do not think so as well as I. Yet that favoured people *could* not have admitted them to communion in some other branches of divine worship, without transgressing the laws of JEHOVAH.[25] If this be allowed, the consequence is plain, and the argument, though analogical, is irrefragable. For the paschal feast and the sanctuary services were not more of a positive nature than the Lord's supper;[26] nor were the former more peculiar to that dispensation that the latter is to this; but preaching and hearing the word are not peculiar to any dispensation of grace, as are baptism and the sacred supper.

Our Lord, though he warned his hearers against the pride and hypocrisy, the unbelief and covetousness, of the ancient Pharisees, and Scribes, and Jewish teachers; yet exhorted the people to regard the truths they delivered.[27] Our opponents, notwithstanding, cannot imagine that Christ would have admitted those ecclesiastics to baptism, had they desired it; nor will they attest that any, who are not proper subjects of that ordinance, should be received into communion. —When the beloved disciple said, "Master, we saw one casting out devils in thy name, and we forbad him, because he followeth not with us:" Jesus answered, "Forbid him not; for he that is not against us, is for us."[28] From which it appears, that we are under obligation to encourage those that fight against the common enemy, and propagate the common truth; though they and we may have no communion

---

[25] Exod. xii. 44, 48. Ezek. xliv. 7.
[26] Ad coenam *typicam,* h.e. ad Pascha, non admittedbatur ullus *paregrinus,* Exod. xii. 43. aut *praeputiatus,* ver. 40. sicut sub N.T. non admititur non-baptizatus. Act. ii. 41, 42. MASTRICH. *Theolog.* Tom. II. p. 843.
[27] Matt. xxiii 1, 2, 3.
[28] Luke ix. 49, 50.

together, in the special ordinances of God's house; which is the very case when we admit our Pædobaptist brethren to preach among us. —We are also informed, that the first Gentiles who were converted by the apostolic ministry, were endued with miraculous gifts immediately upon their believing and before they were baptized; for "they spake with tongues and glorified God."[29] Nor is it improbable but some of them then received gifts for the ministry; and if so, in the fullness of their hearts and the transport of their joy, they also gave the first specimen of their future ministrations, to the pleasing astonishment of Peter and those that were with him. But can our brethren suppose, that the great apostle would have taken equal pleasure in hearing them request a place at the Lord's table, before they were baptized? No; his own conduct opposes the thought. For, having beheld with astonishment the gifts they received, and hearing with rapture the truths they delivered, he COMMANDED them to be baptized in "the name of the Lord;" to be baptized *immediately* in the name of that Lord, who requires a submission to the ordinance from all that believe.

Once more: A very competent judge of all that pertains to the ministerial character, and of all that belongs to a Christian profession, has left his opinion on record concerning the ministry of certain persons, whom he considered as quite unworthy of his intimate friendship. Yes, Paul, that most excellent man, when acting as amaneuensis to the Spirit of wisdom, and when speaking of some who preached the gospel, informs us, that *envy* and *strife* were the principles on which they acted, and the increase of his afflictions the end which they had in view. How carnal and base the principles! How detestable the end at which they aimed!—But was the apostle offended or grieved, so as to wish they were silenced? Or, did he charge his beloved Philippians, and all the sincere followers of Christ, never to hear them? Let his own declaration answer the queries. "What then? notwithstanding every way, whether in pretence, or in truth,

---

[29] Act. x. 44.

CHRIST IS PREACHED; and therein I do rejoice, yea, and will rejoice."[30] When a corrupted gospel is preached; he asserts his apostolic authority, and thunders out anathemas against the propagators of it.[31] Because, as God will not set the seal of his blessing to a falsehood, or sanctify a lye, it can do no good; it is pregnant with mischief. But when the pure gospel is preached, though on perverse principles, as it is THE TRUTH, God frequently owns and renders it useful, whoever may publish it.

Hence the apostle's joy in the text before us. —Now, as we are far from impeaching the sincerity of our Pædobaptist brethren, when preaching the gospel of our ascended Lord; and as Paul rejoiced that Christ was preached, though by persons who acted on the basest principles; we cannot imagine that he would have taken less pleasure in the thought of Pædobaptist ministers publishing the glorious gospel of the blessed God, had there been any such in those days, even though he might have considered them as under a great mistake, in regard to baptism: for our opponents do not believe, any more than we, that Paul knew any thing of infant sprinkling. And if so, we may falsely conclude, that there is nothing inconsistent with our hypothesis, in occasionally admitting Pædobaptist ministers into our pulpits, and hearing them with pleasure. —But will our opponents assert, or can they suppose, that the great apostle of the Gentiles would have encouraged with equal delight such persons as those of whom he speaks, to approach the holy table and have communion with him in all the ordinances of God's house? Persons, who made the glorious gospel of the blessed God, the vehicle of their own pride, and envy, and malice; and in whose conduct those infernal tempers reigned, and had for their immediate object one of the most excellent and useful men that ever lived? Certainly, if on any occasion, we may here adopt the old proverb; *Credat Judareus apella.*

---

[30] Philip. i. 15-18.
[31] Gal. i. 6-9.

An Apology for the Baptists

"CHRIST IS PREACHED, and therein I do rejoice, yea, and will rejoice." Disinterested, noble saying! Worthy of a first rate minister in the Messiah's kingdom; worthy of PAUL; who cared not who opposed him, nor what he suffered, if Christ were but glorified in the conversion of sinners. But though that man of God thus expresses himself, in reference to gospel preaching; I cannot imagine, nor will our brethren affirm, that he would with the same pleasure have admitted any of the Jewish converts to communion, because they supposed themselves to have been baptized, merely on account of their having been washed according to the traditions of the elders. To a request of this kind, his mildest answer, we have reason to think, would have been, "We have no such custom, nor the churches of God." Yet, as Baptists, our opponents must consider infant sprinkling, as having nothing more to recommend it, than *human authority* and *general practice;* which were the grand recommendations of those Jewish washings, and the very basis on which they stood. —Suppose our brethren in the course of their reading, were to find it asserted by some ancient author, "That Paul frequently admitted persons to communion, on such a pretence to baptism;" what would they say? They would, I presume, consider the assertion as a libel on his character. They would execrate the pen which transmitted such a falsehood to posterity; and look on the writer, either as a weak and credulous man, or as a forger of lyes. And, except a predilection for free communion biased their judgment, their opinion and censure would be much the same were they to find it recorded; "He frequently admitted believers to the Lord's table, *before* they were baptized." The utter silence of the New Testament, relating to a conduct of this kind; the many passages, in that infallible code of divine worship, inconsistent with such a practice; and their veneration for the character of the great apostle, would oblige them so to do. Yet, amazing to think! for such a procedure they plead; such a conduct they adopt; and look upon us as greatly injuring the honour and interests of real religion, and not a little contributing to the cause of infidelity; merely because we cannot consider them as the followers of Paul in this particular, nor become their humble imitators!

But why should our brethren so earnestly plead for believers receiving the Lord's supper, while they treat baptism as if it were a mere trifle; an appointment of Christ that might very well have been spared? What is there of obligation, of solemnity, of importance, in the former, that is not in the latter? Have they not the same divine Institutor, and the same general end? Were they not intended for the same persons, and are they not equally permanent in the church of God? And as to baptism, was not the administration of it by John, one of the first characteristics of the Messiah's appearance, and of the gospel dispensation commencing? Did not the King Messiah submit to it, as an example of obedience to all his followers; and most strongly recommend it to their judgment and conscience; their affections and practice, when he said: "THUS IT BECOMETH US TO FULFIL ALL RIGHTEOUSNESS?" Which, by the way, is more than can be asserted concerning the sacred supper; for though he instituted it with great solemnity, yet we do not read that he *partook* of it.[32] Was not the administration of baptism so honoured at the river Jordan, when the great IMMANUEL submitted to it; when the eternal FATHER, by an audible voice, declared his approbation of it; and when the DIVINE SPIRIT descended on the head of Jesus, just emerged from the water, as no other institution ever was? And does not the divinely prescribed form of words that is used in its administration shew, that there is a peculiar solemnity, an excellence, an importance in it? while, at the same time, it suggests arguments of unanswerable force against those Antitrinitarian errors which now so much abound. For no man who has been baptized at his own request, "in the name of the FATHER, and of the SON, and of the HOLY GHOST;" can deny that fundamental doctrine of the Trinity, without giving the lye to his baptism.

---

[32] WOLFIUS *in Luc.* xxii. 18.

~ An Apology for the Baptists ~

Nor is it unlikely that this consideration may have inclined some to oppose the ordinance. "I believe one reason, says Dr. WALL, why SOCINUS had such a mind to abolish all use of baptism among his followers, was, because persons baptized *in the name of the Father, and the Son, and the Holy Spirit,* would be always apt to think those names to express the Deity in which they were to believe; which he did not mean they should do. And some of his followers have been so disgusted with that form of baptism, that they have given profane insinuations that those words were not originally in the scripture; but were taken from the usual doxology into the form of baptism, and then inserted into the text of Matt. xxviii. 19."[33] —The same suspicions, relating to this matter, were entertained by Mr. THOMAS BRADBURY, as appears by the following words: "My friends, I ought to warn you, that the main debate in a little time will be, not *how much water* should be used, but whether *any at* all. They who deny the doctrine of the Trinity are so uneasy at the form of words, that our Saviour has made essential to baptism, that they have a great mind to lay aside the ordinance, as SOCINUS did in Poland. They write and argue that it is not *necessary;* by which if they mean any thing that is worth our heeding, it must be, that it is not *commanded.* For though we dare not say that it's necessary to God's *grace,* yet the question is, whether he has not made it so to our *duty?* And when they ask you, whether a man may not be *saved* without it? Do you ask them whether he is obedient without it? whether he stands compleat in all the will of God? whether he fulfills all righteousness? or whether he neglects to do, what the scripture told him he ought to do?"[34]

It is with peculiar pleasure, on this occasion, that I introduce the following pertinent passage from a little publication written by Mr. JOHN RYLAND. His words are these: "Dr. DANIEL WATERLAND justly observes, that the true doctrine of the Trinity and the atonement of Christ, have

---

[33] *Hist. Inf. Bap.* Part II Chap. VII.
[34] Duty and Doct. p. 52.

been kept up in the Christian church, by the institutions of baptism and the Lord's supper, more than by any other means whatsoever; and, humanly speaking, these glorious truths, which are essential to salvation, would have been lost long ago, if the two positive institutions had been totally neglected and disused amongst professors of Christianity. In this point of view, baptism and the Lord's supper appear to be of *unspeakable importance to the glory of God, and the* VERY BEING *of the true church of Christ on earth.*"[35] — *Again: In* another little piece, to which I have already referred, and of which the same worthy minister of Jesus Christ has expressed his approbation in more ways than one, though it does not bear his name; I find the following strong assertions relating to the importance and utility of baptism. "It is highly incumbent on *all* that love the Lord Jesus Christ in sincerity, and are glad to behold their Saviour in every view in which he is pleased to reveal himself, to consider the *dignity* and *glory* of his holy institutions. These last legacies of a dying Saviour, these pledges of his eternal and immutable love, ought to be received with the *greatest reverence* and the *warmest gratitude.* And as they directly relate to the death of the great Redeemer, which is an event the most interesting; an action the most grand and noble that ever appeared in the world; they ought to be held in the *highest esteem,* and performed with the *utmost solemnity.* Of these institutions, *baptism* calls for our *first* regard, *as it is appointed to be* FIRST PERFORMED: AND HOWEVER LIGHTLY THE INCONSIDERATE PART OF MANKIND MAY AFFECT TO TREAT THIS ORDINANCE, IT OUGHT TO BE REMEMBERED, [I hope CANDIDUS, and especially PACIFICUS, will never forget it] THAT CHRIST HIMSELF CONSIDERED IT AND SUBMITTED TO IT, AS AN IMPORTANT PART OF THAT RIGHTEOUSNESS WHICH IT BECAME EVEN THE SON OF GOD TO FULFIL. As this ordinance is to be *once* performed, and not repeated, every Christian ought to be *particularly careful* that it is done in a

---

[35] *Beauty of Social Relig.* p. 10.

right manner; or the benefit arising to the soul from this institution is *lost,* and lost *for ever.* We ought with the utmost deliberation and care to consider—its own *native dignity,* as an action of the positive, or ritual kind, the *most great and noble in itself, and well pleasing to God,* THAT IS POSSIBLE FOR US TO PERFORM ON THIS SIDE HEAVEN. —In this action, Christians, you behold the counsel of God: it is the result of his wise and eternal purpose: it is clearly commanded in his word: it is enforced by his own example; and honoured in the most distinguished and wonderful manner, by every Person in the adorable TRINITY. This ordinance is no *trivial* affair; it is no *mean* thing; and whoever is so unhappy as to despise it, wants eyes to see its beauty and excellency. —Our great Redeemer seems to have designed this ordinance as *a test* of our sincerity, and *to distinguish his followers* from the rest of mankind. As a captain who, to try a new soldier, employs him at first in some arduous and important service; so our Saviour, to try his own work, and to make the reality of his powerful grace in the hearts of his people manifest to themselves and to the world, calls them out at first to a great and singular action, and requires their submission to an institution that is disgustful to their nature and mortifying to their pride." And the title of the pamphlet, from which these extracts are made, speaks of baptism, "As an act of *sublime worship* to the adorable Persons in the Godhead—As a representation of the *sufferings of Christ,* his death, burial, and resurrection— As *the answer* of a good conscience towards God—As an emblem of *regeneration* and *sanctification* —As *a powerful obligation* to newness of life—And as a lively figure of *the natural death* of every Christian."[36]

Mr. DANIEL TURNER has also born his testimony to the usefulness and importance of baptism. For, speaking of that ordinance, he says; "Christ himself submitted to this rite, as administered by John; not indeed with the same views, or to the same ends, with others; but as pointing out by his

---

[36] *Six Views of Believers Bap.* p. 1, 2, 3, 15.

example, *the duty of Christians in general.* He also gave his ministers a commission and order, to baptize all the nations they taught. —It appears that being baptized, was the *common token* of subjection to Christ, AND NECESSARY TO A REGULAR ENTRANCE INTO HIS VISIBLE CHURCH." And, when describing the qualifications of those that are to be received into communion, he says; "They should be acquainted with the chief design of the rites and positive institutions of Christianity, and *reverently use them; viz.* baptism, and the Lord's supper." Once more: Speaking of that respect which the two positive appointments have to visible fellowship among believers, he says; "*Baptism,* indeed, by which we are first formally incorporated into the visible church, or body of Christ, is the BEGINNING and FOUNDATION of this external communion: but the Lord's supper is best adapted for the constant support and continual manifestation of it."[37] Nay, he mentions "the *reverent use* of the two sacraments," among those things which are "ESSENTIAL to the constitution of a particular visible church."[38]

After such considerations as these, relating to the vast utility and grand importance of baptism, one cannot but wonder at PACIFICUS, CANDIDUS, and others of our opponents that were never suspected of Antitrinitarian error; calling that ordinance, *a non-essential,* an *external rite,* an *indifferent thing, a shadow, a mere outward form;* comparing it with *the antiquated right of circumcision,* in the apostolic age. How different this way of talking from the quotations I have just produced; especially those I have taken from pieces that were either published, or composed and recommended, by my worthy friend Mr. RYLAND! For he looks upon baptism, in connection with the Lord's supper, as of *unspeakable importance* to the glory of God, and the very being of a true church upon earth. He insists upon it, that baptism demands the believer's regard, *prior* to the holy supper, as it was appointed to be first administered: and he severely censures

---

[37] Compend. Social Relig. p. 27. (Note); and p. 63, 120. (Note).
[38] See p. v. Note.

those *inconsiderate mortals,* who treat the ordinance lightly. —Mr. TURNER also, as we have seen, maintains that baptism is *the duty of Christians in general;* that it is the *common token* of our subjection to Christ; that it is *necessary to a regular entrance* into the visible church; and that it is the FOUNDATION of external communion in the house of God. Surely, then, these authors cannot but be greatly grieved, if not offended, with those diluting terms and that degrading comparison, which are used by Messieurs PACIFICUS and CANDIDUS, when speaking of the ordinance! Nay, they will be ready to retort upon them that heavy charge, which those *Peaceful* and *Candid* Gentlemen levelled at us; and to remind them that, by treating baptism in such a manner, they greatly injure "the honour and interest of true religion, and not a little contribute to the cause of infidelity." For they have united in repeatedly calling baptism *a nonessential;* and in comparing it with that obsolete appointment *circumcision,* of which judaizing Christians of old were so fond. This being the case, I am heartily glad that these worthy authors have *reprobated* their conduct, and so *publickly condemned* their way of thinking, in regard to baptism. It may serve, perhaps, as an antidote against the hurtful influence of their *Modest Plea;* nor may it be entirely useless to PACIFICUS and CANDIDUS themselves. But yet, methinks, I could sincerely wish, as Mr. RYLAND and Mr. TURNER are pretty well acquainted with those writers, that they would seriously examine and converse with them *in private,* on the subject about which they *so widely differ.* And I may just hint, that as they are the fittest persons in the world to perform the friendly office, they need not fear provoking their choler. For as their names are, CANDID and PEACEFUL, so is their temper; and it might have a beneficial effect, by making them more careful what they write and publish in future, in regard to free communion. —But I return from this digression.

Mr. BUNYAN, when speaking of baptism, calls it an *outward circumstantial thing—A shadow,* an *outward circumstance—*

WATER—WATER—WATER—WATER—WATER; five times over, in so many lines. And a submission to baptism he describes in equally degrading language. For he represents it, as an *outward conformity to an outward circumstance*—As an *outward and bodily conformity to outward and shadowish circumstances*—And calls it *obedience to* WATER.[39] What depreciating terms! What irreverent language! Is not the reader tempted to think, that I have made a mistake in my author; and that I have been referring to SOCINUS, or BARCLAY, instead of him who penned that immortal work, *The Pilgrim's Progress?* But let me not wrong those authors, by insinuating that they make use of similar language on the same subject. For though the former, when speaking of the ordinance under consideration, frequently calls it, "The external baptism of water," for which his opponent reproves him;[40] and though the latter denominates both the positive institutions of our Lord, "Shadows, and outside things;" yet, so far as I have observed, neither of them ever used such degrading and indecent language concerning baptism, as that produced from Mr. BUNYAN. Nay, I do not remember to have met with any thing of the kind that is equal to it, except what is reported of some ancient heretics, called *Archontici.*[41] Yet had SOCINUS, or BARCLAY, so expressed himself, we should not have been much surprised; because the one maintains, that Christ never required his apostles to baptize in water, but only *permitted* them so to do; and the other expressly says, "That he [Christ] commanded his disciples to baptize with water, I could never yet read."[42] Our brethren, therefore, who plead for free communion, are the only persons professing firmly to believe, that Christ *commanded,* really and solemnly COMMANDED his ministering servants to baptize in water, and *continue the practice* to the end of

---

[39] *Works,* Vol. 1, p. 133, 137, 168, 169, 134, 138, 194.
[40] Baptismum aquae externum. Apud HOORNE. *Socin. Conf.* Tom. *II.* p. 301.
[41] "Who impiously, as THEODORET asserts, Lavacrum exocrant, et mysteriorum participationem, ut quae siat in nomine Sabaoth. Apud, SUICERUM, Thes. Eccles. sub voce Cf. Baptism.
[42] HOORNE, ubi supra, p. 249, 250, 251, 301. BARCLAY's *Apol.* p. 424.

the world; and yet treat the ordinance as if it were a mere circumstance in divine worship; an indifferent thing; and dispense with it just as occasion requires. Consequently, they have the complete monopoly of that honour which arises from the union of *such a creed* and *such a conduct.*

The Lord's supper, however, is considered and treated by them in a different manner; for they speak of it as *a delightful,* an *edifying,* an *important* institution. But what authority have they for thus distinguishing between two appointments of the *same* LORD, intended for the *same persons,* of *equal continuance* in the Christian church, and *alike required* of proper subjects? They have, indeed, the *example* of some Socinians, and the *venerable sanction* of the whole Council of Trent. For the title of one chapter in the records of that Council, is; "Concerning the excellence of the most holy Eucharist, *above the rest* of the sacraments."[43] But, as a good old Protestant writer observes, "That the one sacrament should be so much extolled above the other, namely, the Lord's supper to be preferred before baptism, as the more worthy and excellent sacrament, we find no such thing in the word of God; but that both of them are of like dignity in themselves, and to be had equally and indifferently in most high account."[44] Nay, Mr. RYLAND assures us, of which I would have PACIFICUS take particular notice; That "baptism ought to be considered as glorious an act of worship, *as ever was instituted by God."*[45] —Might not the Jews of old have distinguished, with equal propriety, between circumcision and the paschal supper? Does it become us to form comparisons between the positive appointments of our Eternal Sovereign, in regard to their importance; and that with a view to dispense with either of them, while the very same authority enjoins the one as well as the other? Can such a conduct be pious, humble, or rational? Is it not something like being "partial in God's law," for which the ancient priests were severely censured? Or,

---

[43] Concil. Trident. Sess. XIII. Cap. III.
[44] WILLET's *Synops. Papismi,* p. 556, 557.
[45] *Beauty of Social Relig.* p. 9.

shall we say of our obedience to God, as he says to the mighty ocean; "Hitherto shalt thou come, but no further?"

But supposing it evident, that baptism is *much inferior* to the sacred supper, in point of importance; yet, while it is an ordinance of God, it has an equal claim on our obedience. For it is not the manifest excellence, or the great utility, of any divine appointment, that is the true reason of our submission to it; but the *authority* of Him that commands. "It hath been ever God's wont, says Bp. HALL, by small precepts to prove men's dispositions. Obedience is as well tried in a trifle, as in the most important charge: yea, so much more, as the thing required as less: for oftimes those who would be careful in main affairs, think they may neglect the smallest. What command soever we receive from God, or our superiors, we must not scan the *weight* of the thing, but the *authority* of the commander. Either difficulty, or slightness, are vain pretences for disobedience."[46] Nay, even Dr. PRIESTLEY, though remarkable for his liberal sentiments and rational way of thinking, and far from ascribing too much to God's dominion over the subjects of his moral government; yet strongly asserts Jehovah's prerogative in this respect. These are his words; "Every divine command ought certainly to be *implicitly complied with,* even though we should not be able to discern the reason of it."[47] And has not He who is God over all blessed for ever, said; "Whosoever shall break one of these least commandments, and shall teach men so, he shall be called the least in the kingdom of heaven"? As, in the great concerns of religious worship, nothing should be done that is not required by Jehovah; and as the lawfulness of all positive rites depends entirely on their divine Author and his institution; so he who complies with some, and neglects others that are equally commanded and equally known, may please himself, but he does not obey the Lord.[48]

---

[46] Contemplations, Vol. III, p. 274. Edinb. Edit.
[47] On giving the Lord's Supper to Children, p.6.
[48] Qui in aliq ibus tantum morem Deo gerere instituit, aliqua vero eximit, qua; suo sibi arbitratu agat, is non Deo paret, fed fibi placet. Veræ obedientiac fundamentum est prxcipientis auctoritas; quay quum in omn

Further: These depreciating expressions, *non-essential, external rite, a shadow,* and *a mere outward form,* may be applied to the sacred supper with as much propriety as they are to baptism. Another quotation from BARCLAY will not be displeasing to our opponents; especially when they observe, how nearly his language, in regard to baptism, coincides with theirs. "We," says the plain dealing apologist, "we always prefer the power to the form, the substance to the shadow; and where the substance and the power is, we doubt not to denominate the person, accordingly, though the form be wanting. And, therefore, we always seek first and plead for the substance and power, as knowing that to be indispensably necessary; though *the form sometimes may be dispensed with.*"[49] —*Dispense with the form,* in regard to such persons *as possess the power:* why that is the VERY THING for which our brethren plead. How happily friend ROBERT and they are agreed, in this respect! And what *an honour* it reflects upon them, as *Baptists,* to have such an associate! They, however, will do well to remember, that the principle on which the Quaker proceeds, extends its influence to the holy supper, no less than to baptism; and that he who has a right to *dispense* with a law, may *entirely repeal it,* and enact another whenever he pleases. —Baptism is an *external rite, a mere outward form.* But whatever SOCINUS, or BUNYAN, or any of our brethren, may say in defense of their conduct on this ground, will apply with equal force against a punctual observance of the Lord's supper. This BARCLAY intended. For are not *bread* and *wine* external things, as well as *water?* And has not the act of *baptizing* as much *spirituality* in it, as the acts of *eating* and *drinking?* Besides, an apostle has assured us, that "the kingdom of God is not *meat* and *drink,*" though the latter were the richest of cordials, any more than it is *immersion* in water.[50]

---

bus preeceptis eadem sit, cuncta etiam ex aequo obligare censendum est. WITSII. *Miscel. Sac.* Tom. II. Exercit. XV. § II.
[49] *Apology,* p. 419.
[50] Vid. HOORNBEEK. ubi supra, p. 362.

Once more: When I consider how much *more frequently* baptism is mentioned in the New Testament, than the sacred supper;[51] how often repenting and believing sinners are *exhorted,* by the apostles, to be baptized; how *soon* that ordinance was administered to Christian converts after they believed; what *exhortations* are given to professing Christians on the ground of their being baptized; and when I reflect, that the Holy Spirit *commends* them that were baptized by John, as "justifying God;" while he *severely censures* others, as "rejecting the counsel of God against themselves," because they slighted the solemn appointment; I cannot but wonder at the language and conduct of our opponents. —Their very singular conduct appears to me still more extraordinary, and yet more unwarrantable, when I reflect; That baptism is a divine institution to which a believer submits but *once,* and a branch of divine worship that he is required to perform but *once;* in which respect it greatly differs from every other appointment in the worship of God, under the Christian œconomy. For, this being the case, one should have imagined, if notorious and stubborn facts had not forbidden the thought; that *every minister* of Jesus Christ, and *every church* of the living God, would INSIST on a submission to what they consider as *real* baptism, in all whom they admit to the Lord's table. And, whatever PACIFICUS may have said to the contrary, or however unimportant *he* may suppose the ordinance to be; I have the pleasure to find, that Mr. RYLAND, as before observed, seems to consider it in the same light with myself; if one may venture to form a judgment of his views relating to this institution, from what he has published under his own name. These are his words, and I would warmly recommend them to the consideration of PACIFICUS: "Baptism ought to be considered *as glorious an act of worship as ever was instituted by God.* It is to be performed but *once* in the life of a Christian—but *once* to eternity; and therefore, *it ought to be done* with the utmost veneration and love."[52] Here, then,

---

[51] HOORNBEEK, ut supra, p. 409, 416.
[52] *Beauty of Social Relig.* p. 9.

we have an ordinance appointed by Supreme authority, which requires to be celebrated but *once;* a command given by the Lord Redeemer, that is perfectly satisfied with *one,* yes, with *only one* act of obedience in the whole course of a Christian's life: yet, strange to imagine, but certain in fact, though the authority enjoining is *absolute,* and acknowledged so to be; though the obedience required consists in *a single* instance; and though the duty commanded is generally *easy, very easy* to be performed, where there is a disposition for it; our brethren not only connive at a neglect of it, but severely censure us because we do not adopt their conduct! But whether we, or they, deserve censure, considering the principles we hold in common, I leave the impartial reader, I leave all but themselves, to judge; they not believing, any more than we, the divine authority, or the validity of infant sprinkling; for if they did, they would stand convicted before all the world of *Anabaptism.* My reader will pardon the frequent repetition of this thought, it being of great importance in every dispute of this kind; nor can we suffer our opponents long to forget it.

SECTION VI.

Reflections on the distinguishing Character,
STRICT BAPTISTS,
which our Brethren apply to us.

Our opponents, I observe, repeatedly call us, STRICT BAPTISTS; but whether for so doing they merit commendation, or deserve censure, may, perhaps, be a question with some. If, by the epithet *strict,* they mean *exact, accurate, conscientiously nice;* their candour deserves commendation. In that sense of the term we are not ashamed to be called STRICT *Baptists:* we cheerfully adopt the character.

It may, however, admit of a query, whether we be so fully entitled to possess this honour without a rival, as our brethren seem to insinuate. Is it because we are stricter than the *apostles,* in regard to communion at the Lord's table? That remains to be proved. Is it because we consider baptism as equally the duty of *all* believers? This, indeed, we maintain: and the reason is, those arguments which prove it the duty of one, will apply to all.[1] Or, is it because we consider baptism as *a term* of communion? We, it is true, avow the sentiment; but it is far from being peculiar to us. For it appears from the foregoing pages, that we act on a principle received in common by Christians of almost every name, in every age, and in every nation. When, therefore, we are compared with professing Christians in general, we have

---

[1] Si baptismi significationem et veram rationem respicimus, nulla plane dari potest ratio, cur non omnibus sine discrimine Christianis administrari debeat, sed potius contrarium patet. *STAPFERI Institut. Theolog. Polem.* Tom. *III.* p. 578.

no peculiar claim to the epithet *strict;* whatever right we may have to the denomination of *Baptists,* or whatever may be our distinguishing character, when opposed to our brethren with whom we now contend. —Nor can we be otherwise than *strict,* without violating our own principles and contradicting our own practice. For *we* believe that all who have received the truth, should profess their faith in Jesus Christ and be baptized. And have we not the happiness, in this respect, of agreeing with our brethren? When we made a public declaration of our dependence on Christ, and gave a reason of the hope that is in us, we believed it was *our* duty to be baptized, before we received the sacred supper. Did not our opponents do the same? or had it no place at all in their creed? In consequence of such a conviction, *we* were actually immersed in the name of the Lord, before we approached the holy table. And were not they also? But how came it to be either *our* duty, or *theirs,* thus to proceed? Was it because they or we *believed* that it was required of us? Or, did a full persuasion of this kind constitute that *a duty,* which would not otherwise have been obligatory? If so, a Catholic may lawfully adore the host, a Mussulman revere Mahomet, and a Jew blaspheme the Messiah. No; that which made it our duty to be baptized, and then to receive the Lord's supper, was THE COMMAND OF GOD; which lies on every person so qualified, by the renewing agency of the divine Spirit, as we humbly conceived ourselves to be. Now, can it be supposed that this command extends to none but those among real converts, who feel its force on their own consciences? Or, may we safely conclude, that a believer is no further obliged by any divine precept, or prohibition, than he *sees* and *acknowledges* the obligation, in regard to himself? If so, a believer who has been baptized, may live all his days in the neglect of communion at the Lord's table, and stand acquitted of blame; and covetousness is no crime, in thousands who bow at the shrine of Mammon; for there are comparatively few lovers of money, who acknowledge their guilt in that respect. Nay, on this principle it will follow, that the more ignorant any believer is, and the less tender his conscience, he is under so much the less obligation to obey the divine commands. But the reader will do well to remember, that the GREAT SUPREME does not lie at our courtesy for his claim of obedience upon us, in any instance that can be named. No; it is not our conviction of the propriety, the utility, or the necessity of any command which he has given, that entitles him to the performance of it; but, in all things of a moral nature, our being *rational creatures is* the ground of his claim; and in those of a positive kind, our *being qualified* according to his direction, whether we be so wise and so sincere as to acknowledge the obligation, or no. Thus it appears that the epithet *strict*, if taken in the sense already explained, is no dishonour to *us*.

But if, on the contrary, our brethren mean by the epithet, that we are *bigoted, unnecessarily exact, unscripturally confined;* their forwardness to give us a name calls for our censure. In the former sense, I will venture to affirm, every Baptist *ought* to be *a strict* one, or else to renounce the name. In the latter use of the term, we reject the distinguishing epithet, and require our opponents to prove—I say to *prove*, not to surmise, that it justly belongs to us. And that they use the word in this *obnoxious* meaning appears to me, by the tenour of their arguing; by superadding that harsher epithet *rigorous;* and by that home charge, of greatly injuring "the honour and interest of true religion, and NOT A LITTLE CONTRIBUTING TO THE CAUSE OF INFIDELITY."

But if we be STRICT BAPTISTS, what are they? Our brethren will not be offended, if I again ask; What *are* they, and by *what name* shall we call them? That they are not strict Baptists, is out of all dispute; because from such they expressly distinguish themselves, and have abundant reason, if the charge just mentioned be true, to be *ashamed* of them. I am obliged, therefore, if it be lawful for me to imitate their officiousness, and to give them a name, (for as yet they are *half* anonymous) to search for some significant and descriptive adjective, that will set them at a *wide distance* from the strict Baptists. But what must it be? *Inaccurate,* or *loose,* or *latitudinarian?* I would not, designedly, be guilty of a misnomer; but as all these terms are very different in their meaning from that obnoxious word *strict,* it can hardly be supposed that I am far from the truth. As they profess themselves BAPTISTS, there we agree; but as they hold the ordinance of baptism with a LOOSE HAND, there we differ; and hence the necessity of such oppositely significant epithets, to mark our different conduct. For names, you know, are so much the more perfect, by how much the more they express the nature and properties of persons and things. Yes, the practice of our opponents makes it evident to all the world, that the term *Baptists,* when applied to them, is to be understood in such a latitude of signification, as will comport with receiving persons to communion, who, in their judgment, are *unbaptized.* That is, they are *Baptists,* when the ideas expressed by that name suit the dispositions of their hearers; and they entirely omit the ordinance, from which they take their denomination, when candidates for communion with them do not approve of it. And, which makes their conduct, in this respect, appear exceedingly strange, they do not, like his Holiness of Rome, expressly claim a dispensing power; nor, in the madness of enthusiasm, pretend to any new revelation; nor yet, with the disciples of GEORGE FOX, consider baptism as a temporary institution.

Our character, then, is fixed. Their own pens have engrossed it. And, be it known to all men, we are STRICT BAPTISTS. To this character, as before explained, we subscribe with hand and heart, in the last words of the celebrated Father PAUL, *Esto perpetua.* Theirs I have attempted to draw, in contrast with ours, and will now venture to call them, LATITUDINARIAN BAPTISTS. Whether they will allow the name to be just, and esteem it as we do ours, I am not certain. But of this I make no doubt, that the religious world in general, were they to see and compare it with the opinion and practice of our brethren; would pronounce it descriptive of the persons to whom it is given. STRICT BAPTISTS—they will permit our character to stand first, as it has confessedly the right of primogeniture—STRICT BAPTISTS! LATITUDINARIAN BAPTISTS! These characters, in contrast, sound very oddly, I must confess; and they are but of a novel date. For they do not appear to have had an existence till about the middle of the last century. What a pity it is but something of a similar kind could have been found, in the ancient monuments of the Jewish church, relating to circumcision, as a prerequisite for communion in it! Had it appeared, in any authentic records, that the sons of Abraham, in times of yore, were divided in their judgment about that obsolete rite; and that some of them were called STRICT CIRCUMCISIONISTS, and others LATITUDINARIAN CIRCUMCISIONISTS; it would have given, at least, an *air* of antiquity to our brethren's hypothesis, practice, and character. But—we must take things as we find them.

I just now recollect, what many of my readers must now to be fact, that our Pædobaptist brethren, when they have a mind to shew their wit and be a little merry at our expense, represent the Baptists, without distinction, as *exceedingly fond* of water; as professors that cannot *live* in a church state, without *a great deal of water*. Nay, one of them has very politely called us "WATERY BIGOTS;" and then immediately adds, "Many ignorant sprinkled Christians are often, to their hurt, *pulled by them into the water.*"[2] — According to this Gentleman, then, we are *watery bigots. Well, it does not greatly distress me* to be thus represented by a sneering antagonist; because I really believe that *much water is* necessary to baptism, and am no less confident, that baptism is necessary to communion at the Lord's table. But since I have maturely considered the singular character and peculiar situation of our latitudinarian brethren, I can by no means think it either candid or equitable that they should be

---

[2] Dr. MAYO's *True Scripture Doctrine of Baptism, p. 33.* Poor creatures! How much these "sprinkled Christians' are to be pitied, when treated so rudely by WATERY BIGOTS! Is there no remedy against such an invasion of personal liberty, by appealing to Cæsar? If there be, *a Doctor of Laws* would not spend his time ill in pointing it out, for the benefit of such "*ignorant* sprinkled-Christians,' and to prevent any of them being *hurt,* in future.

thus represented. Because it is evident, evident even to demonstration, that their profession and practice taken together will not admit of it. They, it must be acknowledged, will sometimes declaim aloud on the necessity of a profession of faith, and of immersion in the name of the triune God, to constitute that baptism which is from heaven. So, when they write on the subject, and publish their thoughts to the world at large, they assert these things with the greatest confidence. They will also, with the venerable JOHN, go down into Jordan, and there administer the significant ordinance: so that one would be tempted to think they were *strict* Baptists, *real* Baptists, and that baptism has no *faster friends* upon earth. But when they plead for free communion, they *talk* a different language; they speak of it as an indifferent thing and a mere trifle, that is not worth contending about. And, when they admit communicants, they often *act* in a different way; for, in receiving a Pædobaptist, what they consider as real baptism is entirely set aside. They might, consequently, with equal consistency, admit believers to their communion, who have neither been immersed nor sprinkled; and so, like the Quakers, have nothing at all to do with *water* in the worship of God. Whether, therefore, a person has been immersed in a river, be the waters ever so *many;* or sprinkled with that element from the palm of the hand, be the drops ever so *few;* or has had no concern with water *at all,* it makes no material difference with them, in point of communion. So, then, as they can receive members into their communities, subsist in a church state, and enjoy fellowship at the Lord's table, with either *much* water, or *little* water, or *none at all; I* humbly conceive, that if our bantering opponent would do them justice, while he displays his own wit, he should give them *a different name.* For though they seem, at some times, to be as fond of water as we are; insisting upon it, that where there is no immersion there is no baptism; yet, at others, they warmly contend, that believers of ALL denominations, (*i.e.* Baptists, with *much* water; Pædobaptists, with *little* water; and Katabaptists, without *any water* at all) have a right of communion with them in the sacred supper. It behooves the Doctor, therefore, if ever he favour us with another address, to search for a new, distinguishing epithet, to connect with the term *bigots,* that shall include and express these various ideas. But whether our own language be able to furnish an adjective comprehensive enough, on such an occasion, I dare not assert: very probably, however, among those numerous compounds contained in the language of ancient Greece, he may find one that is fit for the purpose. And as it is not every one, no, nor every Doctor, who could have thought of that elegant phrase, "WATERY BIGOTS;" I doubt not but the fertility of his invention, and the well known accuracy of his pen, when handling the Baptists, will enable him to give our brethren a descriptive character, that shall be equally polite and perfectly suitable.

Though I am far from suspecting that our brethren want sincerity, or from thinking that they violate the dictates of conscience, in maintaining their very singular hypothesis; yet their conduct, in regard to baptism, has such an *ambiguous* appearance, and looks so much like holding *both sides* of a contradiction, that I should not wonder if one or another of our Pædobaptist opponents, were to apply to them, with a little alteration, the spirited remonstrance of Bp. HALL to Abp. LAUD. The latter being strongly suspected of a predilection for Popery, and the former intending to deal roundly with him on that subject, addressed him in the following language: "I would I knew where to find you—To day you are in the tents of the Romanists; to morrow in ours; the next day between both, against both. Our adversaries think you ours; we theirs—This of yours is the worst of all tempers. Heat and cold have their uses; lukewarmness is good for nothing but to trouble the stomach—How long will you halt in this indifferency? Resolve one way, and know, at last, what you do hold; what you should. Cast off either your wings or your teeth; and, loathing this bat-like form, be either a bird or a beast. If you must begin, why not now? — God crieth with Jehu, *Who is on my side, who?* Take you *peace;* let me have *truth,* if I cannot have both."[3] Thus the acute and the good Bishop HALL, to one who halted between two opinions; who was neither an uniform Papist, nor a consistent Protestant.

And now, before I conclude, our brethren will suffer me also to remonstrate; and the reader may rest assured, that I do it without the least impeachment of their integrity: If infant sprinkling be a human invention, disown it, renounce it, entirely reject it, and no longer let it hold the place of a divine institution, in any of your churches. But if it be from Heaven, embrace it, profess it, practise it in the face of the sun, and lay the other absolutely aside, as destitute of a divine warrant. For as there is but ONE GOD, and ONE FAITH, so there is but ONE BAPTISM. Divine truth is consistent; divine ordinances are consistent, for they are not yea and nay; and all the Christian world are consistent with themselves, relating to baptism; be ye, therefore, consistent in this, as you are in other respects. That is, be either consistent *Baptists,* or *Pædobaptists;* for, according to your present practice, all thinking and impartial men must pronounce you an *heterogeneous mixture* of both.

FINIS.

---

[3] Bp. HALL's *Epistles,* Decad. III. Epist. 5.

BOOK II

AN ESSAY ON THE KINGDOM OF CHRIST

An Essay

on the

Kingdom of Christ

BY ABRAHAM BOOTH

LONDON:

HOULSTON AND STONEMAN

65, PATERNOSTER ROW

1788

he Baptist Standard Bearer, Inc.

NUMBER ONE IRON OAKS DRIVE • PARIS, ARKANSAS 72855

Thou hast given a *standard* to them that fear thee;
that it may be displayed because of the truth.
— *Psalm 60:4*

PREFACE.

The kingdom of Christ is a subject of great importance: for, according to the views we have of that kingdom will our conclusions be, respecting various branches of religious conduct. If those views be imaginary, these conclusions must be false. By the former, the glory of Messiah's regal character will be obscured; by the latter, his worship will be corrupted whereas, the true doctrine concerning this holy empire, may not only be the mean of preserving from those evils, but of presenting us with *data* for the decision of many disputes among the professors of Christianity. A competent acquaintance, therefore, with its nature and laws, its emoluments and honours, is closely connected with our duty and happiness: which acquaintance must be derived from divine revelation.

Important, however, as the subject manifestly is, it has been but seldom professedly discussed. This consideration was a leading motive to the present attempt. To illustrate the nature of our Lord's kingdom, and to infer the conclusions flowing from it, constitute the design of this essay.

The author has expressed his thoughts with great freedom; yet without intending the least offence to any party of Christians, or to any person, from whose notions and practices he conscientiously differs. In the course of discussion he animadverts, indeed, on some particulars, with a degree of severity: but then they appear to him in the light of *political artifices,* which either impeach the dominion of Christ in his own kingdom; or degrade and corrupt that worship which he requires, Now, ice cases of this kind, the writer is of opinion, that allegiance to the king Messiah, and true benevolence to man, demand the language of marked opposition.

Such is the nature of our Lord's empire, that few of his loyal subjects can seriously reflect upon it, without feeling themselves both delighted and reproved. *Delighted;* because it is for the honour of their Mediator, to be the sovereign of a spiritual monarchy. A character of this kind apparently suits the dignity of his person, the design of his mediation, and the riches of his grace. *Reproved;* because they daily find a want of that spirituality in their affections, and of that heavenly mindedness, which become the professed subjects of such a kingdom. When meditating on the characteristics of this holy empire, they stand convicted before its divine sovereign of much carnality and worldly mindedness, over which they sincerely mourn: while merely nominal subjects of the King Messiah, or superficial professors of the gracious gospel, are but little concerned about the state of their hearts, in reference to heaven; or with regard to the spirituality of their worship.

This being the case with multitudes, the author would not be much surprised, were various particulars in the following pages to prove disgusting to the taste of numbers professing godliness. But facts are stubborn things; and the sayings of Jesus Christ must not be explained *away,* that conscience may rest in false peace, or that the public taste may be gratified. For, when thinking of our sublime sovereign, "Thy kingdom come," is the language of every upright heart, let carnal professors and the profligate world say what they please.

A. BOOTH.
Goodman's Fields, July 30, 1788.

AN ESSAY ON THE KINGDOM OF CHRIST

It having been revealed by ancient prophets that the Lord Messiah should be a king, and have universal empire, the chosen tribes in every age expected his appearance under the regal character. While, however, the general idea of that expectation was fully warranted by the Spirit of prophecy, the bulk of Abraham's natural posterity were under a gross mistake, respecting the true design of their Messiah's appearance, and the real nature of his kingdom: which mistake had the most pernicious influence upon their temper and conduct, when the gracious promise of his coming was fulfilled.

The sense which they affixed to prophecies respecting the great Redeemer, was manifestly such as flattered their pride and fostered their carnality. This gave it a decided advantage, in their estimation, over that for which our Lord and his apostles contended; and led them to overlook whatever in the ancient oracles opposed their secular views. Ignorant of their spiritual wants, and flushed with a false persuasion of interest in Jehovah's peculiar favour, on the ground of carnal descent from Abraham, and of the covenant made at Horeb; the doctrine, example, and claims of Christ, were extremely offensive. Not appearing as a temporal prince, discovering no disposition to free them from the Roman yoke, and frequently addressing their consciences with keen reproof, on account of their pride and hypocrisy, superstition and covetousness; they rejected with determined opposition all the evidences of his divine mission, treated him as an impostor, and procured his crucifixion. After he was risen from the dead, and ascended to heaven, multitudes of them indeed believed, and professed the Christian faith; but a great majority of the nation continued in hardened impenitence, and persecuted the Apostles with unrelenting malevolence. Thus they proceeded till, divine forbearance being exhausted, "wrath came upon them to the uttermost," in the total subversion of their civil and ecclesiastical polity.

This mistake of the Jews, respecting the kingdom of their Messiah, lying at the foundation of all the opposition with which they treated him, and of their own ruin; it behoves us to guard with diligence against every thing which tends to secularize the dominion of Christ; lest, by corrupting the Gospel œconomy, we dishonour the Lord Redeemer, and be finally punished as the enemies of his government. Our danger of contracting guilt, and of incurring divine resentment in this way, is far from being small. For we are so conversant with sensible objects, and so delighted with exterior show, that we are naturally inclined to wish for something in the religion of Jesus to gratify our carnality. Under the influence of that master prejudice, *the expectation of a temporal kingdom,* Jewish depravity rejected Christ; and our corruption, if we be not watchful, may so misrepresent his empire, and oppose his royal prerogatives, as implicitly to say, "We will not have him to reign over us.

Among the numerous admirable sayings of Jesus Christ, and of his apostles, that stand recorded in the New Testament, and are adapted to instruct us in this important subject; there is one which deserves peculiar notice. The saying to which I advert, is part of that "good confession" which our Lord witnessed before Pontius Pilate; "MY KINGDOM IS NOT OF THIS WORLD." A concise, but comprehensive declaration, and worthy of him that made it! This capital saying may be considered as the grand maxim on which he formed his conduct when among men; and it is pregnant with needful instruction to all his disciples, respecting the new economy and the Christian church. Relative to matters of that kind, there is not, perhaps, a more interesting passage in all the New Testament; nor one which is better adapted to rebuke the pride and carnality of millions who bear the

An Essay on the Kingdom of Christ

Christian character. To approve of Christ as a spiritual monarch, agreeably to the meaning and tendency of this emphatical text, requires a degree of heavenly mindedness which comparatively few possess.

"My kingdom is not of this world," says Messiah the Prince, when standing before the Roman governor, and questioned about his claim of dignity. He boldly avows himself a king; yet, while advancing his title to the honours of royalty, he tacitly informs Pilate, that the civil rights of Cæsar had nothing to fear from him; and that his own disciples had no advantages to expect, of a secular kind, as the result of embarking in his cause, Our Lord, a little while before, had implicitly conveyed the general idea of this declaration, by receiving from a surrounding multitude the acclamations due to his royal character, when "riding upon an ass:" for while he accepted the honours of royalty, the poverty and meanness of his appearance plainly implied that his kingdom was not of a temporal kind. Zechariah had foretold that the children of Zion should loudly rejoice in this humble manifestation of the king Messiah, and that their joy should kindle into rapture. An incontrovertible evidence that he predicted, the public inauguration of a Sovereign, whose "kingdom is not of this world." For the loyal and affectionate subjects of a political monarch never thought it matter of exultation, that he appeared among them, when proclaimed king, with all the marks of meanness and of poverty. Yet so it was in respect of the king Messiah.

It is generally allowed, if I mistake not, that the kingdom of Christ is no other than the gospel Church;[1] which is both distinguished from the world, and opposed to it. Relative to this kingdom, and its divine Sovereign, Jehovah says, "I have set my King upon my holy hill of Zion." This prophetic oracle was fulfilled when our Lord, leading captivity captive, ascended on high and sat down on the right hand of the

---

[1] Regnum Dei in evangelia, says Witsius, vix alia significatione venit, quam ut notet statum eximium et vere liberum Ecclesia Testamenti Novi sub Rege *Messia.* —*Exercitat, in Orat. Dominic.* Exercit. ix. § 11.

eternal Father. Then was he most solemnly inaugurated and proclaimed King of the New Testament church, amidst adoring myriads of attendant angels, and the "spirits of just men made perfect." In pursuance of which most grand investiture with his regal office, he distributed royal donatives, at the feast of Pentecost, among his devoted subjects—such donatives, as perfectly suited the majesty of his Person, and the nature of his kingdom. Yes, that wonderful assemblage of spiritual gifts and heavenly graces, which he bestowed upon his disciples at the Jewish festival, was a glorious first-fruit of his ascension, and of his being "a priest upon his throne." The gospel church, which is the subject of his laws, the seat of his government, and the object of his care, being surrounded with powerful opposers; he is represented as ruling in the "midst of his enemies." Nor shall his mediatorial kingdom and administration cease, till all those enemies become his footstool.

The empire of Christ, indeed, extends to every creature: for all authority in heaven and on earth is in his hands, and he "is Head over all things to the church." But the kingdom of which we treat, stands distinguished from that of general Providence, as well as from every political state. It must be considered, therefore, as consisting of those persons whom he bought with his blood, whom he calls by his grace, and over whom he reigns as a spiritual monarch. These constitute what is frequently called, the Catholic Church, wherever the favoured individuals may reside. Of such also, or of those who make a credible profession of being such, all those particular churches consist, which constitute our Lord's visible kingdom—that kingdom of which we speak. Into the principal characteristics of this holy empire, and into the genuine consequences of those criteria, we shall now inquire.

The gospel church is a kingdom not of this world, in regard to its origin. From the time of Nimrod to the present age, secular empires have generally originated in the vile passions of their first founders: for, in almost every instance, avarice and pride, ambition and a lust of dominion, have been conspicuous. Not so, in the kingdom of Christ. The remote foundation of his dominion was laid in the counsels of heaven before time commenced, by all comprehending wisdom and infinite goodness, for the glory of God and the benefit of man and the immediate basis on which it stands, is his own vicarious obedience to divine law; both as to its precepts, and as to its penalty. Justice and goodness, therefore, are the foundation of his throne: mercy and truth attend the whole of his administration.

The kingdom of Christ is not of this world, respecting the subjects of his righteous government. The generality of people in all countries, were *born* subjects of those governments under which they lived. No sooner, for instance, were we capable of reflecting upon our civil connections, than we found ourselves freeborn subjects of the British crown: and thus it commonly is in the sovereignties of secular princes. Their dominion being confined to the exterior of, human conduct, and not reaching the heart; natural birth and local circumstances constitute subjects of the state, put them under the protection of law, and invest them with civil rights. Such subjects are perfectly well suited to the kingdoms of this world, and to the character of their sovereigns. For, considered as men, kings and subjects are on a level: and, as distinguished by political characters, their obligations are mutual; allegiance on the one part, and protection on the other. Besides, temporal kingdoms respect the present world. The mutual duties of sovereigns and of subjects, as such, regard the happiness of civil society, and of that only. As an investiture with political sovereignty does not constitute a lord of conscience, it gives no claim to authority in spiritual things, but is entirely confined to the concerns of this world. It is, indeed, the indispensable duty of secular princes, and of their people, to love and adore God: yet that obligation does not arise from any political relation subsisting among them, but from their being reasonable creatures. It is also their happiness to be the subjects of Jesus Christ: but that felicity does not result from any thing short of divine mercy exercised upon them, as depraved and guilty creatures.

The kingdom and claims of Christ being very different from those of Caesar, the qualifications and obedience of his real subjects must be so too. For persons may be good subjects of a temporal sovereign, and enjoy the rights of such a character, while they are so far from bearing true allegiance to Jesus Christ, as to be quite inimical to his dominion, and entire strangers to the privileges of his kingdom. The empire of Christ "is not of this world:" it is not a temporal, but a spiritual kingdom. Our Lord, therefore, is a spiritual Sovereign; whose dominion extends to the mind, conscience, and heart, no less than to the external behaviour. Consequently, all the subjects of his government must have spiritual dispositions, and yield spiritual obedience— obedience, proceeding from an enlightened understanding, an awakened conscience, and a renewed heart. For, as is the sovereign, such are the subjects, and such the allegiance required. A spiritual Sovereign, and subjects yielding an obedience merely external, are manifestly inconsistent.

As all mankind are born in a state of apostasy from God; as the natural turn of the heart, or "the carnal mind, is not subject to the law of God, neither indeed can be;" we must be born again— "born, not of blood, nor of the will of the flesh, nor of the will of man, but of God," before we are permitted to consider ourselves, or to be considered by others, as the subjects of Him whose kingdom is of a spiritual kind. Remarkable are the words of our Lord, when speaking of his loyal subjects: "They are not of the world, even as I am not of the world." No: they are described by the apostles, as being "of the truth;" "of faith;" and "of God."[2] "Of the truth:" enlightened, converted, and sanctified by the gospel. "Of faith;" living by it; deriving peace and holiness from Jesus Christ, through believing in him. "Of God;" born of him; or "begotten again to a lively hope, by the resurrection of Jesus Christ from the dead." Such are the subjects of our Lord's kingdom: in opposition to whom, the New Testament represents the rest of our apostate race, as being "of the

---

[2] John xviii. 17; Gal. iii. 7, 9; 1 John. iv. 4, 6.

works of the law;" "of the world;" "of darkness;" and "of the devil."[3] "Of the works of the law:" seeking acceptance with God by their own imperfect obedience, which leaves them under a curse. "Of the world;" carnally minded, and in a state of enmity to God. "Of darkness:" ignorant of their perishing state, and unacquainted with Jesus Christ. "Of the devil:" partakers of his image, subjects of his dominion, and performers of his will.[4] So great is the contrast formed by scripture, between those who are under our Lord's government, and the rest of mankind! Agreeably to which, real Christians are further described, as "delivered from the power of darkness," or the tyranny of Satan, and translated into the kingdom of God's dear Son: and as being "of God," while all the rest of the "world lies in wickedness." None, therefore, but those who are born from above, are the subjects of Jesus Christ: for if the heart be not under his dominion, he reigns not at all as a spiritual monarch.

That none but real Christians are subjects of our Lord's kingdom, is yet further apparent from the descriptive characters of those that were members of the apostolic churches. We find them described in the New Testament, as "gladly receiving the word" of grace, as "the called of Jesus Christ," and as "called to be saints." The apostles denominate them "brethren;" "faithful brethren," "holy brethren," "saints," and "lively stones" in the spiritual temple.[5] These and similar characters are frequently applied to members of the primitive churches in general; and of those churches the visible kingdom of Christ then consisted. We may therefore say, with Vitringa; "The kingdom of grace; in which Christ is king upon Mount Zion, is properly and emphatically "the kingdom of Christ:" of which none are subjects, except those who are chosen, called, faithful, peaceable, and humble; in

---

[3] Gal. iii. 10; John viii. 23; 1 John iv. 5; 1 Thess. v. 5; John viii. 38, 41, 44; 1 John iii. 8, 12.
[4] Rom. viii. 6, 7, 8; Eph. v. 8; John viii. 44; Eph. ii. 2.
[5] Acts ii. 41; Rom, i. 6; 1 Cor. i. 2; Eph. i. 1; Philip. i, 1; Col. i. 2; 2 Thess. i. 3; Heb. iii. 1; 1 Pet. i. 2, 3, and ii. 5; 2 Pet. i. 1.

whom Jesus Christ lives by his Spirit, as in the members of a mystical and spiritual body, of which he is the Head."[6]

This view of our Lord's subjects is perfectly agreeable to the nature and genius of the new covenant, with which, the Messiah's kingdom is closely connected because it appears, that subjects of any other description, have no reason to consider themselves as covenantees; and it is plain that a divine covenant must suit the kingdom to which it belongs, whether Jewish or Christian. When, "in the fulness of time," God performed his gracious and comprehensive promise of blessing all nations, it was by the intervention of a new and better covenant than that which was made at Sinai. For thus it is written: "Behold, the days come, with the Lord, that I will make a new covenant with the house of Israel, and with the house of Judah: *not according to the covenant that I made with their fathers, in the day that I took them by the hand to bring them out of the land of Egypt;* which my covenant they brake, although I was an husband unto them, with the Lord but this shall be the covenant that I will make with the house of Israel; After those days, with the Lord, I will put my law in their inward parts, and write it in their hearts, and will be their God; and they shall be my people. And they shall teach no more every man his neighbour, and every man his brother, saying, Know the Lord: for they shall all know me, from the least of them unto the greatest of them, with the Lord: for I will forgive their iniquity, and I will remember their sin no more."[7]

This admirably gracious covenant is completely suited to a spiritual kingdom, and to the subjects we have been describing: for it announces no designs, makes no provisions, confers no blessings, but those that are spiritual, internal, and everlasting. The true knowledge of Jehovah, writing his law in the heart, forgiveness of all sin, and perpetual relation to God, are the blessings for which it engages; but there is

---

[6] Observat. Sac, lib. v, c, iv. § 8. See Dr. Erskine's Theolog. Dissertat, p. 111-115.
[7] Jer. xxxi. 31-84; Heb. viii. 8, 9.

not a word respecting *temporal* blessings, nor concerning any merely *external relation* to the Great Supreme, though these were the grand articles in the covenant made at Horeb. Covenantees, therefore, under the Christian economy, can be no other than the spiritual seed of Abraham: and such are the subjects of this kingdom. Hence the gospel covenant is called *new,* and is expressly opposed to the Sinai confederation, from which it is extremely different. It is also pronounced *a better* covenant than that which Jehovah made with the ancient Israel: and so it is, whether we consider its objects, its blessings, its confirmation, or its continuance. Its *objects:* for they are the spiritual seed of Abraham, gathered out of all nations. Its *blessings:* for they are all spiritual and internal. Its *confirmation:* for it was ratified by the death of Christ. Its *continuance:* for it is "an everlasting covenant, ordered in all things and sure." Yes, it is as much better than the covenant made at Sinai, as being the children of God by regeneration, is preferable to carnal descent from Abraham: as the number of God's elect in all nations, exceeds that of the chosen tribes: as blessings entirely spiritual and immortal, are more excellent than those of an earthly kind and of short duration: as redemption from spiritual bondage and eternal ruin, is greater and nobler than deliverance from temporal slavery: as the ratification of this covenant, by the blood of Immanuel, is more sacred than that which the old covenant received by the slaughter of brute animals: as the Son of God, the Mediator of it, is greater than Moses, who appeared under that character at Horeb: and as a covenant of everlasting efficacy, that secures the final happiness of all to whom it relates, is better than one of a temporary nature, which was violated by the covenantees, and is become for ever obsolete. Hence we read, not only of a better *testament,* but also of better *promises,* on which the new covenant is established; of a better *hope,* introduced by it; of better *sacrifices,* by which guilt is expiated; of better *things* provided for the Christian, than were enjoyed by the Jewish church; and of a better *country* for an inheritance,[8] than the

---

[8] Heb. viii. 6, vii. 19, ix. 23, xi. 16. 40.

earthly Canaan. Nay, we are assured by an inspired writer, that the Sinai covenant and the Mosaic dispensation had no glory attending them, compared with that of the new covenant and of the Messiah's œconomy.[9] Now, to this more glorious covenant, the kingdom of Christ, and the subjects of it, must agree. As, therefore, none but spiritual blessings are contained in that covenant, so none but real saints are the subjects of our Lord's dominion.

Very different, then, is the kingdom of Christ from the ancient Israelitish theocracy. For, of that theocracy, all Abraham's natural descendents were true subjects, and properly qualified members of the Jewish church; such only excepted, as had not been circumcised according to the order of God, or were guilty of some capital crime. To be an obedient subject of their civil government, and a complete member in their ecclesiastical state, were manifestly the same thing; because, by treating Jehovah as their political sovereign, they avowed him as the true God, and were entitled to all the emoluments of their national covenant. Under that œconomy, Jehovah acknowledged all those for "his people," and himself, as "their God," who performed an external obedience to his commands, even though in their hearts disaffected to him.[10] These prerogatives were enjoyed; independent of sanctifying grace, and of any pretension to it, either in themselves, or in their parents.

The state of things, however, under the new œconomy, is extremely different. For the great Proprietor and Lord of the Christian church, having absolutely disclaimed a kingdom that is "of this world," cannot acknowledge any as the subjects of his government, who do not know and revere him—who do not confide in him, and sincerely love him. Having entirely laid aside those ensigns of political sovereignty, and those marks of external grandeur, which made such a splendid appearance in the Jewish theocracy; he

---

[9] 2 Cor. iii, 7-11
[10] Judges viii. 23; 1 Sam. viii. 6, 7, and xii. 12; 1 Chron. xxviii. 5; xxix. 23; 2 Chron. ix. 8.

disdains to be called the King, or the God, of any person who does not obey and "worship him in spirit and in truth." Appearing as the head of his church, merely under the character of a spiritual monarch, over whomsoever he reigns, it is in the understanding, by the light of his truth; in the conscience, by the force of his authority; and in the heart, by the influence of his love: for as to all others, his dominion is that of providence, not that of grace. The New Testament affords no more ground for concluding, that our being descended from parents of a certain description, constitutes us the subjects of our Lord's kingdom; than it does to suppose that carnal descent, in a particular line of ancestry, confers a claim to the character and work of ministers in the same kingdom.

It is of great importance to the right interpretation of many passages in the Old Testament, that this particular be well understood and kept in view. Jehovah is very frequently represented as the Lord and God of all the ancient Israelites; even where it is manifest that multitudes of them were considered as destitute of internal piety, and many of them as enormously wicked. How, then, could he be called *their* Lord, and *their* God, in distinction from his relation to Gentiles, (whose creator, benefactor, and sovereign he was) except on the ground of the Sinai covenant? He was *their* Lord, as being the sovereign whom, by a federal transaction, they were bound to obey, in opposition to every political monarch, who should at any time presume to govern them by laws of his own. He was *their* God, as the only object of holy worship; and whom, by the same national covenant they had solemnly engaged to serve according to his own rule, in opposition to every pagan idol. But that national relation between Jehovah and Israel being long since dissolved, and the Jew having no prerogative above the Gentile; the nature of the gospel economy, and of the Messiah's kingdom, absolutely forbids our supposing that either Jews or Gentiles are warranted to call the Great Supreme *their* Lord, or *their* God, if they do not yield willing obedience to him, and perform spiritual worship. It is, therefore, either for want of understanding or of considering, the nature, aspect, and influence of the Sinai constitution, that many persons dream of the new covenant, in great numbers of places, where Moses and the prophets had no thought about it; but had the convention at Horeb directly in view. It is owing to the same ignorance, or inadvertence, that others argue from various passages in the Old Testament, for justification before God by their own obedience, and against the final perseverance of real saints. Because, to be entitled to national happiness, by performing the conditions of the Sinai covenant, and to lose that right by backsliding into profligacy of manners; are very different things, from obtaining justification before God, and forfeiting an interest in the great Redeemer—so different, that there is no arguing from the one to the other.

Again, as none but real Christians are the subjects of our Lord's kingdom, neither adults, nor infants, can be members of the gospel church, in virtue of an *external* covenant, or of a *relative* holiness. A striking disparity this, between the Jewish and the Christian church. Of this difference we may be assured by considering, that a barely relative sanctity, supposes its possessors to be the people of God in a merely external sense: that such an external people, supposes an external covenant, or one that relates to exterior conduct and temporal blessings: and an external covenant, supposes an external king. Now an external king, is a political sovereign: but such is not our Lord Jesus Christ, nor yet the divine father. Once, indeed, it was otherwise: for, concerning the Israelitish nation, it is thus written; "I, Jehovah, will be thy king. Gideon said unto them, I will not rule over you, neither shall my son rule over you: Jehovah shall rule over you. Jehovah, your God, was your king."[11] It was the peculiar honour and happiness of Israel, to have a Sovereign who was the only object of their worship. For thus the Psalmist sings, "Blessed is the nation, whose (king) Jehovah is their God!"[12]

---

[11] Hosea xiii. 10; Judges viii. 23; 1 Sam, xii. 12.
[12] Psalm xxxiii. 12, and cxliv. 15. Heb. See the Septuagint Version, and that of Junius and Tremellius; together with Poli Synops. and Venemæ Comment, in loc.

Hence Jehovah's complaint; "They have rejected me, that I should not reign over them."[13] Yes, Jehovah, as a temporal monarch, stood related to the ancient Israelites, and entered into a federal transaction with them at Sinai, not only as the object of their worship, but as their King. Their judicial and civil institutes, their laws of war and of peace, various orders respecting the land they occupied, and the annual acknowledgments to the great Proprietor of it, were all from God, as their political sovereign. Hence all the natural posterity of Abraham were Jehovah's people, on the ground of an external covenant made with the whole nation.

The children of Israel, being distinguished from the Gentile world, by a system of ceremonial precepts, and their divine Sovereign residing among them, were denominated "a holy nation:" for that external sanctity which they possessed, seems to have arisen, partly from their national covenant, and partly from their having the divine presence among them. By the former, they renounced idolatry in all its forms, and gave up themselves to Jehovah, in opposition to the false objects of pagan worship; which separation to the service of God, is denominated *holiness.* By the latter, they had a kind of local nearness to God, which conferred a relative sanctity, as appears by various instances. When, for example, Moses with astonishment beheld the burning bush, the ground on which he stood was pronounced *holy,* because of Jehovah's peculiar presence there. Thus it was in the case of Joshua: and so in regard to the place of our Lord's transfiguration; for Peter calls it the *holy* mount.[14] And why was part of the ancient sanctuary called "the most holy place," but because Jehovah in a singular manner, and under a visible emblem, dwelt there? Hence it is manifest, that the divine presence, whether under the form of an august personage, as in the case of Joshua; or under the emblem of devouring fire, as in the bush, and upon mount Sinai;[15] or, under the milder appearance of a luminous cloud, as over the mercy-seat, and

---

[13] 1 Sam, viii. 7.
[14] Exod. iii. 5; Josh. v. 15; 2 Pet. i. 18.
[15] Exod. xix. 18.

at our Lord's transfiguration, confers a relative holiness. It is also equally plain, that this miraculous presence of God being withdrawn from the several places to which we have just adverted, they have now no more holiness than any other part of the earth.

So the Israelites, being separated from all other nations for the worship of Jehovah as their God, to the exclusion of all idolatry; avowing subjection to him as their King, in contradistinction to all other sovereigns; and he residing among them, in the sanctuary, as in his royal palace; there was a relative holiness attending their persons, and almost every thing pertaining to them. For not only Jehovah's royal pavilion, with all its utensils and services; the ministers of that sanctuary, and their several vestments; but the people in general, the metropolis of their country, the houses of individuals, the land cultivated by them, and the produce of that land, were all styled *holy*.[16] —The divine presence residing among them, appears to have had an extensive influence upon the people, with regard to relative sanctity and external purity. So, in cases of corporal pollution by disease, the patients were to be excluded from the common intercourses of society, that they might not defile the camp, in the midst of which their sublime Sovereign dwelt.[17] Nay, divine law expressly required, that even the surface of the ground on which they trod should be preserved from one species of defilement; and the injunction is enforced by this consideration, "For Jehovah thy God walketh in the midst of the camp."[18]

Remarkably to our purpose is the declaration of God, when speaking of the ancient sanctuary; "There I will meet with the children of Israel, and Israel (not the tabernacle) shall be sanctified by my glory."[19] For, as Venemx observes, "neither

---

[16] See Exod. xxviii. 2, 4, xxix. 1; Lev. xix. 23, 24, xx. 28, xxv. 2; 4, xxvii. 14, 30; Numb. xvi. 3, 38, xxxv. 34; Deut. vii. 6.
[17] Numb. v. 2, 3, xxxv. 34.
[18] Deut. xxiii. 12, 13, 14.
[19] Exod, xxix. 43. —Vid. Junium et Tremell. in loc.

the *tabernacle,* nor the *altar,* is to be understood; but the *Israelites themselves,* as appears by the connection and series of the discourse. Because, in the immediately following verse, the sanctification of the tabernacle, and of the altar, is expressly mentioned. Besides, it is plain that the external symbol of Jehovah's presence, was a sufficient indication of God's glory in the tabernacle. Thus the holiness of the people, equally as that of the places, was derived from the external presence of God."[20] Now, as the divine presence had a local, visible residence over the mercy-seat, which was the throne of Jehovah; as that presence among the Israelites had such an extensive operation upon their state, both in respect of privilege and of duty; as the whole nation was a typical people, and a great part of their worship of a shadowy nature; we need not wonder, that in such an ecclesiastico-political kingdom almost every thing should be esteemed, in a relative sense *holy.*

Under the gospel dispensation, however, these peculiarities have no existence. For Christ has not made an external covenant with any people; He is not the king of any particular nation. He dwells not in a palace made with hands. His throne is in the heavenly sanctuary: nor does he afford his visible presence in any place upon earth. The partition wall between Jews and Gentiles has long been demolished: and, consequently, our divine Sovereign does not stand related to any people, or to any person, so as to confer a relative sanctity, or to produce an external holiness.

While the Sinai covenant continued in force, the Son of God was the king of the Jews: for though, by Saul and others bearing the regal character, the Divine government was obscured; yet it was not abolished. The kingdom of Israel, "in the hands of the sons of David," being denominated "the kingdom of Jehovah;" the throne on which Solomon sat being called "the throne of Jehovah;"[21] and the laws of the state being still divine, we are, led to view the Jewish kings as the

---

[20] Dissertat. Sac. lib, ii. cap. iii. § 6.
[21] 2 Chron. xiii. 8; 1 Chron, xxviii. 5, and xxix. 23.

vicegerents of Jehovah.[22] In this light the queen of Sheba considered Solomon when she said, "Blessed be the Lord thy God, which delighted in thee to set thee on *his throne,* to be king *for the Lord thy God."*[23] Of the Jewish magistrates it is also written, "Ye judge not for man, but for Jehovah."[24] Now so long as a political relation subsisted between the Son of God and the seed of Abraham, an external holiness continued, as resulting from that relation. But though this foundation of relative sanctity was not removed till the death of Christ, there is no intimation in the evangelical history of any one being entitled to a New Testament rite, or to the character of a subject in the Messiah's kingdom, in virtue of that holiness. Nay, the reverse appears in the conduct of John toward the Jews.[25]

The covenant made at Horeb having long been obsolete, all its peculiarities are vanished away: among which, relative sanctity made a conspicuous figure. That national constitution being abolished, Jehovah's political sovereignty is at an end. The covenant therefore now in force, and the royal relation of our Lord to the church, are entirely spiritual. All that external holiness of persons, of places, and of things, which existed under the old economy, is gone for ever: so that if the possessors of Christianity do not possess a real, internal sanctity, they have none at all. The national confederation at Sinai is expressly contrasted, in holy scripture, with the new covenant:[26] and though the latter manifestly provides for internal holiness, respecting all the covenantees, yet it says not a word about relative sanctity. And indeed, how should it? since, by its commencement, the whole Sinai constitution became obsolete; the partition wall was broken down; the special relation between God and Abraham's natural seed ceased, and left no difference of a

---

[22] Vid.Witsii Miscell. Sac. tom. 2, p. 920-936. Venemæ Hist. Eccles. Vet. Test. Tom. 1. sect. 198. Dissertat. Sac. lib. 2, chap, iv.
[23] 2 Chron. ix. 8.
[24] 2 Chron, xix. 6.
[25] Matt, iii. 7-12.
[26] Jer. xxxi. 31-34; Heb. viii. 7-13.

AN ESSAY ON THE KINGDOM OF CHRIST

religious kind between Jews and Gentiles; no difference in respect of nearness to God and communion with him, except that which regeneration and faith in Christ produce. For, under the present dispensation, "Christ is all in all." We may therefore safely conclude, that were the Jews converted and resettled in Palestine, both they and their infant offspring would be as entirely destitute of the ancient relative holiness, as those Mohammedans are who now reside in that country.

But did an external holiness now exist, we should be obliged to consider it as very different from that of the ancient Israelites: for it appears, by what has been said, that the grounds of their exterior sanctity make no part of the Christian economy. Besides, their holiness extended to the whole nation: but in what Utopia shall we find all the inhabitants possessed of this relative purity? Theirs continued as long as they lived; except they committed some enormous crime, by which they forfeited their lives, or were cast out of the congregation: for it did not wear out by age, nor was it lost merely by continuing in a state of unregeneracy. Whereas, that external holiness for which so many plead, is not generally considered by them as extending beyond the time of infancy. But why should any contend for the relative holiness of infants, who deny a sanctity of that kind, to places of worship, clerical habits, and various other things? for it is plain that the Jewish external purity, whether of persons, of places, or of things, originated in the same national covenant, and in the same relation of God to Israel: and, consequently, must have the same duration in one case, as in another. We may therefore justly conclude, that the federal and relative holiness of which so many speak, neither agrees with the laws of Judaism, nor with the nature of Christianity. But if so, it cannot belong to the kingdom of Christ.

Further, if all the subjects of Christ be real saints, it may be justly queried, whether any *national religious establishment* can be a part of his kingdom. That multitudes of individuals belonging to such establishments are subjects of the king

Messiah, is cheerfully granted but is it not plain, that a national church is inimical to the spirit of our Lord's declaration, "my kingdom is not of this world?" Does not that comprehensive and important saying compel us to view the church and the world in a *contrasted* point of light? And does not the idea of a national church lead us to *confound* them? Does it not manifestly confound "the church of the firstborn, which are written in heaven;" with "the world, that lies in wickedness," whose names are entered in parish registers?[27] The subjects of our Lord's kingdom are born of God, are called out of the world; but natural birth and local circumstances are considered, either as giving membership, or as entitling to a positive rite which confers membership in a national church. The church of England, for instance, includes all English subjects of the British crown, whether they be moral or profligate, pious or profane: such only excepted, as have not been baptized, or as lie under a sentence of excommunication. Nay, so tenacious is the English church of this idea, as to consider numbers within its pale, who never considered themselves in that light. For, in certain cases, well known to the doctors in canon law, Protestant dissenters, and even Popish recusants, are cast out of its communion—cast *out,* with dreadful penalties annexed, though they never acknowledged themselves to be *in!*

The church of England, indeed, is manifestly a secular kingdom. For it is established by human laws, and

---

[27] It has been well observed by a sensible writer, that "when Jesus told Pilate "the sole end of his kingdom, and of his coming into the world, was *truth,* and the propagation of it;" Pilate says, "What is truth?" He knew very well that truth had little or nothing to do with the maxims of worldly policy: that he, that is, Jesus, was not at all likely to be a competitor with Cæsar: that a kingdom of truth could not interfere with the claims of his master: that it was trifling to accuse him as an enemy to Cæsar. But then, had Jesus said that he was setting up a kingdom that claimed an alliance with the state, and which pretended to a supremacy, Pilate would have had whereof to accuse him." —Comment on *Bishop Warburton's Alliance between Church and State,* page 9.

AN ESSAY ON THE KINGDOM OF CHRIST

acknowledges a political head; nor is it esteemed material whether that head be male or female. It is a creature of the state, supported by the state, incorporated with the state, and governed by a code of laws confirmed by the state—a code, very different from the sacred canons of the New Testament; those being quite foreign to its constitution. Its principal officers are appointed by the crown; and, in virtue of ecclesiastical station are lords of Parliament.[28] Nay, even the doctrines professed, and the worship performed in that

---

[28] That our first Reformers did not approve of secular grandeur, power, and employments, being annexed to the character of bishops, is very apparent. Thus Mr. Tyndal, for instance: "Is it not a shame above all shames, and a monstrous thing, that no man should be found able to govern a worldly kingdom, save bishops and prelates, that are taken out of the world, and appointed to preach the kingdom of God? To preach God's word is too much for half a man; and to minister a temporal kingdom is too much for half a man also. Either other requireth a whole man. One therefore cannot well do both. Wherefore if Christ's kingdom be *not of this world,* nor any of his disciples may be otherwise than he was; then Christ's vicars, which minister his kingdom in his bodily absence, and have the oversight of his flock, may be none emperors, kings, dukes, lords, knights, temporal judges, or any other temporal officer; or, under any false names, have any such dominion, or minister any such office, as requireth violence." Thus Bishop Latimer, in his Sermon of the Plough, "This much I dare say, that since *lording* and loitering bath come up, preaching hath come down, contrary to the apostles' times. For they preached, and *lorded* not: and now they *lord,* and preach not. Ever since the prelates were made *lords* and nobles, the plough standeth, there is no work done, the people starve. They are other wise occupied (than in preaching): some, in king's matters; some are ambassadors; some, of the privy council; some, to furnish the court; some, are *lords of the parliament;* some are presidents, and comptrollers of mints. Well, well. Is this their duty? Is this their office? Is this their calling? Should we have ministers of the church comptrollers of the mints? Is this a meet office for a priest, that hath cure of souls? Is this his charge? I would here ask one question: I would fain know who comptrolleth the devil at home in his parish, while he comptrolleth the mint? If the apostles might not leave the office of preaching to be deacons, shall we leave it for minting?" Thus Bishop Hooper, "Our bishops have so much wit, they can rule and serve, as they gay, in both states: in the church, and also in the civil policy. When one of them is more than any man is able to satisfy, let him do always his best diligence. They know that the primitive church had no such bishops, as be nowa-days." In Mr. Peirce's *Vindicat, of Dissent.* Part iii, chap. 1.

establishment, are all secularized. Its creeds and forms of prayer, its numerous rubrics and various rites, are adopted and used under the sanction of civil authority. Its liturgy, therefore, may be justly considered as an act of parliament respecting religious affairs. It must therefore be considered as a kingdom of this world.

The tenor of the New Testament, however, agreeably to our Lord's maxim, leads us to consider particular churches, as congregational; and as consisting of those who make a credible profession of repentance and faith.

Such congregations, wherever they be, constitute the visible kingdom of Christ. That the apostolic churches were congregational, is clear from the sacred records; and that there was no national church for the first three hundred years, is equally evident. Because there could not be any such establishment, till the civil government of some nation or other professed christianity; which was not the case before Constantine ascended the imperial throne. Then, indeed, a kind of political christianity came into fashion, which has continued ever since, and is yet in great repute. Nor are national churches likely to fail, while the policy of sovereign princes, and the pride of aspiring prelates can support them. But, being established by human laws, and each of them acknowledging a visible head, either civil or ecclesiastical, either prince or pontiff; they are secular kingdoms, and unworthy the name of Christian churches.

Once more: as none but regenerate persons belong to the kingdom of Christ, no one is a better subject of his dominion, or a more honourable member of his church, on account of wealth or power, of parts or learning. These things though useful in their places, of much reputation to a secular empire, and of great consequence to it; neither pertain to the true glory of a Christian church, nor to the sterling worth of a Christian character. For what concern have worldly wealth and civil power, in forming a spiritual character, or in adorning a spiritual kingdom? The greatest affluence and the highest authority that mortals can enjoy, add nothing to any one's moral worth. No one is a better man, because he is rich and powerful; nor the worse, because he is poor and in a low station. These things are all exterior to moral character. For the most licentious are often exalted and wealthy, while the most upright and amiable are lost in obscurity and oppressed with want. Besides, when wealth, or power, is possessed by a true subject of our Lord's kingdom, the honour attending his character does not arise from his riches, or his authority; but from the holiness of his life, or his likeness to Jesus Christ.

As our British sovereign is the fountain of honour to all his subjects, even so is the king Messiah to all that are under his dominion. The only way however to be great and honourable in his kingdom, is to be humble, diligent, and useful, in promoting the happiness of our fellow Christians and fellow creatures. For among the fundamental laws of Messiah's empire, the following is one, and it relates to comparative honour: "Whosoever will be great among you, let him be your minister; and whosoever will be chief among you, let him be your servant. Even as the Son of man came not to be ministered unto, but to minister, and to give his life a ransom for many."[29] This being the law of honour, and the rule of promotion, in the kingdom of Christ, we may safely conclude, that the meanest domestic may be a dignified character in a gospel church, and "adorn the doctrine of God our Saviour;" while his wealthy and powerful master, professing the same faith, may disgrace the name of a Christian, and bring reproach on the congregation to which he belongs. If the former be diligent and faithful in his menial station; if he be "sound in the faith," zealous for God, and heavenly minded; he is an honourable subject of Jesus Christ, and high in the estimation of heaven. If, on the contrary, the latter be formal in his religious profession; if he be unjust or haughty, voluptuous or covetous; he does not belong to the kingdom of Christ but is manifestly a subject of Satan.

---

[29] Matt. xx. 26, 27. Mark x. 42-45.

Nor do the most shining mental accomplishments, or literary acquisitions, enter into the true glory of this kingdom. Genius and learning, like wealth and power, are frequently possessed by the worst of moral characters. They cannot, therefore, make any part of that excellence by which the subjects of Jesus Christ are distinguished from those of secular princes. It is not by the gifts of common providence, among which parts and learning make a conspicuous figure; but by the graces of the Holy Spirit, that any person, as a christian, is worthy of regard. —Yes, it is faith in Christ, and obedience to him; love to God, and benevolence to man; humility, patience, and resignation; spirituality, and heavenly-mindedness, which adorn the subjects of our Lord's kingdom—which distinguish them from the children of this world. These, and similar things, respect the state of the conscience, and of the heart. They form a character for eternity, and savour of the heavenly world. Whereas, learning and parts, equally as wealth and power; are quite of a different nature. The distinction they make between one and another is entirely superficial, and often disgraced by a profligate heart—belongs only to this world, and has no connection with heaven. But, as will appear in its proper place, the kingdom of Christ is nearly allied to heaven—is a state of preparation for that sublime blessedness, an introduction to its employments, and gives an earnest of its fruitions. Consequently, the true glory of that kingdom cannot but consist in the lively exercise of holy tempers and heavenly affections. The more there is of a likeness to heaven, in the heart and life of any christian; the more there is of that "honour which comes from God," and the more is the cause of Christ adorned. To be a real subject of this kingdom, is a much greater honour than merely to be a prophet, or an apostle. For Balaam was the former, and Judas was the latter; yet both of them were base and wicked. "Rejoice not that the devils are subject to you; but rather rejoice that your names are written in heaven." "Though I speak with the tongues of men and of angels, and though I have the gift of prophecy, and understand all mysteries and all knowledge; and though I have all faith, so that I could remove mountains, and have no charity, I am nothing," in the estimate of a spiritual Sovereign, or in reference to the heavenly state.

No minister of the word, therefore, when performing his public work, should ever think of exalting himself as an officer in this kingdom, by displaying his learning, his genius, or his eloquence; for that would be to preach himself, not "Christ Jesus the Lord:" but, as "in the sight of God," he should honestly aim at "commending himself to every man's conscience, by manifestation of the truth." Then will he imitate a first-rate minister in the Messiah's kingdom, and obtain the approbation of his divine Sovereign. Besides, in the displays of profound learning, by critical disquisitions; of great acumen, by metaphysical speculations; or of a sparkling genius, by agreeable turns of wit, Christ and conscience feel their interests but little concerned. The former is too observant of the preacher's motives, and too jealous of his own honour, to be pleased with such a procedure; and the latter is either too sleepy to be aroused, or too much pained to receive relief, by those means. If our Lord consider himself as honoured by the preacher's labours, and if the minister have any reason to expect success, it must be by a faithful and simple promulgation of revealed truths—those truths which regard supreme authority in the divine law, and saving grace in the glorious gospel—those truths, I will add, which lie open to common capacities. If the conscience receive advantage, it is by the operation of the same truths; either as convincing of sin and enforcing duty, or as revealing pardon and affording peace. But the honour of Christ and the tranquillity of conscience are seldom promoted, in a public ministry, by the researches of learning or the refinements of genius: for they are too sacred, and too spiritual, to acknowledge their obligations to such things.

The kingdom of Christ is not of this world, with regard to the means he employed in its first establishment, and those he appointed for its enlargement and support.

Craft and violence, injustice and cruelty, have been commonly used in the founding, supporting, and extending of secular kingdoms. The Roman empire was founded, and grew to its height, in blood. Even the Jewish republic was established, enlarged, and defended by force of arms. The Canaanitish nations, on account of their enormous wickedness, were exterminated by the sword of Israel; or, if spared by the chosen tribes, became tributary to them. This, though according to Jehovah's appointment, as the great Proprietor of the whole earth; and though a righteous execution of punishment, for acts of rebellion against the eternal Sovereign; was a plain indication that, in various respects, the Israelitish church was a kingdom of this world. Such also was that kingdom of the Messiah which the carnal Jews in our Lord's time vainly expected, whenever the great promise made to their fathers should be fulfilled: for they dreamed of being exalted to the highest pitch of political grandeur, and of having all other nations under their control. —The principal instruments employed by princes, to establish, maintain, and extend their dominions, are not persons the most remarkable for integrity and benevolence, for piety and philanthropy; but those who are most eminent for political prudence, or martial bravery; for secret intrigue, or open hostility—those who are best qualified to persuade by eloquence, to circumvent by cunning, or to subdue by force.

But the most illustrious instruments employed by our anointed Prince in the erecting of his monarchy, were of a character quite the reverse. They were chiefly selected from the lower orders of life, and called from occupations esteemed mean. Uneducated in the courts of royalty, in the schools of learning, or in the field of war; they were strangers to the finesse of politicians, little acquainted with Gentile philosophy, and unpractised in the art of eloquence. It may be justly presumed, therefore, that a strong degree of rusticity appeared in their dress, their aspect, and their accent: for they were apparently "unlearned and unpolished men."[30] So ignorant were they of sciences called liberal, so unpolite in their address, and so uncanonical in their garb, that multitudes called Christians, it is highly probable, would be ashamed to give them a hearing, were they now present among us; unless the public attention were first excited, by the exercise of their miraculous powers. —Yes, by the instrumentality of those unlettered and plain men did our Lord erect his kingdom, or establish the Gospel Church. In making war upon Satan's empire, evangelical truth and spiritual gifts, laborious preaching and ardent prayer, fortitude, patience, and a holy example, were the arms they used. Such were the militia, and such the armour, employed by our divine Sovereign; yet perfectly suited to the nature of his kingdom. For it is an empire, not of secular power and external pomp; but of truth and of righteousness, of love and of peace.

Were the Messiah's kingdom of this world, his loyal subjects might lawfully take the sword, to repel assailants and subdue his enemies; for without the liberty of such defence, no secular state can long subsist. This, however, he absolutely prohibited: which prohibition is founded in the peculiar nature of his kingdom. For thus he speaks, to one who thought of defending his person and cause by force; "Put up thy sword into the sheath." Soon after, on another occasion, he said; "If my kingdom were of this world, then would my servants fight, that I should not be delivered to the Jews: but now is my kingdom not from hence."[31] As by the particle *now,* our spiritual Sovereign apparently refers to his kingdom among the Jews; so he seems to distinguish his dominion in the Gospel Church, from that over the Israelitish nation.

In former times, the Holy Spirit frequently came upon the subjects of Jehovah's government, to inspire them with martial courage for the defence of his kingdom, and to destroy his enemies. Hence, among the ancient worthies, we

---

[30] Αγφαμματοι και ιδιωται, Acts iv. 13.
[31] John xviii. 11. 36.

read of those who "subdued kingdoms, waxed valiant in fight, and put to flight the armies of the aliens." But the disciples of Christ being called to a different kind of conflict, divine energy is granted for a different purpose. The military service of a Christian, as such, is entirely of a spiritual nature. It is a "good fight of faith:" a "striving against sin," in himself, and in the world around him: a "holding fast the profession of his faith," in spite of all opposition. The Christian hero is conformed to the Captain of salvation, in maintaining the truth, and in bearing the cross; in enduring the contradiction of sinners, and in despising the shame that is cast upon him. His accoutrements are, as Paul informs us, "the girdle of truth, and the breast-plate of righteousness; the shield of faith, the helmet of hope, and the sword of the Spirit."[32] Such is the armour provided by the King Messiah for his devoted subjects; by which they are enabled to defend themselves, and to promote the general interests of his kingdom. This holy empire depends not upon power, wealth, or learning, either for ornament or support. "Not by might, nor by power, but by my Spirit, saith Jehovah."

Neither the force of secular power, nor the arts of carnal policy, ought therefore to be used in promoting the cause of Christ: such things being quite abhorrent from his intention, and from the nature of his kingdom. The great design of our Lord in founding a Spiritual empire was, to display the perfections of God in the holiness and happiness of his chosen people. The kingdom of Christ, as before observed, is a dominion of truth and of rectitude, of love and of peace. Now the interests of such a monarchy, and the end, proposed by it, cannot be promoted by any other than spiritual means, and those of divine appointment. It is only so far as the minds of men are enlightened by heavenly truth, their consciences impressed with God's authority, and their hearts engaged on spiritual things, that the cause of Christ is advanced. But in what way shall persecuting force be applied, to irradiate the dark understanding, to arouse the

---

[32] Eph. vi. 10-18; 1 Thess. v. 8; 2 Cor. x. 3, 4, 5.

stupid conscience, and to sanctify the depraved heart? It is only by the fruits of an adoring affection for God, of sincere love to the brethren, and of cordial good-will to all mankind, that our Lord is honoured, or his end answered, by the subjects of his dominion. How, then, shall coercive measures increase those fruits of holiness? Or how shall malevolence, in any of its infernal forms, be employed to support a kingdom of love and of peace?

Nor are the contrivances of carnal policy less foreign to the nature of this kingdom, than the exertions of secular power. For what has the policy of princes, or of prelates, to do in maintaining, or in extending, an empire of truth and of rectitude? Truth seeks no subterfuge, and rectitude fears no examination: but the operations of policy are subtle, and its first designs are latent. Thee policy of great men may form civil establishments of Christianity, and adorn the exterior of public worship. It may dignify ministers of the word with pompous titles, unknown to the New Testament, and invest them with temporal power, till their claim of succeeding to the apostles becomes an insult upon common sense. These and similar things may be effected by it, under the fair pretext of rendering religion respectable, and of making it more general: but the empire of Jesus Christ disdains them all, because they belong to the kingdoms of this world.

But though our Lord neither needs, nor accepts, the puny arts of men, to advance his cause and support his interests; yet various methods have been devised by ecclesiastics, to obviate the offence of the cross, to render themselves respectable, and to promote something called Christianity. That they might not be thought, like the fishermen of Galilee, unlearned and ignorant persons, they have eagerly sought literary titles, and to be called rabbi. To adorn the ministerial office, and to sanction their administrations, they have been as careful as Jewish priests to appear in canonicals. To prevent the pride of their hearers being disgusted, certain humiliating truths have been kept out of sight; and that the consciences of others might not be pained, softening interpretations of divine precepts have been given. To stand free from a suspicion of bigotry, the importance of capital truths has been surrendered; and to keep fair with something called charity, it has been agreed that human inventions should hold the place of divine institutions. Many of the clerical character, in our national establishment, have deliberately subscribed what they did not believe; solemnly professed their consent to what they could not approve; and frequently practised as part of their public devotions, what they were constrained to wish had never existed.[33] Nay, as if the ministers of that Establishment possessed a righteous monopoly of publishing evangelical truth, and of administering divine institutions, numbers of them have sworn to persecute their Protestant dissenting neighbours, for daring to hold separate assemblies.[34]

---

[33] For can any man upon earth really believe all that is contained in the Thirty Nine Articles, and cordially approve of every thing contained in the Book of Common Prayer?

[34] Thus runs part of an oath which is taken by graduates in the University of Oxford. Item specialiter to jurabis, quod inter nullas communitates, vel personas istius Universitatis, impedies pacem, concordiam et amorem-Nec Conventiculis interesse debes, nee eis tacite vel expresse consentire; *sed ea potius, modis quibus poteris, impedire.* —*Excerp. e Corp. Statut. Uniuersit. Oxon. Tit. IX. Sect.* vi. § 1. That is, "You shall in a particular manner swear, that you will not obstruct peace, harmony and love, among any communities, or persons, of this University—Nor ought you to he present in Conventicles, nor either expressly nor tacitly consent to them; *but rather hinder them by any means in your power."* —How any man, at all acquainted with the rights of conscience, can take this oath; or, having taken it, can treat dissenters as Christian brethren, without renouncing his own Conformity, I cannot imagine. A more shocking dilemma can scarcely be conceived: for it is persecution on the one hand, and perjury on the other. Of a similiar complexion is the eleventh Canon of the Church of England, which is entitled, *Maintainers of Conventicles censured,* and it reads thus: "Whosoever shall hereafter affirm or maintain, that there are within this realm other meetings, assemblies, or congregations of the king's born subjects, than such as by the laws of this land are held and allowed, which may rightly challenge to themselves the name of true and lawful churches: let him be excommunicated, and not restored, but by the archbishop, after his repentance, and public revocation of such his wicked errors." —I will here subjoin the following remark of Dr. Owen: "There is in this (ecclesiastical) conformity required a renunciation of all other ways

An Essay on the Kingdom of Christ

Thus multitudes have subscribed and consented, trimmed and sworn, to promote the interests of a spiritual kingdom—a kingdom of truth, of love, and of peace!

Some, of different communions, have deliberately acted as if the preachers work were a mere trial of skill, and as if a pulpit were the stage of a harlequin. To display the fertility of their invention, they have selected for texts mere scraps of scripture language; which so far from containing complete propositions, have not, in their dislocated state, conveyed a single idea. Upon these they have harangued; while the ignorant multitudes have been greatly surprised that the preacher could find so much, where common capacities perceived nothing. Sometimes these men of genius will choose passages of scripture expressive of plain historical facts, which have no connection with the great work of salvation by Jesus Christ; and handle them (not professedly by way of accommodation, for then it might be admitted) but as if they were sacred allegories. Such historical facts being spiritualized, as they love to call it, doctrines, privileges, duties, in abundance, are easily derived from them. Nay, so ingenious are preachers of this turn, that it is no hard matter for them to find a great part of their creed in almost any text they take. Thus they allegorize common sense into pious absurdity. It might, perhaps, be too barefaced, though it would certainly suit the vanity of such preachers, were they frequently to address their hearers on the pronominal monosyllable I: and there are two passages of sacred writ where it occurs in the most apposite manner. The former

---

of public worship, or means of edification, that may be made use of. For they are all expressly forbidden in the rule of that conformity. No man, therefore, can comply with that rule, but that a renunciation of all other public ways of edification as *unlawful*, is part of the visible profession which they make. *Video melinra prohoque, deteriora sequor,* is no good plea in religion. It is uprightness and integrity that will preserve men, and nothing else. He that shall endeavour to cheat his conscience by distinctions, and mental reservations, in any concernments of religious worship, I fear he bath little of it, if any at all, that is good for aught."—*Enquiry into the Orig. Nature, Institut. and Common, of Evano. Churches,* p. 228, 229.

would make an admirable text; the latter, a noble conclusion: and they are as follow: "Such a man as *I*,"— "Is not this great Babylon that *I* have built?"[35]

Others, and often the same persons, frequently use the gestures of the theatre, and the language of a mountebank: as if their business were to amuse, to entertain, and to make their hearers laugh. Extravagant attitudes and quaint expressions, idle stories and similies quite ludicrous, appear in abundance, and constitute no small part of the entertainment furnished by such characters. But in what a state must the consciences of those preachers be, who can deliberately and with premeditation act in this manner! Or, what must we think of their petitions for divine assistance, in addressing the people, when they intend thus to treat them! I called it *entertainment;* and, surely, they themselves do not consider it in a religious point of light. For can any man, who is not insane, deliberately adopt measures of this kind, when really aiming, either to produce, or to promote, a devotional and heavenly temper in the hearts of his hearers? Yet that is the general end of preaching. Or can the preacher have any devotion, while showing the airs of a mountebank; and when, if the bulk of his auditory bad no more decency than himself; there would be a burst of laughter through the assembly? Whatever such declaimers may think, where there is no solemnity, there is no devotion; and, we may venture to add, that a person habitually destitute of devotion in his own heart, while pretending to teach others the doctrine of

---

[35] Mr. G. Gregory, when animadverting on the conduct which is here censured, says; "It is dangerous on any occasion to depart from the plain track of common sense; and there is no attempt at ingenuity so easy as that which borders upon nonsense: It is one of the mean artifices of barren genius, to surprise the audience with a text consisting of one or two words. I have heard of a person of this description, who preached from Jehovah Jireh; and another, from the monosyllable, But. These are contemptible devices, more adapted to the moving theatre of the mountebank than to the pulpit, and can only serve to captivate the meanest and most ignorant of the vulgar." *Sermons,* Introduct. p. 14, 15. 18. Mr. Claude says, "Never choose such texts as have not a complete sense; for only impertinent and foolish people will attempt to preach from one or two words, which signify nothing." *Essay on Composition of a Sermon,* vol. i. p. 3.

An Essay on the Kingdom of Christ

Christ, is a wretched character in the sight of God, and has reason to tremble. Such a man serves not our Lord Jesus Christ, but his own interests, in some form or other. He may wish for popularity, and perhaps may obtain it from the ignorant multitude; but people of sense and of piety will consider him as disgracing his office, as affronting their understandings, and as insulting the majesty of that divine presence in which he stands. For where, upon earth, are we to expect solemnity, if not in the pulpit? There, a man should be serious and solemn as death.

It may perhaps be said, "this kind of trifling has its use. It is a mean of exciting curiosity, and of drawing many to hear the gospel, who might not otherwise have the least inclination so to do." Such, I presume, is the chief reason by which preachers of this cast endeavour to justify themselves at the bar of their own consciences. In answer to which, a repetition of that capital saying, "my kingdom is not of this world," might be sufficient for that must be a wretched cause, even of a secular kind, which needs buffoonery to support it. To trifle in the service of God, is to be profane. It is, therefore, an impious kind of trifling: and "shall we do evil that good may come?" Through the interference of providence, and the sovereign grace of God, various instances of enormous wickedness have issued in the highest good to mankind. Of this we have undoubted evidence in the selling of Joseph by his envious brethren. We have a still more striking instance in the death of Christ, through the treachery of Judas and malice of the Jews. Nay, persecution has frequently been an occasion of spreading the gospel: yet few, I take it for granted, have persecuted for that end, or attempted to justify the practice upon that principle. Were the farcical conduct, here censured, lawful, there would be reason to think that the cause of Christ, and the interests of harlequin, are very nearly allied; because the same kind of means is adapted to promote them.

The seraphim, however, in Isaiah's vision, and the apostles of Christ, appear to have had a very different view of the case.

The *former* (who seem to be an emblem of apostolic ministers),[36] are presented to notice, as performing the service of their sublime Sovereign with profoundest awe. Struck with the majesty of his appearance, and penetrated by the authority of his commands, they adore and obey with all humility, and with all solemnity. Agreeably to which, the *latter* give it as divine law, that those who would perform acceptable worship, must do it "with reverence and godly fear." This law of devotion, they further inform us, is founded in the nature of things; as appears by the reason assigned to enforce the precept, "for our God is a consuming fire." Such is the Christian's God, with regard to his purity, his jealousy, and his justice.[37]

Conformable to this idea of that sublime Being whom every preacher professes to serve, was the conduct of Paul when dispensing the gospel. For, in opposition to some who "handled the word of God deceitfully," to amuse the carnal and win their affections; he laboured, "by manifestation of the truth, to commend himself to every man's conscience, as in the sight of God." Truth, conscience, and God! What sacred and solemn ideas! Yet Paul, as a preacher, habitually acted under their influence. That evangelical truth might be displayed, that the human conscience might be impressed, and that the will of God might be performed, were all included in his design. How foreign are these particulars from every thing of a farcical nature! Nor can any person who considers himself, when preaching the word, as having eternal truth for the subject of his discourse, the consciences of men for the objects of his regard, and the omniscient God for a witness of his conduct, be otherwise than solemn: for such an one will speak, as knowing that he "must give an account." When hearing a minister who acts in character, and copies the example of Paul, we are led to reflect on that ancient oracle; "I will be sanctified in them that come nigh me," to perform sacred service. But when sitting under the effusions of a pulpit buffoon, the language of an Egyptian

---

[36] Vid. Vitringam in loc.
[37] Heb. xii. 28, 29; Deut. iv. 24, ix. 3.

tyrant occurs to remembrance; "Who is Jehovah, that I should obey him?" or what is his worship, that I should treat it with reverence?

When a sermon was expected from Peter, by Cornelius and his friends, the centurion expressed himself thus "We are all here present before God, to hear all things that are commanded thee of God." These gentiles it is manifest, were penetrated with devout solemnity, and filled with holy expectation. Not being assembled for carnal amusement, but in order to know and perform the will of God; they considered themselves as in the divine presence: and so did their inspired teacher. A worthy example for us to follow when convened to preach and to hear the word of truth. But how contrary to this is that pulpit drollery, which is the object of our censure! For it converts the solemn service of God (shocking metamorphosis!) into carnal amusement: upon which numbers indeed attend with pleasure, but with no more devotion than if they were in a playhouse.

Is there any reason to be surprised that men of sense, who are already prejudiced against the genuine gospel, should have their disaffection to evangelical truths increased, when they find those truths avowed, and their importance loudly urged, by merry-andrews? If, instead of sound speech which cannot be condemned, they meet with extravagance and nonsense, what will they say? Is there any reason to wonder that infidels should thence take occasion to ridicule the scripture, as calculated to serve the meanest purposes; or that they should contemptuously call preaching, *priestcraft?* If those who profess to love revealed truths dress them up in a fool's coat, for the entertainment of their hearers, will deists forbear to laugh? If, where the *man of God* should be heard, with all solemnity warning sinners *to flee from the wrath to come,* and intreating them *to be reconciled to God,* a farcical droll appear, spouting low wit and provoking risibility, will not the infidel say, "the preacher himself does not believe the Christian ministry to be a divine appointment, nor the exercise of it a devotional service; but he finds it convenient for secular purposes to make pretences of that kind?" Among all the devices of carnal policy for the support and enlargement of our Lord's kingdom, there are none more contemptible, and few more detestable, than that of converting the pulpit into a stage of entertainment. Of this mind was an old nonconformist minister, when he said; "of all preaching in the world I hate that most, which has a tendency to make the hearers laugh; or to affect their minds with such levity as stage-plays do, instead of affecting them with an holy reverence for the name of God. We should suppose, as it were, when we draw near him in holy things, that we saw the throne of God, and the millions of glorious angels attending him; that we may be awed with his majesty, lest we profane his service, and take his name in vain." To the pulpit harlequin we may therefore apply the following lines

>"If angels tremble, "tis at such a sight
>More struck with grief, or wonder, who can tell?"

The kingdom of Christ is not of this world, in regard to the laws by which it is governed. —Secular kingdoms are under the direction of human laws, which are frequently weak, partial, and unjust—of laws which, when least imperfect, extend their obliging power no further than the exterior behaviour: for it would be vain and foolish in a temporal sovereign, to think of giving law to the thoughts, or desires, of any subject. Civil penalties are the sanction of human laws, and external force gives them their energy. Not so the laws of this holy empire. For, proceeding from him, in whom *are all the treasures of knowledge,* they must be consummately wise: being enacted by him who is inflexibly just and supremely kind, they cannot but be perfectly good; being given by him who searches the heart and is Lord of conscience, their obligation extends to the latent desire, and the rising conception. Controlling the thoughts and binding the conscience, their sanction is entirely spiritual. The motives enforcing obedience to them, are the smiles, or the frowns of him who has our everlasting all at his disposal.

❧ An Essay on the Kingdom of Christ ❧

As is the kingdom, such is the sovereign: and as is the sovereign, such are his laws. If the kingdom be of this world, it must have a political sovereign; whose laws must be coercive, and confined to exterior behaviour. But if the kingdom be of a spiritual kind, the sovereign must be so too. His laws must extend no less to the conscience, than to the conversation, and be enforced by sanctions of a spiritual nature. Such is the king Messiah, and such are the laws of his kingdom.

The subjects of our divine Sovereign may be considered, either as detached individuals, or as united in distinct societies, and visibly professing their subjection to his authority. Hence the execution of those laws by which they are governed, comes under a twofold consideration. *As detached individuals,* the application of his laws to particular cases, is entirely with him, and with the conscience of each individual. *As united in distinct societies,* which are called particular churches, his laws of admission, of worship, and of exclusion, are to be applied by the community—applied, not under the influence of carnal motives, but under the operation of his authority, and for purposes entirely spiritual.

By the laws of this kingdom, a credible profession of repentance and faith is required of all, previous to baptism. Such profession being considered as an evidence of their "fellowship in the gospel," and of willing subjection to the authority of Christ, they are entitled to membership in a particular church. On this ground they are admitted: nor do they forfeit any membership, except by some capital departure from *that* gospel, or some flagrant offence against *this* authority. But as, by the laws of our heavenly Sovereign, their admission to visible fellowship was entirely for spiritual purposes, their exclusion from it does not include any temporal disadvantages. Their situation as men, and as the subjects of a political state, not being altered by their church-relation commencing; they should not be affected, in those respects, by the dissolution of that relation. For as the laws of Christ say nothing about the admission of one or another, on account of his domestic or civil connections; nor yet for his wealth or influence, his parts or learning; so they are equally silent about pecuniary fines and satisfactory penances, about civil disabilities and corporal punishments, attending the exclusion of any offender. The former being quite foreign to qualifications for a spiritual kingdom, the latter must be utterly abhorrent from the laws by which it is governed; being manifestly the inventions of antichrist, and the supporters of his cruel throne. Civil penalties, in this case, are adapted to generate fear, and promote hyprocrisy; to suppress truth, and render Christianity itself suspicious.

Here we perceive another disparity between the Jewish and the Christian church. For under the old economy, the laws of religion were sanctioned by temporal penalties, and frequently those of the severest kind.[38] To be cast out of the congregation, to be forbidden access to the sanctuary worship, (except for ceremonial pollution) was to be deprived, not only of ecclesiastical privileges, but also of civil rights. The church and the state being co-extended, and including the same persons, an exclusion from the former was an expulsion from the latter; whether it was by a sentence of capital punishment, or in some other way. But this, like many other things, was peculiar to that dispensation. It was founded in the national form of their church-state, and in their theocracy. Thence it was that blasphemy and idolatry were punished with death, as being high-treason against their divine Sovereign. That economy being abolished, the church of God has taken a new form. "The priesthood being changed, there is of necessity a change also of the law," relating to the constitution, members, and government of the church. The laws of admission, and of exclusion, must therefore be very different; as well as those pertaining to public worship. Now, to understand these laws, we must study, not the Pentateuch of Moses; much less the

---

[38] See Exod. xii. 15. 19, xxx. 33. 38, xxxi. 14; Lev. vii. 20-27, xvii. 3-9, xix. 8, xxiii. 27, 28, 29; Numb. ix. 13, xv. 30, 31, xix. 13. with many other similar places.

An Essay on the Kingdom of Christ

Provinciale of Lyndwood, or the Codex of Gibson, but the New Testament of Jesus Christ. To reason from the constitution and form, the laws and government, the privileges and rites of the Jewish, to those of the Christian church; is to adopt a capital principle of papal depravity, and grossly to corrupt our holy religion.

Our divine Sovereign has also provided for the edification of his loyal subjects, by ordinances and rites of worship, no less than for the government of his kingdom. As King of the Christian church, it constitutes a distinguished part of his royal prerogative, to prescribe the whole of that spiritual service which is to be performed. Of this prerogative Jehovah was always jealous: nor, under the former economy, did he ever more instantly, or more severely punish, than when his orders about the affairs of religion were disregarded; even though, as in the case of Uzzah, the motive appeared laudable. What is religion, in its various branches, but that obedience which is due to God? And what is obedience, but submission to his authority? Now, as authority exerts itself in commands, there cannot be obedience, there cannot be holy worship, where there is no divine command, either explicit or implied. "Who hath required this at your hands? In vain do ye worship me, teaching for doctrines the commandments of men:" exclude and condemn a great number of things, winch millions esteem ornamental and useful in the worship of God.

Strange, that any Protestant church should avowedly claim a "a power to decree rites or ceremonies" in the solemn service of our divine Lord! As if he were not the legislator in his own kingdom! Or as if, though possessed of authority, he had not wisdom enough to provide for his own honour; or were defective in goodness, respecting his faithful subjects! But whatever the compilers and the subscribers of a national creed may think, to perform rites which Christ did not appoint, and to alter those which he enjoined, are vile impeachments of his royal character, and must expose to his resentment. The former usurps his throne: the latter annuls his *laws*. *Strange,* did I say? the expression must be recalled. For there is no reason to wonder that a national religious establishment, with a political sovereign for its head, should make the claim I have just mentioned. Who can doubt whether the same authority which constitutes, governs, and supports a community for any particular purpose, may not prescribe to that community with a view to the end intended by it? But things should not be called by wrong names; and to denominate such an establishment a church of Christ, is a gross misnomer.

The kingdom of Christ is not like the empires of this world, in regard to external splendour. —The grandeur of a temporal kingdom chiefly consists, in the number and affluence of its nobility, the titles and pompous appearance of its various magistrates, the flourishing state of its trade and commerce, the wealth of its yeomanry, and the elegance of its public buildings. Magnificent palaces and royal robes are quite in character for secular princes. Ensigns of honour, splendid equipages, and stately mansions, are suitable to the nobles: while a more solemn kind of exterior pomp is very becoming the ministers of public justice. These and similar things give an air of dignity, and of importance, to political sovereignties; but they are all foreign to the kingdom of Christ, the glory of which is entirely spiritual. The Christian church is dignified and adorned, by being the depositary of divine truth in its unadulterated state, and by practising divine appointments in their primitive purity; by possessing the beauties of holiness, and by enjoying the presence of God. Such is the true glory of our Lord's kingdom, which renders it incomparably superior to every temporal monarchy.

It must therefore be very absurd to think of doing honour to Christianity, by erecting pompous places of worship, by consecrating those places, and by adorning ministers with showy vestments, in the performance of public worship. Let the palaces of princes, and the mansions of the mighty, be magnificent and richly ornamented: let the nobles and judges of the land, when acting agreeably to their different characters, appear in robes of state and in robes of magistracy; as those things belong to the kingdoms of this world, nor pretend to any thing more, there is nothing amiss, nothing inconsistent with station or profession. But confine them there, and by no means think of decorating the kingdom, or of promoting the cause of Christ, by any thing similar. Were any man to lacquer gold, and paint the diamond, to increase their lustre, he would certainly be considered as insane. Yet the conduct of those persons is more absurd, who borrow the trappings of secular kingdoms, to adorn the spiritual kingdom of Jesus Christ.

As to places of worship, conveniency is all that is wanted, and all that becomes the simplicity of Christianity. To lay the first stone of such an edifice with solemn formalities, is Jewish:[39] to dedicate it, when completed, to any particular saint, is manifestly superstitious: to consecrate it by any solemn form, looks as if it succeeded to the honours of Solomon's temple; as if the Deity were expected to reside in it, rather than grant his presence to the congregation worshipping there; and as if it were to possess a relative holiness, like that of the ancient sanctuary. I may venture to add, that any religious parade at the first opening of such a place, is apparently inconsistent with the idea of all distinction of places, in regard to worship, being abolished, and too much resembles a Jewish, or a popish consecration.[40]

---

[39] Ezra iii. 10, 11.
[40] I will here subjoin a few particulars mentioned by Mr. James Owen, relative to Consecrations. Ile shows, that the Israelites dedicated not only the tabernacle and temple, but also their private houses, and their cities (Deut. xx. 5. Psalm xxx. *title.* Nehem. xii. 27.)-That the Jewish synagogues were not consecrated, nor esteemed holy, as the temple was-that the consecration of places for Christian worship was invented in the time of Constantine-that Christians had not long been in possession of consecrated temples before they thought it expedient to furnish them with altars; and being provided with altars, they afterwards invented the sacrifice of the mass—that the Papists, like the old Pagan Romans, first consecrate the ground, and then the edifice erected upon it—that Durandus argues for the consecration of churches, from the example of Nebuchadnezzar dedicating his golden image—that Roman Catholics consecrate, with various and solemn formalities, the first foundation stone of a building intended for

In regard to *ministers,* when attending to any branch of their holy function, let them not think of heightening their own importance, or of promoting the cause of Christ, by imitating Jewish or Pagan priests, adorned with peculiar habits, when performing their different rites. If Christian ministers be decently clothed, when in their own families, when visiting their friends, or when walking the streets; why should they not be considered as properly habited for the performance of their sacred office? What reason can be assigned for the use of any particular dress, when engaged in public service, that would not militate against the spirituality of our Lord's kingdom, and the simplicity of his worship?

It may, perhaps, be said, "Clerical habits are indifferent and harmless things, except when they are imposed." But if so, the idea of imposition being excluded, the canonical dress of a popish priest, the red hat of a cardinal, and the triple crown of a pontiff, may all be justified; for, in themselves, they are equally harmless as the gown, the surplice, or the band. Innocent, however, as all these peculiarities are, detached from the ministerial character, and from holy worship; the reason or motive of wearing them in sacred service, may be carnal, base, and sinful. In some, there is too much ground of suspicion, a desire of being esteemed by the vulgar, either as persons of learning, or as episcopally ordained, when they are not so; and, in others, a lust of increasing their learned and priestly importance, are the latent reasons of wearing those idle badges of clerical distinction. But when illiterate men assume the garb of learning, their vanity is contemptible: when they intend, by so doing, to obtain that

---

public worship—that they consecrate bells, priests'-garments, and almost every thing belonging to their corrupted worship—that though in England, since the Reformation, it does not appear that any form for the consecrating of churches, and of burying grounds, has received the sanction of public authority; yet various forms for those purposes have been published and used-that the consecrating bishop blesses the church or chapel, and prays "° that the blessed Spirit would send down on the place, his sanctifying power and grace."-That he consecrates the font, the pulpit, the reading-desk, the communion table, the paten, the chalice, and so on. —*Hist, of Consecration of Altars, Temples, and Churches,* passim.

respect from the ignorant, of which they know themselves unworthy, their practical falsehood is detestable: and when any minister thinks of magnifying his office, by pomposity in the pulpit, he betrays his ignorance relating to the nature of that kingdom in which he professes to be an officer. Do the laws of this holy empire forbid the subjects to affect shining and costly apparel, as not becoming those who "profess godliness,"[41] and will not the principle of that prohibition apply with increasing force to the case before us? Is it inconsistent with that spiritual-mindedness, of which every avowed disciple of Christ makes an implicit profession, to be fond of a showy dress in the intercourses of common life; and can it be suitable to the simplicity of Christian worship, to the character of its Lord, or to the example of his apostles, for ministers to make a more grand appearance, and take more state upon them, when performing their solemn service, than at any other time? Let those who understand the Christian system, and are heavenly-minded, form the determination.

It must indeed be acknowledged, that the ancient people of God had a splendid sanctuary, and a sumptuous temple; that the Jewish priests, when performing sacred service, appeared in holy garments; and that the high-priest, on certain occasions, was richly adorned, in a manner peculiar to his office. But then it is plain, that those things were expressly appointed by Jehovah; that the dispensation to which they belonged was of a typical nature; that they were suited to the church while in a state of minority; that the whole Jewish nation was then the visible church; that Jehovah was not only the God, but also the King of that nation; that the ancient sanctuary was a palace, where political royalty resided,[42] as well as a temple, where Deity was adored; and that the priests were officers in the state, as well as ministers of religion. To such a politico-ecclesiastical kingdom the splendour of the sanctuary, and the dress of the priests, were manifestly adapted. Hence the tabernacle is

---

[41] 1 Tim, ii. 9, 10; 1 Pet. iii. 3, 4.
[42] Matt. v. 35.

called "a worldly sanctuary," and the rites performed there "elements of the world."[43] To these, the heavenly sanctuary, into which our great High Priest is entered, and the spiritual worship of the Christian church, stand opposed. It should not be forgotten, that though the Son of God, when displaying his glory as King of the Jewish state, took up his abode in the sanctuary, as in a royal palace; yet, when "he came into his own country,"[44] as King of the Gospel Church, he had not "where to lay his head."

What, then, have the splendour, the laws, or the rites of Judaism, to do in the new economy; except we mean to convert the Christian church into the Jewish temple? Grandeur and show, whether as pertaining to places of worship, or to ministers of the word, are abhorrent from the gospel dispensation: nor, under the present economy, have they any other tendency, than to gratify that pride from which they originate, and to give the kingdom of Christ a secular appearance. The new economy being intended for all nations and all succeeding ages, is equally fitted for the rich and the poor; nor, does it make any distinction, in regard to places, where its worship should be performed. That God be adored "in spirit and in truth," according to his own rule, is all it requires of one congregation or of another. It disdains, therefore, to borrow any part of its glory, from the grandeur of an edifice, or from the garb of a minister. Though far from supposing rusticity, illiteracy, and meanness, to be characteristics of a gospel church; yet I may venture to assert, that an assembly of princes in a splendid cathedral, with an arch prelate appearing in canonical pomp, may insult the Divine Majesty, and be utterly unworthy the name of a church; while a congregation of day-labourers, with an illiterate minister in the meanest habit, convened in a barn, may be a spiritual temple, enjoy the Divine presence, and perform the Christian worship in all its glory. It has been well observed, by a certain author, that "the presence of God

---

[43] Heb. ix. 1; Gal, iv. 3. 9; Col. ii. 8. 20.
[44] John i. 11. εις τα ιδια ηλθε. See Dr. Doddridge in loc.

confers dignity and importance:" but that "he can receive none from created, much less from artificial pomp and magnificence." To which I will add, in the words of Dr. Owen, "If the whole structure of the temple, and all its beautiful services, were now in being on the earth, no glory would redound unto God thereby: he would receive none from it. To expect the glory of God in them, would be a high dishonour unto him."[45]

If secular grandeur, however, must needs attend the religion of Him who was born in a stable, and lived in poverty; who received the acclamations of royalty, when riding upon an ass, and quickly after expired on a cross;—if, I say, it *must* appear in the worship of any who pretend to follow the fishermen of Galilee, those prime ministers in the Messiah's kingdom, let it be confined to such as avow themselves members of a national establishment. For, with regard to those who maintain that particular churches are congregational, consisting of such as make a credible profession of repentance and faith; pomp and show in the worship of God are quite unbecoming their principles. Yes, let those monopolize the splendour in question, who consider the church and the state as of equal dimensions; who acknowledge a visible head of political royalty; and who must search, not the New Testament, but a code of canons and constitutions larger than the whole Bible,[46] if they would know on what foundations their ecclesiastical fabric stands, and by what laws it is governed. The national form of the Jewish church being their model, and a temporal monarch being their head, why should not they have magnificent cathedrals, and consecrate them like Jewish temples? Why should not ancient Judaism be imitated in these particulars,

---

[45] On the Person of Christ, p. 354, 355.
[46] Referring to Gibson's Codex. "When," says Sir Michael Forster, "Christianity became the established religion of the empire, and church and state became one body, considered only in different views and under different relations, the ecclesiastical and civil laws of the empire flowed from one and the same source, *imperial rescripts.*" *Examinat. of Bp. Gibson's Codex,* p. 122. Third Edition.

as well as in other things? As the head of the English church is adorned with royal robes; as the principal *officers* in it are appointed by him, and are lords in the legislature; and as it is established by laws of the state, who shall forbid the various orders of its ministers being adorned with sounding titles, and with pompous canonicals? There is no reason to wonder that, in such a constitution and such a polity, almost every thing should wear a secular appearance. For, political authority pervading the whole ecclesiastical frame, it would be inconsistent with itself if its various parts had not an air of external grandeur. As a kingdom of this world, it is respectable; but it should not pretend to any thing more.

But, however it may be with a national establishment, let not Protestant dissenters behave as if they envied, either its magnificence, or its emoluments. No; let not those who consider the church and the world as opposite ideas; who maintain, that Christ only is the head of Christian communities; and that the New Testament contains the whole of their ecclesiastical polity, be desirous of external grandeur in any thing pertaining to public worship: lest they practically deny their own principles, and implicitly reproach primitive Christianity for being too simple and too spiritual. It is frequently much easier for people, and much more desired by them, to assemble in an elegant edifice, and for their minister to appear in canonical fashion; than to perform a spiritual worship, and to shine in the beauties of holiness. The splendour of a place for assembling, and the pageantry of clerical dress, are procured by money; but the graces of real sanctity, and internal devotion, are of heavenly origin: nor is the exercise of them to be expected, unless by those who are habitually aiming at it. I will add, whatever kind of succession to the apostles may be claimed by diocesan bishops,[47] yet let not Protestant dissenting ministers implicitly arrogate an apostolic mission, powers, and authority, by calling themselves *ambassadors* of Christ. For that character, it is plain, belonged to the first-rate

---

[47] Dr. Owen's *Nature of a Gospel Church, and its Government*, p. 33.

~ An Essay on the Kingdom of Christ ~

messengers of our divine Sovereign. Or, if any of those who publish the gospel of peace consider a title of that high importance as quite suitable to the dignity of their ecclesiastical station, their credentials must be produced.

By this characteristic of our Lord's kingdom, and by the general nature of it, we are further taught, that *simplicity* and *spirituality* must constitute the chief glory of that worship which he requires. This forms another striking disparity between the Messiah's government and the ancient theocracy. It has been observed, by Dr. Erskine, that "the respect paid to God, under the old Testament dispensation, corresponded to his character as a temporal monarch; and in a great measure consisted in external pomp and gaiety, dancing, instrumental music, and other expressions of joy usual at coronations or triumphs. But the hour is now come, in which the true worshippers must worship the Father in spirit and in truth; not with external show and pageantry."[48] Yes, numerous rites, and ceremonious pomp, were appointed by Jehovah in the first establishment of the Jewish church: to which various additions were made, by divine order, in the time of David.[49] These things were undoubtedly suited to the nature of that Dispensation, and to the church of God, while in a state of minority.[50] On worship, so various in its branches, and so splendid in its appearance, multitudes attended, and found amusement in it, who were in their hearts disaffected to God. In hearing the temple music, vocal and instrumental, there is no doubt but numbers of ungodly people were much delighted. Such a concert, by persons trained to the employment, and under the direction of skilful masters, must produce very pleasing emotions in the attending multitude: a great majority of whom, it is highly probable, considered their system of worship as the best that could be appointed, it being so grand and so delightful.

---

[48] Theological Dissertations, p. 69.
[49] 1 Chron, xvi. 4, 5, 6; 2 Chron, xxix, 25.
[50] Gal. iv. 1-7.

But though that system was fitted both to the people, and to the times; though it was of great utility, and answered the purpose of Jehovah, under a shadowy dispensation; yet the New Testament informs us, that its numerous rites were the mere elements of spiritual knowledge and of holy worship. Nay, compared with appointments and services of the Christian church, that they were beggarly elements and carnal ordinances.[51] Why, then should any professors of Christianity be so fond of ceremonious pomp in the worship of God? Why so attached to the language and forms of Judaism, or practise a ritual nearly akin to the rubrics of Moses? Why call the holy supper a sacrifice, the Lord's table an altar, and the administrator a priest? Why have recourse to the temple worship for musical instruments, and for a set of singers distinct from the congregation at large? Why should responsive singing, and tunes more fit for a theatre than for the worship of God, be heard in religious assemblies? Why, without an appointment for alternate singing, should one part of a congregation suspend an act of social worship, while the other carries it on? To these and similar queries the answer must be; because things of this nature amuse and please the carnal mind because the simplicity and spirituality of New Testament worship have no charms for the multitude—and because the generality love to perform something called religious worship, in a way of their own devising. To save appearances, however, as many things in the Jewish ritual were pretty well adapted to please the carnally minded, they will be contented with having the christian worship reformed, in various particulars, according to the ancient model, as completed in the time of David. Who, that enters a splendid edifice, where he beholds a minister in his canonicals, and meets with such entertaining worship, can forbear to think of the temple service? Such, through a course of ages, has been the predilection of multitudes for ancient Judaism, that a number of its peculiarities, which were either honourable and profitable to the priests, or amusing and pleasing to the

---

[51] 1 Gal. iv. 9; Heb, ix. 10.

people, have been incorporated with Christianity, notwithstanding the mischiefs produced by similar conduct in the apostolic churches.

I said, honourable and profitable to the priests—amusing and pleasing to the people. But here they stop for those branches of Judaism that were of a different kind, are treated as entirely obsolete. So, for instance, though numbers of christian ministers are fond enough of priestly vestments, and of tithes, *jure divino;* yet they are not inclined always to wash their feet, before they perform sacred service;[52] much less to perform it barefoot.[53] As to the people, though multitudes of them are greatly delighted with pompous appearances and musical sounds, they are far from being in raptures with circumcision. For notwithstanding that Abrahamic rite retained its obligation and utility, as long as any Jewish ceremony did; and though, in apostolic times, judaizing Christians had the highest opinion of its importance; yet, like the ancient baptismal immersion, it is now considered as too painful and too indelicate for polished persons to regard. Thus the worship of the new economy is become a compound, unknown to the Bible, of Judaism and Christianity: and it is treated by too many ministers, as a trade, not a divine service; by numbers of people, as an article of decent amusement suitable to the Lord's day, not as duty to God, and as a mean of preparing for heaven. "Men run to church," says Erasmus, "as to a theatre, to have their ears tickled."[54] "The prophets prophesy falsely, and the priests bear rule by their means, and my people love to have it so: and what will ye do in the end thereof?"[55]

But though the magnificence of places intended for public worship, the consecration of those places, canonical habits, and various amusing ceremonies, are now defended (if

---

[52] Exod. xxx. 17-21.
[53] See Dr. Lightfoot's *Temple*. Service, chap. I, and X. and Dr. Gill on Exod, iii. 5.
[54] 1 Cor. xiv. 19.
[55] Jer. v. 31.

defended at all by Scripture) on the ground of Old Testament customs; yet we are taught by the most respectable ecclesiastical historians, that they originated in a perverse imitation of Paganism. Christians being surrounded with heathens, of whose conversion they were desirous; and the latter having been accustomed, in performing their idolatrous worship, to the external pomp of temples and of ceremonies; Constantine had no sooner abolished the superstitions of his ancestors, than magnificent places of worship were erected, and consecrated with great parade; it being considered as unlawful, except in extraordinary cases, to perform any part of public worship in them, previous to their consecration. Heathens having often reproached Christianity, for the poverty and simplicity of its appearance, the Christians of the fourth century adopted many of the pagan rites. Ministers of the word, for example, when performing their office, appeared in canonical habits, and with priestly pomp. Their newly erected temples were consecrated, by singing of such hymns as were thought suitable to the occasion, by prayers, and by thanksgivings. Then, in the eastern churches, the responsive singing of David's psalms was introduced; precentors were appointed, and laws were framed by different councils to direct the singers in the performance of their service.[56] Such was the origin of those gaudy appearances, which, to amuse the carnal mind, have so long corrupted the worship of God, and secularized the kingdom of Christ! "Vain man would be wise;" and, in his great wisdom, thinks it necessary to add a few ornaments and supports to this heavenly empire, of which it was entirely destitute when the apostles left the earth. This was thought expedient, in order to render the religion of Jesus a little more pleasing, respectable; and edifying, than it was in its native state. But well may he demand, with the aspect of incensed majesty, "who hath required this at your hands?"

---

[56] Vid. Spanhemii Hist. Eccles, Secul. IV. p. 851-854. Venemæ Hist. Eccles. Secul. IV. § 128.

An Essay on the Kingdom of Christ

The kingdom of Christ is not of this world, in respect of its immunities, its riches, and its honours. Wealth, titles, and authority, are frequently conferred by secular princes: but they are all external things. A patent of peerage, or a lucrative office, gives no wisdom to the mind, no peace to the conscience, no holiness to the heart. The possessor, notwithstanding his plentiful income and splendid title, may be a fool, a wretch, and a disgrace to the human species. The highest honours and the greatest emoluments which the subjects of an earthly kingdom can enjoy, are all of them unsatisfactory; and, therefore, the first favourites of temporal princes are sometimes the most unhappy. Of this we have a remarkable instance in Haman, the prime favourite of Ahasuerus. Great privileges and exalted honours are enjoyed by comparatively very few subjects of any temporal monarch; the nature of the case forbidding them to become general, among the inhabitants of any country. Dukedoms, marquisates, and grants from the crown, are but seldom bestowed, how loyal soever the subjects may be. Besides, those distinguished favours are of short duration, and quite uncertain.

Whereas, the immunities, emoluments, and honours of our Lord's kingdom, are all of them spiritual and eternal. They are suited to the state of an enlightened mind, to the feelings of an awakened conscience, and to the desires of a renewed heart. Pardon of all sin, and complete acceptance with God; adoption into the heavenly family, and a title to future glory, are some of the privileges and honours enjoyed by the subjects of this kingdom. Blessings, these, of infinite worth, because of their spiritual nature and immortal duration. Nor are they confined to a few distinguished favourites of our celestial Sovereign; for they are common to all his real subjects. Yes, they are all enriched, and all ennobled, with "righteousness, peace, and joy in the Holy Ghost."

Now, as the immunities, grants, and honours, bestowed by the King Messiah, are all of a spiritual nature; his faithful subjects have no reason to wonder, or to be discouraged, at any persecutions, afflictions, or poverty which may befall them. Were his empire of this world, then indeed it might be expected, from the goodness of his heart and the power of his arm, that those who are submissive to his authority, zealous for his honour, and conformed to his image, would commonly find themselves easy and prosperous in their temporal circumstances. Yes, were his dominion of a secular kind, it might be supposed that an habitually conscientious regard to his laws, would secure from the oppression of ungodly men, and from the distresses of temporal want. Thus it was with Israel under their theocracy. When the rulers and the people in general were punctual in observing Jehovah's appointments, the stipulations of the Sinai covenant secured them from being oppressed by their enemies, and from any remarkable affliction by the immediate hand of God. Performing the conditions of their national confederation, they were, as a people, warranted to expect every species of temporal prosperity. Health and long life, riches, honours, and victory over their enemies, were promised by Jehovah to their external obedience.[57] The punishments also, that were denounced against flagrant breaches of the covenant made at Horeb, were of a temporal kind.[58]

In this respect, however, as well as in other things, there is a vast difference between the Jewish, and the christian œconomy. This disparity was plainly intimated, if I mistake not, by the opposite modes of divine proceeding, in establishing Jehovah's kingdom among the Jews, and in

---

[57] See Exod. xv. 25, 26, xxiii. 25-28; Lev. xxvi. 3-14; Deut. vii. 12-24, viii. 7, 8, 9, xi. 13-17, xxviii. 3-13.
[58] Lev. xxvi. 14-39; Deut. iv. 25, 26, 27, xi. 27, xxviii. 15-68, xxix. 22-28. See Dr. Erskine's Theolog. Dissertat. p. 22-29. *External obedience—* Punishments of a *temporal* kind. These and similar expressions in this Essay are to be understood, as referring to the Sinai covenant strictly considered, and to Jehovah's requisitions as the king of Israel. They are quite consistent, therefore, with its being the duty of Abraham's natural seed, to perform *internal* obedience to that sublime Sovereign, considered as God of the whole earth; and with final punishment being inflicted by him, in failure of that obedience.

An Essay on the Kingdom of Christ

founding the empire of Jesus Christ. To settle the Israelitish church, to exalt the chosen tribes above surrounding nations, and to render the ancient theocracy supremely venerable, the divine Sovereign appeared in terrible majesty. Wasting plagues and awful deaths were often inflicted by eternal justice, on those who dared to oppose, or to oppress, the people of God. An angel was commissioned to destroy the Egyptian firstborn; Pharaoh, with his mighty host, were drowned in the Red sea; and the Canaanitish nations were put to the sword, that the subjects of Jehovah might possess their fertile country. Manifest indications these, in connection with express promises, that the special providence of God would exalt and bless the natural seed of Abraham with temporal felicity; provided they did not violate the Sinai covenant.

But when the Prince Messiah founded his kingdom, all things were otherwise. No marks of external grandeur attended his personal appearance: and, instead of executing righteous vengeance on those who opposed him, his language was; "The Son of man is not come to destroy men's lives, but to save them." "Father, forgive them, for they know not what they do!" After a life of labour and of beneficence, of poverty and of reproach, he fell a victim to persecution, and a martyr to truth. Such was the plan of Divine Providence, respecting Christ our King, and such was the treatment with which he met from the world! Striking intimations, these, that his most faithful subjects would have no ground of discouragement, in any sufferings which might await them; and that, considered as his dependants, spiritual blessings were all they should have to expect.

It must indeed be acknowledged, that as vicious tempers and immoral practices have a natural tendency to impair health, distress the mind, and waste the property; so the exercise of holy affections, and the practice of true godliness, have the most friendly aspect on a Christian's own temporal happiness (except so far as persecution intervenes) and on the welfare of society. But then it is evident that this arises from the nature of things and from the superintendency of common providence; rather than from the dominion of Christ, as a spiritual monarch. For, so considered, spiritual blessings are all that they have to expect from his royal hand.

By the prophetic declarations of our Lord himself, and by the history of this kingdom, it plainly appears, that among all the subjects of his government, none have been more exposed to persecution, affliction, and poverty, than those who were most eminent for obedience to his laws, and most useful in his empire. The most uniform subjection to his authority, and the warmest zeal for his honour, that ever appeared upon earth, were no security from bitter persecution, from pinching poverty, or from complicated affliction. Our divine Lord, considered as a spiritual sovereign, is concerned for the spiritual interests of those that are under his government. His personal perfections and royal prerogatives, his power and wisdom, his love and care, are therefore to be regarded as engaged, both by office and by promise, not to make his dependants easy and prosperous in their temporal concerns; but, to strengthen them for their spiritual warfare; to preserve them from finally falling by their invisible enemies; to make all afflictions "work together for their good;" to render them, in the final issue, more than conquerors over every opposer; and to crown them with everlasting life.

Our Lord has promised, indeed, that their obedience to his royal pleasure, shall meet with his gracious regards in the present life. Not by indulging them with temporal riches, or by granting them external honour and ease, but by admitting them into more intimate communion with himself, and by rejoicing their hearts with his favour.[59] Yes, to deliver from spiritual enemies, and to provide for spiritual wants; to indulge with spiritual riches, and to ennoble with spiritual honours, are those royal acts which belong to Him whose "kingdom is not of this world." In the bestowment of these blessings, the glory of his regal character is much concerned.

---

[59] John xii. 26. and xiv. 21. 23.

☙ An Essay on the Kingdom of Christ ☙

But millions of his devoted subjects may fall by the iron hand of oppression, starve in obscurity, or suffer accumulated affliction in other ways; without the least impeachment of his power, his goodness, or his care, as the sovereign of a spiritual kingdom.

The kingdom of Christ is not like the dominions of secular princes, with regard to its limits and its duration. The widely extended monarchies of antiquity were confined to certain parts of the habitable globe, and in the course of a few centuries they came to an end. Not so, the empire of Jesus Christ: for thus run the prophetic oracles, respecting him and his kingdom. "He shall have dominion from sea to sea, and from the river to the ends of the earth. All kings shall fall down before him: all nations shall serve him." "There was given him dominion, and glory, and a kingdom, that all people, nations, and languages should serve him. His dominion is an everlasting dominion, which shall not pass away, and his kingdom that which shall not be destroyed." "He shall reign over the house of Jacob for ever, and of his kingdom there shall be no end."[60] Concerning the gradual enlargement and universal extent of this kingdom, our Lord speaks in his parable of "a grain of mustard seed;" and in that of leaven, pervading the whole mass of meal. This holy empire shall issue in the ultimate glory: and though the present form of its administration will cease, when "God shall be all in all;" yet the glorified subjects of it shall never die, never be disunited, nor ever withdraw their allegiance from Jesus Christ. Such are the foundations of his dominion, and such the excellence of his government, that each of his real subjects will from the heart say; "Let the King live! and let him reign, till all his enemies become his footstool!"[61]

Once more; *The empire of Christ, or the Gospel Church, is called "The kingdom of heaven."* —As our Lord, in the most emphatical manner, is denominated, "the King of kings;" we may with propriety consider his holy monarchy, as the

---
[60] Psalm lxxii. 8. 11; Dan. vii. 14; Luke i. 33.
[61] Psalm lxxii. 15. and c. 1; 1 Cor. xv. 25.

Kingdom of kingdoms. This appellation, "the kingdom of heaven," manifestly sets the New Testament church at the greatest distance from every secular monarchy, and teaches us to consider it as nearly allied to the heavenly state.[62] The subjects of it are described, as born from above; as the heirs of glory. They are governed by laws, indulged with privileges, and invested with honours, which are entirely spiritual, and all from heaven. The truths they believe, the blessings they enjoy, the obedience they perform, and the expectations they entertain, have a regard to heaven. It is the authority of a divine Sovereign under which they live, and his approbation at which they aim. The pleasures which they enjoy, considered as the subjects of Jesus Christ, are all of a spiritual nature, and all savour of the heavenly world.

As Christ is a spiritual monarch, his dominion respects the understandings, the consciences, the hearts of men; and is a preparation for that sublime state, where knowledge and rectitude, where obedience and love, where harmony and joy, are all in their full glory. The foundation of this government, as it respects individuals, is laid in regeneration. There the preparation for heaven begins: and all the genuine fruits of that important change, which is made by divine influence, in the mind, conscience, and heart of a sinner, have a tendency toward heaven; and many of them are anticipations of it. That worship which is performed by the subjects of Christ, is no further spiritual, and agreeable to the New economy, than it is animated with such affections as abound in heaven. For the time is come, when those that worship the Father, "must worship him in spirit and in truth." Knowledge and reverence of God, as revealed by the Mediator; confidence in him, and love to himself—abasement in his presence, and acquiescence in his dominion; are the principal ideas included in spiritual worship, whether as performed by the subjects of Christ here, or by the saints made perfect in glory.

---

[62] Ecclesiam Christi Jesu vere esse Βασιλειαν των ουρανων Regnum Ccelorum, et inter ejus statum et conditionem ecclesiae coelestis maximam intercedere affinitatem et conjunctionem. *Vitringa in Apocalyps. p.* 885. Amstelod. 1719.

An Essay on the Kingdom of Christ

It is manifest from this characteristic of our Lord's kingdom, that a profession of allegiance to him is entirely vain, if not attended with spiritual mindedness: because it is natural for good subjects to seek the prosperity of that kingdom to which they belong. Now the interests of Messiah's empire are all of a spiritual nature. In the spread of evangelical truth, and the purity of divine worship; in the exercise of love, and the practice of holiness, the interests and honour of this kingdom chiefly consist. Indifference about these is an evidence of the heart being disaffected to our divine Sovereign; but allegiance to him will manifest itself by an habitual regard to them. In whomsoever this holy Monarch reigns, there is a relish for spiritual riches, honours, pleasures. To enjoy his favour, and bear his image; to perform his will, and behold his glory, are things of the highest importance in the esteem of real saints. Nor is it a mere dictate of the understanding and conscience, that it should be so. It is matter of choice: for their hearts are engaged on those objects.

It is common for subjects to imitate a sovereign whom they love and revere; especially, if they have derived signal benefits from his administration. Now such is the nature of our Lord's government, that it is impossible for any one to be under it, without sincerely loving and profoundly revering him—without seeing an excellence in his example, which commands esteem and excites imitation. But if we be fond of wealth, or emulous of grandeur and show; if we pursue preeminence, and grasp at power; we imitate the children of this world, not Jesus Christ. Those things are eagerly sought, and highly prized, by the subjects of Satan, because they are carnally minded; but he is unworthy to be called a disciple of Christ, who is not habitually striving to copy his example. Nor can any pretend, that he ever encouraged, by word or deed, the pursuit of secular distinctions, the acquisition of wealth, or the pleasures of sensuality, but quite the reverse: Far from seeking "the honour which comes from men," he neither courted the smiles of the rich, nor the patronage of the mighty: for "the friendship of this world, is enmity with God." So our Lord esteemed it, and so must his disciples. To be the subjects of a spiritual kingdom, and to have our hearts on temporal enjoyments, are inconsistent. "To be carnally minded is death; but to be spiritually minded is life and peace."

As Christ is a spiritual sovereign, and his church a spiritual kingdom, all the subjects of his government must be considered, as *in a state of preparation for heaven.* The prevailing dispositions of their hearts are in favour of heavenly things: and to promote the exercise of spiritual affections, the new economy, in all its branches, is much better adapted than was the Mosaic system. For as it is the most perfect dispensation of divine grace, that ever was, or ever will be enjoyed on earth; so it makes the nearest approaches to heaven.

It has been justly remarked by a certain author, "that the legal economy introduced that of grace, by the gospel, and then vanished away. The dispensation of grace, in like manner, is now performing its work, fulfilling its day, announcing, unfolding, introducing the kingdom of glory: and when that which is perfect is come, then that which is in part shall be done away." Yes, the old œconomy, and the Jewish theocracy, were manifestly introductory to the Christian dispensation, and the Messiah's kingdom. Those, being typical and shadowy, led to these, and in them received their final completion. But the new dispensation, and the kingdom of Christ, have no completion short of heaven. Thither they lead, and there they terminate. No worship is agreeable to the Messiah's kingdom, which is not animated by heavenly affections. All the external services of religion are only so many means of exciting those holy affections, of promoting communion with God, and of cultivating a heavenly temper. Consequently, the worship of those who rest in exterior services, is quite superficial, and has nothing spiritual, nothing heavenly in it.

Jehovah, under the former dispensation, having chosen the holy of holies for the place of his residence, the Jews were directed to address him in prayer, considered as on his throne "between the cherubim."[63] They knew, indeed, that he inhabited celestial mansions; and therefore, when bending the knee before him, their hands were extended toward heaven:[64] but yet he was more immediately regarded by them, as residing in the earthly sanctuary. For, notwithstanding their desire to be heard in heaven, "the cry of their prayer, and the eye of their faith, were directed first to the mercy-seat." The most eminent saints, under that economy, looked to God in both; did homage to him in both; nor could they have neglected him in respect of either, without being culpable. Whereas, when Christians pray, they look directly to their "Father who is in heaven," and as on a throne of grace in the celestial temple; without the least regard to any place upon earth, or to any visible object.[65]

"God," says Dr. Erskine, "as husband of the gospel church, claims from his people inward affection and love, and accepts them only who worship him in spirit and in truth. In the Mosaic covenant it was otherwise. There he appeared chiefly as a temporal prince, and therefore gave laws intended rather to direct the outward conduct, than to regulate the actings of the heart. Hence everything in that dispensation was adapted to strike his subjects with awe and reverence. The magnificence of his palace, and all its utensils; his numerous train of attendants; the splendid robes of the high-priest, who, though his prime minister, was not allowed to enter the holy of holies, save once a year, and, in all his ministrations, was obliged to discover the most humble veneration for Israel's king; the solemn rites with which the priests were consecrated; the strictness with which all impurities and indecencies were forbidden, as things which, though tolerable in others, were unbecoming the dignity of the people of God, especially when approaching to him: all these tended to promote and secure the respect due to their glorious sovereign." It was, however, foretold, by one of the

---

[63] 1 Kings viii. 27-30, 38, 42, 44, 48; 2 Kings xix. 15; Psalm xxviii. 2, lxxx. 1; Dan. vi. 10.
[64] I Kings viii. 22. 1.
[65] See Dr. Goodwin on *Christ the Mediator*, book vi. chap, iii.

minor prophets, "that in gospel times men should not call God, *Baali, i.e.* my Master, but *Ishi, i.e.* my Husband. The passage imports at least thus much, that God, who in the Jewish dispensation had chiefly displayed the grandeur, distance, and severity of a master, would in the Christian dispensation, chiefly display the affection and familiarity of a husband and friend." [66]

Yes, under the Mosaic system, the high-priest only, and he but once in a year, was admitted to the mercy-seat, or throne of Jehovah, in "a worldly sanctuary." That appearance of the Jewish pontiff before the Lord, though grand and solemn, was a mere emblem of spiritual things, and of that holy intercourse which all the subjects of this kingdom have with God, in the performance of spiritual worship. For as Jesus is entered into the heavenly sanctuary, "with his own blood; "as he is there "a priest upon his throne," uniting the sacerdotal censer with the regal sceptre; he ever lives, not only to govern his widely extended empire, but likewise to intercede for all his followers, and to be the medium of their access to the divine Father. In virtue of his atonement made on the cross, and of his appearance in the heavenly world, the meanest subjects of his dominion, when performing sacred service, "have boldness to enter into the holiest." Each of them, in the exercise of faith, of hope, and of love, has access to the divine Majesty on a throne of grace; and each has reason to expect a condescending audience from the King eternal. Hence we find, that New Testament saints are called *the domestics of God;* which "may have some relation to that peculiar nearness to God, in which the Jewish priests were: and refer to that great intimacy of unrestrained converse to which we, as Christians, are admitted. In which respect our privileges seem to resemble, not only those of the people praying in the common court of Israel; but of the priests, worshipping in the house itself."[67]

---

[66] Theological Dissertations, p. 4, 5, 6.
[67] Dr. Doddridge's *Note*, on Ephesians ii. 19.

~ An Essay on the Kingdom of Christ ~

The superior advantages of believers under the Christian economy, in regard to communion with God, and the sanctifying influence which that holy intercourse has on their minds, are strongly expressed in the following remarkable words: "but we all, IN an unveiled face beholding as in a glass the glory of the Lord, are changed into the same image, from glory to glory, even as by the Spirit of the Lord."[68] The apostle here plainly alludes to that glory which appeared in the face of Moses, after his intimate converse with Jehovah on the mount. So dazzling was the lustre of his countenance, that the children of Israel "were afraid to come nigh him." He therefore put a veil upon his face, that they might have familiar intercourse with him:[69] which veil was an emblem, not only of Jewish blindness, but also of the darkness of that dispensation. Now, in contrast with these throbs, Paul informs us, that the glory of the divine perfections appears and shines in the *unveiled* face of Jesus Christ; that this glory is *beheld* by New Testament believers; and that, by beholding it, they are gradually "transformed into the glorious image of God." What an illustrious view does the apostle here give us of the new œconomy! He not only represents the state and privileges of the gospel church, as greatly superior to those of the Jewish people; but as nearly approaching to the employments, and the fruitions of the celestial world. For we cannot easily form a more exalted idea of the business and blessedness of heaven, than that of contemplating the glory of God, and of making continual advances in likeness to him.

---

[68] 2 Cor. iii. 18. *In an unveiled face. So,* I humbly conceive, ανακεκαλυμμενῳ προσωπῳ should here be rendered. Compare 2 Cor. iv. 6. where the inspired writer speaks of the light of the knowledge of the glory of God, εν προσωπῳ, IN THE FACE of Jesus Christ." That ανακεκαλυμμενῳ προσωπῳ will admit the supplemental preposition *in,* as well as *with,* cannot, I presume be doubted and that the whole scope of Paul's reasoning in the context leads us to think of the face of *Christ,* rather than that of *believers,* being unveiled, is, if I mistake not, solidly proved by the learned Ikenius, in his Dissertat. Philolog. Theolog. Dissert. xxvi. § 4, 5, 6.
[69] Exod. xxxiv. 28-35.

As, in the person of our Mediator, the nature of God and the nature of man were not united, till just before the commencement of this kingdom; as God was not "manifested in the flesh," but with an immediate view to this holy and spiritual empire; so there is no reason to wonder that the favoured subjects of Messiah's government, have a more intimate communion with Jehovah, than was ever enjoyed by the Jewish church. Under the old covenant, Israel in general had a kind of local nearness to God, in the performance of religious worship; and real saints had spiritual communion with him. But then it was by means of priests, who had infirmities; of sacrifices, that were imperfect; and of services, that were mere shadows of heavenly things: all which were confined to an earthly sanctuary. Whereas the subjects of Jesus Christ have access to the Father of mercies, without regarding any priest, besides their Sovereign; any sacrifice, besides his death; any incense, besides his intercession. All these they regard as appearing, as operating, as efficacious on their behalf, in the heavenly sanctuary. Yes, their Highpriest, who is of infinite dignity; their sacrifice, which is of boundless worth; and their incense, which is consummately fragrant, are for ever in the immediate presence of God—for ever deserving, and for ever obtaining the divine approbation. On these, therefore, in all their approaches to Eternal Majesty, their dependence fixes. Hence their worship is performed, through the aids of grace, with reverence and with confidence, with love and with delight. "We have access with confidence, by the faith of Christ."

Now, to worship God with profound reverence, yet without a slavish fear; with steady confidence, connected with deep humility; with submission to his will, as the most high Lord; with love to his excellence, as the Infinite Beauty; and with joy in his all-sufficiency, as the Chief Good; is to perform a spiritual service, and to adore in a heavenly manner. In the performance of such worship, we have communion with "the spirits of just men made perfect"—we enter within the veil—we have fellowship with God—we anticipate the business of heaven, and taste its refined pleasures. In these holy exercises of the mind, conscience, and heart, we feel ourselves near to God, as the fountain of all blessedness, and are trained for the heavenly world. Thus we are habituated to a kind of celestial service, by which our likeness to Christ is promoted, and our desires after heaven increased. In these things the very life of spiritual worship and of real religion consists. He therefore is not worthy to be called a subject of our Lord's kingdom, who is not habitually aiming, in his devotional services, at this delightful and solemn intercourse with God. Nor is he deserving of that exalted character, whose thoughts and cares, whose hopes and fears, whose joys and sorrows, are not principally concerned about the government and grace of Christ, considered in their connexion with the heavenly state.

It must, indeed, be admitted, that this communion with heaven is extremely imperfect in the present life. Because, though every true subject of the King Messiah be in a state very different from that of a merely nominal Christian, and though he is thankful for that difference; yet he is not, he cannot be satisfied, either with what he knows, or with what he enjoys; with what he is, or with what he does. Not with what he *knows:* for he knows but in part, and he feels the deficiency. His acquaintance with the greatest and best of beings—with the character and perfections, with the works and ways of God, is extremely small. His knowledge of the adorable Jesus—of his person and *offices,* of his grace and work, of his kingdom and glory, is very contracted. Nay, the knowledge he has of himself, and of his final destination in the heavenly world, is exceedingly scanty: for "the heart is deceitful above all things:" and "it does not yet appear what we shall be." He cannot therefore be contented with such a pittance of spiritual knowledge.

Not with what he *enjoys:* for his enjoyment of spiritual pleasure is, at the highest, comparatively low. Besides, it is frequently interrupted by the insurrections of indwelling sin, and by the incursions of outward temptation. Though he sometimes exults in the light of God's countenance, partaking of joy that is "unspeakable and full of glory;" yet he frequently mourns the want of that exalted pleasure, and "groans, being burdened."

Not with what he is: for he feels much depravity, and laments over it, as affecting his mind with darkness; his conscience with guilt, or with stupidity; and his passions with carnality. So far from perfectly bearing the image of Christ, that his language frequently is; "O wretched man that I am! who shall deliver me from the body of this death!"

Not with what he *does:* for though he sincerely desires to perform the will of God, as revealed in divine precepts, and illustrated by the example of Christ; yet he perceives that his obedience is very imperfect. Does he, for instance, address himself to God in prayer? in that devout exercise his whole soul should be engaged. Reverence of the divine Majesty, and an abasing sense of his own guilt; faith in the great atonement, and confidence in paternal mercy; the ardour of petition, and the comfort of expectation, should be all united. But frequently, alas! his thoughts wander, and his pious affections are dull, if not dormant. His prayer seems little besides a conflict with his own corruption. He rises from his knees with sorrow and with sighs. Ashamed of the manner in which he has treated the omniscient object of his worship, he cannot forbear exclaiming; "God be merciful to me a sinner!" and this, perhaps, is the only petition over which he does not mourn, as destitute of holy animation. Or, if he enjoy liberty in his converse with the Father of all mercies, how often does he find secret pride, and self-gratulation, arise in his heart? as if the Most Holy would regard his confessions, petitions, and thanksgivings for the sake of their own excellence! Aware of the latent poison, he is almost confounded. For well he knows, that Christianity is the religion of sinners—of depraved, of guilty, of unworthy creatures; and that nothing is more inconsistent with evangelical truth, or more detestable in the sight of our Maker, than self-applause respecting acceptance with God. Knowing himself to be a polluted worm that deserves to perish, he trembles to think of ever supposing that the majesty of the Most High, and the

An Essay on the Kingdom of Christ

purity of the Most Holy, will accept his imperfect services for their own sake. In the most emphatical manner he, therefore, with Job exclaims; "Behold, I am vile! I abhor myself!" So various and so great are the defects in our devotional services, that we might well despair, were it not for a High-priest who bears the iniquity of our holy things. For we "find a law, that when we would do good, evil is present with us."

To such imperfections and such complaints, is a real subject of our Lord's dominion liable in the present life. But, looking forward to the separate state, when he shall "be with Christ, which is far better," and to the resurrection of the righteous; with joy he adopts the language of David and says, "I shall be satisfied, when I awake with thy likeness." Yes, when that ultimate and everlasting economy commences, his mind being all irradiated with divine truth, be shall be satisfied with what he *knows:* perfectly possessing the chief good, he shall be satisfied with what he *enjoys;* conscious of complete rectitude, he shall be satisfied with what he is: and knowing his obedience to be consummate, he shall be satisfied with what he *does*. Delightful, ravishing thought! To have all our immortal powers expanded and filled, with knowledge of the supreme Truth, and with love to the supreme Beauty; with reverence of the supreme Lord, and with delight in the supreme Good, must constitute complete happiness. Yet such is the grand result of our Lord's dominion in the hearts of men! To this, therefore, we must look, upon this our affections must be placed, if we would behave as the subjects of Jesus Christ, and finish our course with honour. For as this life is the seed-time of an eternal harvest; as no one "gathers grapes of thorns, or figs of thistles;" and as "whatever a man sows, that shall he also reap;" so we have no reason to expect heaven as our final residence, if we be not habitually desirous of communion with God in all our worship, and of making it our business to perform his will.

It is one of the noblest and most delightful employments of the human mind, to contemplate the gradual revelation of Jehovah's will, and the growing display of his eternal favour, from the fall of our first parents, to the consummation of the divine economy. It is both pleasing and improving to reflect on the patriarchal dispensation introducing the Mosaic system; on the Sinai confederation making way for the new covenant; on the Jewish theocracy leading to the kingdom of Christ; on the government of that kingdom as a preparation for celestial mansions; on the performance of holy worship, by the subjects of Christ here, as the mean of communion with "saints in light;" and on the present state of worship and of blessedness in the heavenly sanctuary, as preparing for the ultimate glory.

In reference to the communion of believers with "the spirits of just men made perfect," in the performance of spiritual worship; and respecting the consummation of all things, Dr. Owen speaks as follows, with whose words I shall conclude. "Were all that die in the Lord immediately received into that state wherein "God shall be all in all," without any use of the mediation of Christ, or the worship of praise and honour unto God by him, without being exercised in the ascription of honour, glory, power, and dominion unto (Christ,) on the account of the past and present discharge of his office; there could be no communion between them and us. But whilst they are in the sanctuary, in the temple of God, in the holy worship of Christ, and of God in him, and we are not only employed in the same work in sacred ordinances suited unto our state and condition, but in the performance of our duties do by faith "enter in within the veil," and approach unto the same throne of grace in the most holy place; there is a spiritual communion between them and us. So the apostle expresseth it, in the twelfth of Hebrews—as we are here, in and by the word and other ordinances, prepared and made meet for the present state of things in glory; so are they, (the spirits of the just made perfect) by the temple worship of heaven, fitted for that state of things when Christ shall "give up the kingdom unto the Father, that GOD MAY BE ALL IN ALL."[70]

---

[70] *On the Person of Christ*, chap. xx. p. 365, 366.

BOOK III

PASTORAL CAUTIONS

PASTORAL CAUTIONS:

AN ADDRESS TO THE LATE MR. THOMAS HOPKINS WHEN ORDAINED

PASTOR OF THE CHURCH OF CHRIST, IN EAGLE STREET,
RED LION SQUARE, JULY THE 13TH, 1785

Sepius animum meum mirifice adfecit paulini illius moniti, attende tibi ipsi, recordatio: et hæc causa east, quamobrem aliis etiam libentissime illiud in animum revocem. — *A.H. Franck*

We must, in the first place, take heed to ourselves, if we intend to take heed to the flock as we ought. — *Dr. J. Owen*

BY ABRAHAM BOOTH

LONDON
BY THE AUTHOR, 1805

The Baptist Standard Bearer, Inc.
NUMBER ONE IRON OAKS DRIVE • PARIS, ARKANSAS 72855

Thou hast given a *standard* to them that fear thee;
that it may be displayed because of the truth.
-- Psalm 60:4

PASTORAL CAUTIONS

As you, my brother, are now invested with the pastoral office in this church, and have requested me to address you on the solemn occasion; I shall endeavour to do it with all the freedom of a friend, and with all the affection of a brother; not as your superior, but as your equal.

The language of divine law on which I shall ground my address, is that memorable injunction of Paul, in his charge to Timothy

Take heed to thyself. 1 TIMOTHY iv. 16.[1]

Very comprehensive, salutary, and important is this apostolic precept. For it comes recommended to our serious and submissive regard, as the language of a saint, who was pre-eminent among the most illustrious of our Lord's immediate followers; as the advice of a most accomplished and useful Minister of the Gospel, when hoary with age, rich with experience, and almost worn down by arduous labours; and as the command of an apostle, who wrote by the order and inspiration of Jesus Christ, This divine precept I shall now take the liberty of urging upon you in various points of light.

Take heed to yourself, then, with regard to the reality of true godliness, and the state of religion in your own soul. —That you are a partaker of regenerating grace, I have a pleasing persuasion: that you have some experience of those pleasures and pains, of those joys and sorrows, which are peculiar to real Christians, I make no doubt. But this does not supersede the necessity of the admonition. Make it your daily prayer, and your diligent endeavour, therefore, to *feel* the importance

---

[1] See also, Acts xx. 28.

of those truths you have long believed—of those doctrines you now preach. Often inquire at the mouth of conscience, what you experience of their comforting, reproving, and sanctifying power? When you have been preaching the promises of grace, or urging the precepts of duty, earnestly pray that their practical influence may appear in your own dispositions and conduct. Endeavour to realize the force, and to comply with the requisition of that precept, "Grow in grace, and in the knowledge of our Lord and Saviour Jesus Christ."

In proportion as the principles of true piety are vigorous in your heart, may you be expected to fill up the wide circumference of pastoral duty. For there is no reason to fear that a minister, if tolerably furnished with gifts, will be remarkably deficient, or negligent, in any known branch of pastoral obligation, while his heart is alive to the enjoyments and to the duties of the *christian* character. It is from the pastor's defects considered under the notion of *a disciple,* that his principal difficulties and chief dangers arise. For, my brother, it is only on the permanent basis of genuine christian piety, that your pastoral character can be established, or appear with respectability, in the light of the New Testament. I called genuine christian piety *permanent,* because every thing essential to it will abide, and flourish in immortal vigour: whereas the pastoral office, though honourable and important when connected with true godliness, must soon be laid aside, as inconsistent with the heavenly state.

Take heed to yourself, lest you mistake an increase of gifts for a growth in grace. —Your knowledge of the Scriptures, your abilities for explaining them, and your ministerial talents in general, may considerably increase, by reading, study, and public exercise; while real godliness is far from flourishing in your heart. For, among all the apostolic churches, none seem to have abounded more in the enjoyments of spiritual gifts, than the church at Corinth: yet few of them appear to have been in a more unhappy state, or more deserving of reproof. I have long been of opinion, my brother, that no professors of

❦ Pastoral Cautions ❦

the genuine gospel have more need to be on their guard against self-deception, respecting the true state of religion in their own souls, than those who statedly dispense the gracious truth. For as it is their *calling* and their *business*, frequently to read their Bibles, and to think much upon spiritual things—to pray, and preach, and often to converse about the affairs of piety; they will, if not habitually cautious, do it all *ex officio*, or merely as the work of their ministerial calling, without feeling their own interest in it.

To grow in love to God, and in zeal for his honour; in conformity to the will of Christ, and in heavenly-mindedness, should be your first concern. Look well, therefore, to your internal character. For it is awful to think of appearing as a minister, without being *really* a Christian; or of any one officially watching over the souls of others, who is habitually unmindful of his own immortal interests.

In the course of your public ministry, and in a great variety of instances, you may perhaps find it impracticable to enter into the true spirit of a precept, or of a prohibition, so as to reach its full meaning and its various application, without feeling yourself *convicted by* it. In cases of this kind, you must fall under the conviction secretly before God, and pray over it with undissembled contrition: agreeably to that saying, "Thou that teachest another, teachest thou not thyself?" When ministers hardly ever make this practical application of their public admonitions and cautions, as if their own spiritual interests were not concerned in them; their consciences will grow callous, and their situation with regard to eternity, extremely dangerous. For, this being habitually neglected, how can they be considered as *walking* HUMBLY *with God,* which, nevertheless, is of such essential importance in the Christian life, that, without it, all pretences to true piety are vain. Hence an author, of no small repute in the churches of Christ, says, "He that would go down to the pit in peace, let him keep up duties in his family and closet; let him hear as often as he can have opportunity; let him speak often of good things; let him leave the company of profane and ignorant men, until he have obtained a great repute for religion; let him preach, and labour to make others better than he himself; and in the mean time, neglect to humble his heart to walk with God in a manifest holiness and usefulness, and he will not fail of his end."[2]

Take heed that your pastoral office prove not a snare to your soul, by lifting you up with pride and self importance. — Forget not, that the whole of your work is ministerial; not legislative—that you are not a lord in the church, but a servant—that the New Testament attaches no honour to the character of a pastor, except in connexion with his humility and benevolence, his diligence and zeal, in promoting the cause of the Great Shepherd—and, that there is no character upon earth which so ill accords with a proud, imperious, haughty spirit, as that of a Christian pastor.

If not intoxicated with a conceit of your own wisdom and importance, you will not, when presiding in the management of church affair, labour to have every motion determined according to your own inclination. For this would savour of ecclesiastical despotism; be inconsistent with the nature and spirit of congregational order; and implicitly grasping at a much larger degree of power, and of responsibility, than properly falls to your share.

Nor, if this caution be duly regarded, will you consider it as an insult on either your ministerial wisdom, or your pastoral dignity, if now and then, one or another of your people, and even the most illiterate among them, should remind you of some real or supposed inadvertency or mistake, either in doctrine or in conduct; no, not though it be in blunt language, and quite unfounded. For a readiness to take offence on such occasions, would be a bar to your own improvement; and, perhaps, in articles, relatively considered, of great importance. Nay, in such cases, to be soon irritated, though not inconsistent with shining abilities, nor yet with great success in the ministry; would, nevertheless, be an evidence

---

[2] Dr. Owen's *Sermons and Tracts*, p. 47, folio, London, 1721.

of pride, and of your being, *as a christian,* in a poor, feeble state. For, to be easily shoved out of the way, pushed down, as it were, with a straw, or caused to fall into sin, by so feeble an impulse, must be considered as an undoubted mark of great spiritual weakness.[3] Because the health of the soul, and the vigour of the spiritual life, are to be estimated, not by our knowledge and gifts, but by the exercise of Christian graces, in cheerfully performing arduous labours; in surmounting successive difficulties; and in patiently bearing hardships, for the sake of Jesus. Yes, and in proportion to the degree of your spiritual health, will be your meekness and forbearance under those improprieties of treatment, by one and another of your people, which you will undoubtedly meet.—On examining ourselves by this rule, it will plainly appear, I presume, that though many of us in this assembly might, with regard to the length of our Christian profession, be justly denominated *fathers;* yet, with reference to spiritual stature and strength, we deserve no better character than that of *ricketty children.* —Think not, however, that I advise you always to tolerate ignorant, conceited, and petulant professors, in making exceptions to your ministry, or in calling you to account for your conduct, without reason, and without good manners but endeavour, with impartiality and prudence, to distinguish between cases of this kind. Then the simple and sincere, though improperly officious, will not be treated with resentful harshness; but with some resemblance of what is beautifully denominated, "the meekness and and gentleness of Jesus Christ."[4] But alas! how poorly we imitate our Perfect Pattern!

It is of such high importance, that a pastor possess the government of his own temper, and a tolerable share of prudence, when presiding in the management of church affairs; that, without these, his general integrity, though undisputed, and his benevolence, though usually considered as exemplary, will be in danger of impeachment among his

---

[3] Rom. xv. 1.
[4] 2 Cor. x. 1.

people. Nay, notwithstanding the fickleness and caprice of many private professors with regard to their ministers, it has long appeared probable to me, that a majority of those uneasinesses, animosities, and separations, which, to the disgrace of religion, take place between pastors and their several churches, may be traced up, either to the unchristian tempers, to the gross imprudence, or to the laziness and neglects of the pastors themselves.

Take heed to yourself, respecting your temper and conduct in general. —Every one that calls himself a Christian should fairly represent, in his own dispositions and behaviour, the moral character of Jesus. The conversation of every professor should not only be free from gross defects; it should be worthy of general imitation. But though each member of this church be under the same *obligations* to holiness, as yourself; yet your spiritual gifts, your ministerial office, and your pastoral relation, suggest a variety of *motives* to holiness, which your people do not possess. Make it your diligent concern, therefore, to set your hearers a bright example, formed on that perfect model, the temper and conduct of Jesus Christ.

Yes, my brother, it is required that pastors, in their own persons and conduct, especially in the discharge of ministerial duties, give a just representation of the doctrine they preach, and of Him in whose name they dispense it. But, in order to do this, though in an imperfect manner, what integrity, benevolence, humility, meekness, and zeal for the glory of God; what self-denial and readiness for bearing the cross; what mortification of corrupt affections and inordinate desires of earthly things; what condescension and patience; what contempt of the world, and heavenly-mindedness, are necessary; not only the scripture declares, but the nature of the thing shows.

Persons who are not acquainted with the true nature and genius of evangelical doctrine, will be always disposed to charge the gospel itself with having a strong tendency to encourage those immoralities" which appear in the character

❦ Pastoral Cautions ❦

of its professors, and especially of those that preach it. Hence an apostle says, "Giving no offence in any thing that the ministry be not blamed." For what can persons, otherwise uninformed, with more appearance of reason conclude, than that the example of those who propagate the doctrine of salvation by grace, through Jesus Christ, is an authentic specimen of its genuine tendency in the hearts and lives of all those who believe and avow it? In the ministry of religious teachers, there is an implicit language, which is commonly considered by their hearers as importing, that what they *(lo and are,* if disgraceful, is the effect, not of their natural depravity, or of peculiar temptations; but of their doctrinal principles. Hence the ministers of Christ are commanded "in all things to show themselves patterns of good works. To be examples to believers in word, in conversation, in charity, in spirit, in faith, in purity." Yes, my brother, the honour, and preferment, to which our divine Lord calls his ministers, are, to give a just representation, in their own conduct, of the graces of his person, and the holiness of his doctrine, to others. For whatever apparently splendid advantages a man may have, with reference to the ministry; if they do not enable him the more effectually, in his Christian course and ministerial work, to express the humility, the meekness, the self-denial, and the zeal of the Chief Shepherd, together with the holiness of the doctrine he teaches; will redound but little to his account another day.[5]

I will now adopt the words of our Lord, and say, *Take heed and beware of covetousness.* That evil turn of heart which is here proscribed with such energy and such authority, is, through the false names it assumes, and the pleas which it makes, to be considered extremely subtle, and equally pernicious. It evidently stands opposed, in scripture, to contentment with the allotments of Providence;[6] to spiritual mindedness;[7] and to real piety.[8] It is an extremely evil

---

[5] See Dr. Owen's *Nature of Apostasy,* p. 441-444.
[6] Heb. xiii. 5.
[7] Luke xii. 15-21.
[8] Col. iii. 5; Eph. v. 5; 1 Cor. v. 11.

disposition of the heart; of which, notwithstanding, very little account is made by the generality of those who profess the gospel of divine grace; except when it procures the stigma of penuriousness, or the charge of injustice. But, whatever excuses or palliatives may be invented, either to keep the consciences of covetous professors quiet, or to support a good opinion of others respecting the reality of their piety; the New Testament declares them unworthy of communion in a church of Christ, and classes them with persons of profligate hearts and lives.[9] The existence and habitual operation of this evil, therefore, must be considered as forming a character for hell.[10] Nor need I inform you, that, for a long course of ages, myriads of those who assumed the appellation of Christian ministers, have been so notorious for an avaricious disposition, for the love of secular honours, and for the lust of clerical domination, as greatly to promote infidelity, and expose Christianity to contempt.

Take heed, then, and beware of covetousness. For neither the comfort, the honour, nor the usefulness of "a man's life consisteth in the abundance of the things which he possesseth." "Let your conversation be without covetousness;" and, possessing the necessaries of life, without being indebted to any man, "be content with such things as you have: for He, who governs the world, hath said, I will never leave thee nor forsake thee." For as a man's happiness *does not consist in* THINGS, but in THOUGHTS, that abundance after which the carnal heart so eagerly pants, is adapted to gratify not the demands of reason; much less the dictates of conscience; nor yet the legitimate and sober claims of appetite; but a fond imagination; pride of show; the love of secular influence; the lust of dominion: and a secret desire of lying as little as possible at the mercy of Providence. I have somewhat seen it reported of Socrates, the prince of pagan philosophers, that on beholding a great variety of costly and elegant articles exposed to sale, he exclaimed, "How many things are here that I do not want!" So, my brother, when

---

[9] 2 Cor, v. 11; 2 Cor. vi. 9, 10.
[10] Psalm, x. 3; 1 Cor. vi. 10.

༄ Pastoral Cautions ༅

entering the abode of wealth we behold the stately mansion, the numerous accommodations, the elegant furniture, the luxurious table, the servants in waiting, and the fashionable finery of each individual's apparel; with what propriety and emphasis ought each of us to exclaim, "How many things are here which I do not want; which would do me no good: and after which I have no desire!" For we should not forget who it was that said, "How hardly shall a rich man enter the kingdom of heaven!"

I said, *Possessing the necessaries of life, without being indebted to any man.* —For this purpose, resolutely determine to live, if practicable, within the bounds of your income; not only so as to keep out of debt, but, if possible, to spare something for the poor. Supposing, my brother, that, either through the afflicting hand of God, or the criminal neglect of your people, unavoidable straits approach; be not afraid of looking poverty in the face, as if it were, in itself considered, a disgraceful evil. For poverty is a very innocent thing, and absolutely free from deserved infamy; except when it is found in scandalous company. But if its forerunner and its associates be pride, laziness, a fondness for good living, a want of economy, and the contracting of debts without a probability of paying them; it deserves detestation, and merits contempt—is inconsistent with virtuous conduct, and must gradually sink the character of any minister. If, on the contrary, it be found closely connected with humility and patience, with diligence, frugality, and integrity—such integrity as impels, for instance, to wear a thread-bare coat, rather than run into debt for a new one; to live on the meanest wholesome food, or to go with half a meal, rather than contract a debt which is not likely to be discharged; such penury will never disgrace, either the minister himself, or the cause of Jesus Christ. *Not the minister himself.* Because, in the purest state of Christianity, the most eminent servants of our divine Lord were sometimes distressed with want of both decent apparel and necessary food.[11] *Not the cause of Jesus Christ.* For his kingdom not being *of this world,* but of a spiritual nature; it cannot be either adorned by riches, or disgraced by poverty. Besides, the ministers of evangelical truth must be poor indeed, if in humbler circumstances than Jesus himself was, when proclaiming the glad tidings of his kingdom. It must, however, be acknowledged, that, so far as a faithful pastor is reduced to the embarrassments of poverty, merely by his people withholding those voluntary supplies which they were well able to have afforded, and to which, in common justice, equally as by the appointment of Christ, he had an undoubted right;[12] the best of causes is disgraced, and the offenders are exposed to severer censure.

Were a pastor driven to the painful alternative, of either entering into some lawful secular employment; or of continuing his pastoral relation and stated ministrations, in a course of embarrassment by debts which he could not pay; the former would become his duty. Not only because we ought never to "do evil that good may come;" but also because it is much more evident, that he ought to "owe no man any thing;" than it is, that the Lord ever called him to the ministry, or qualified him for it. But, if necessity do not impel, the following passage seems to have the force of a negative precept, respecting the Christian pastor: "No man that warreth entangleth himself with the affairs of this life; that he may please him who bath chosen him to be a soldier." A pastor should be very cautious, not only of entering, unnecessarily, into stated secular employment; but also of accepting any trust, though apparently advantageous, in which the preservation and the management of property are confided to his integrity and prudence. For so critically observed is the conduct of a man that has the management of another's pecuniary affairs, and so delicate is a minister's character; that he is in peculiar danger of exposing himself to censure, and of injuring his public usefulness, by such engagements.

---

[11] 2 Cor. xi. 27; Acts iii. vi.
[12] 1 Cor, xi. 1.

~ Pastoral Cautions ~

Take heed, I will venture to add, *take heed to your second-self, in the person of your wife. As* it is of high importance for a young minister in single life, to behave with the utmost delicacy in all his intercourse with female friends, treating with peculiar caution those of them that are unmarried; and as it behoves him to pay the most conscientious regard to religious character, when choosing a companion for life; so, when in the conjugal state, his tenderest attention is due to the domestic happiness and the spiritual interests of his wife. This obligation, my brother, manifestly devolves upon you; as being already a husband and a father. Next after your own soul, therefore, your wife and your children evidently claim the most affectionate, conscientious, and pious care.

Nor can it be reasonably doubted, that many a devout and amiable woman has given her hand to a minister of the gospel, in preference to a private Christian, though otherwise equally deserving, in sanguine expectation, by so doing, of enjoying peculiar spiritual advantages in the matrimonial relation. But, alas! there is much reason to apprehend, that not a few individuals among those worthy females, have often reflected to the following effect.

I have, indeed, married a preacher of the gospel; but I do not find in him the affectionate domestic instructor, for either myself, or my children. My husband is much esteemed among his religious acquaintance, as a respectable Christian character; but his example at home is far from being delightful. Affable, condescending, and pleasing, in the parlours of religious friends; but, frequently, either trifling and unsavoury, or imperious and unsocial, in his own family. Preferring the opportunity of being entertained at a plentiful table, and of conversing with the wealthy, the polite, and the sprightly; to the homely fare of his own family, and the company of his wife and children; he often spends his afternoons and evenings from home, until so late an hour, that domestic worship is either omitted, or performed in a hasty and slovenly manner, with scarcely the appearance of devotion. —Little caring for my soul, or for the management of our growing offspring; he seems concerned for hardly any thing more, than keeping fair with his people: relative to which, I have often calmly demonstrated, and submissively entreated, but all in vain. Surrounded with little ones, and attended with straits; destitute of the sympathies, the instructions, the consolations, which might have been expected from the affectionate heart of a pious husband, connected with the gifts of an evangelical minister; I pour out my soul to God, and mourn in secret." Such, there is ground of apprehension, has been the sorrowful soliloquy of many a minister's pious, dutiful, and prudent wife. Take heed, then, to the best interests of your *Second-self*.

To this end, except on extraordinary occasions, when impelled by duty, *spend your evenings at home*. Yes, and at an early hour in the evening, let your family and your study receive their demands on your presence, in the lively performance of social and secret devotion. Thus there will be reason to hope, that domestic order and sociability, the improvement of your own understanding, and communion with God, will all be promoted.

Guard, habitually, against every appearance of imprudent intercourse, and every indelicate familiarity with the most virtuous and pious of your female friends. Be particularly cautious of paying frequent visits to any single woman who lives alone: otherwise, your conduct may soon fall under the suspicion of your neighbours, and also of your own wife, so as to become her daily tormentor; even while she believes you innocent of the great transgression. —In cases of this kind, it is not sufficient that conscience bears witness to the purity of your conduct, and the piety of your motives: for, in matters of such a delicate nature, there should not be the least shadow of a ground, either to support suspicion, or to excite surmise. There is need for us, my brother, to watch and pray against the greatest sins—even against those to which, perhaps, we never perceived ourselves to be much inclined. For, alas! we have sometimes heard of apparently pious and evangelical ministers falling into such enormous crimes, as not only disgrace religion, but degrade humanity.

～ Pastoral Cautions ～

Of late, I have been much affected with the following reflection: "though, if not greatly deceived, I have had some degree of experimental acquaintance with Jesus Christ for almost forty years; though I have borne the ministerial character for upwards of twenty-five years,[13] though I have been, perhaps, of some little use in the church of God; and though I have had a greater share of esteem among religious people than I had any reason to expect; yet, after all, it is possible for me, in one single hour of temptation, to blast my character—to ruin my public usefulness—and to render my warmest Christian friends ashamed of owning me. Hold thou me up, O Lord, and I shall be safe!" Ah! brother, there is little reason for any of us to be high-minded; and, therefore, "Happy is the man that feareth always."

Take heed to yourself, with regard to the diligent improvement of your talents and opportunities, in the whole course of your ministry. It behoves you, as a public teacher, to spend much of your time in reading and in study. Of this you are convinced, and will act, I trust, agreeably to that conviction. For suitable means must be used, not only in your public ministry, "in season and out of season," for the good of others; but with a view to the improvement of your own mind, in an acquaintance with divine truth. Yes, my Christian friend, this is necessary, that your ability to feed the flock "with knowledge and understanding," may be increased; that your own heart may be more deeply tinctured with evangelical principles; that you may be the better prepared for every branch of pastoral duty, and for every trying event that may occur. For who can reasonably deny the necessity of diligence in the use of means, adapted, respectively, to promote your own ministerial improvement, and to obtain the great objects of your pastoral office; any more than to a rational prospect of success, in the management of secular business? Be, then, as careful to improve opportunities of both obtaining and imparting spiritual benefits, as the

---

[13] Forty years—twenty-five years. These dates were given July 13, 1785.

prudent and assiduous tradesman or mechanic is, to promote the legitimate designs of his professional calling.

If a minister of the gospel behave with Christian decorum, possess tolerable abilities for his work, and, having his heart in it, be habitually industrious; there is reason to conclude that, in the common course of Providence, he shall not labour in vain. As nobody, however, wonders that a merchant, or a manufacturer, who, having no pleasure in his employment, neglects his affairs, and behaves as if he thought himself above his business, does not succeed, but becomes bankrupt; so, if a minister be seldom any further engaged, either in the study of truth, or in the public exercises of religion, than seems necessary to his continuance, with decency, in the pastoral station; there is no reason to wonder, if his public devotion be without savour, and his preaching without success. The church of which such a minister is the pastor, seems completely warranted to cry in his ears, "Take heed to the ministry which thou hast received in the Lord, that thou fulfil it."[14]

Take heed to yourself, respecting the motives by which you are influenced in all your endeavours to obtain useful knowledge. For if you read and study, chiefly that you may cut a respectable figure in the pulpit; or to obtain and increase popular applause; the motive is carnal, base, and unworthy a man of God. Yet, detestable in the sight of Him who searches the heart as that motive is, there will be the greatest necessity for you to guard against it as a besetting evil. It is, perhaps, as hard for a minister habitually to read and study with becoming diligence, without being under this corrupt influence; as it is for a tradesman prudently to manage a lucrative business, without seeking the gratification of a covetous disposition; yet both the minister and the tradesman must either guard against these pernicious evils, or be in danger of sinking in final ruin.

---

[14] Col, iv. 17. Compare chap, i. 2.

Pastoral Cautions

Besides, whatever be the motives which principally operate in your private studies, it, is highly probable those very motives will have their influence in the pulpit. If, when secretly studying the word of God, it was your chief concern to know the divine will, that you might, with integrity and benevolence, lay it before your people for their benefit; it is likely the same holy motive will attend you in public service. But if a thirst of popularity, or a lust of applause, had the principal influence in the choice of your subject, and in your meditations upon it; there will be no reason for surprise, if you should be under the same detestable bias, when performing your public labour.

Study your discourses, therefore, with a devotional disposition. To this you are bound by the very nature of the case, as a Christian minister. For, when the bible is before you, it is the word of God on which you meditate, and the work of God you are preparing to perform. It is reported of Dr. Cotton Mather, "that in studying and preparing them, he would endeavour to make even that an exercise of devotion for his own soul. Accordingly his way was, at the end of every paragraph, to make a pause, and endeavour to make his own soul feel some holy impression of the truths contained in it. This he thought would be an excellent means of delivering his sermons with life and spirit, and warming the hearts of his people by them: and so he found it."[15]

It is, indeed, an easy thing for a preacher to make loud professions of regard to the glory of God and the good of immortal souls, as the ruling motive in his ministerial conduct: but experience has taught me, that it is extremely difficult for any minister to act suitably to such professions. For as that pride which is natural to our species, impels the generality of mankind to wish for eminence, rather than usefulness, in this or the other station; so it is with ministers of the word. Forty years ago I saw but little need of this caution, compared with that conviction of its necessity which I now have. A preacher of the real gospel, I am fully

---

[15] *Abridgment of Dr. C. Mather's Life*, p. 38.

persuaded, may appear exceedingly earnest and very faithful in his public labours, as if his only design were to promote the cause of truth, the happiness of men, and the honour of God; while, nevertheless, he is more concerned to figure away at the head of a large body of people in the religious world, than to advance the genuine interests of Jesus Christ, and the felicity of his fellow mortals. What is it but this detestable pride, that makes any of us ministers take more pleasure in perceiving our labours made useful to the rich, the learned, and the polite; than to the poor, the illiterate, and the vulgar? It is, I presume, principally, because it adds consequence to our own characters, to have wealthy, well-educated, and polished persons in our churches. Jesus, however, in the time of his personal ministry, was far from being influenced by any such motive; and equally far from showing the least predilection for persons of promising dispositions, on any such grounds. Witness his behaviour to Nicodernus, to the young ruler, and to the nobleman at Capernaum.[16]

I will add, what is it but the same depravity of heart, which frequently renders us much more attentive to our wealthy friends, than we are to our poor brethren; in times of affliction? even though we be well assured, that there is little danger of the rich being overlooked in their sorrows. Hoary as I now am[17] in the ministry, and accustomed as I have been to hear conscience cry out against me, for this, that, and the other omission of duty; I do not recollect that it ever charged me with neglecting any person in plentiful circumstances, when deeply afflicted, and requesting my visits. But, alas! I do recollect having frequently heard conscience, with a frowning aspect, and an angry tone, either demanding, "Wouldst thou be thus backward to undergo some little inconvenience, in visiting a wealthy patient?" Or declaring, "That afflicted brother would not, through mere forgetfulness, have been recently disappointed of thy presence, conversation, and prayers, had he not been an

---

[16] John iii. 1-12; Mark x. 17-22; John iv. 46-50.
[17] A.D. 1805.

PASTORAL CAUTIONS

obscure and a poor man. Had be been less deserving of thy compassionate regard, he would have been favoured with it." Alas, my brother, there is reason to fear, that few ministers, on this ground, stand perfectly free from censure, at the bar of a tender conscience!

As you should take heed to yourself, respecting the principles on which you act, and the ends at which you aim, in your preparations for the pulpit; so it behoves you to be still more careful in these respects, when you enter on public service. For then you professedly appear, as a guilty creature, to adore at the feet of Eternal Majesty; as a minister of the Divine Jesus, to perform his work; and as the servant of this church, to promote the happiness of all its members. Endeavour, therefore, always to enter into your pulpit under the force of this conviction: "I am an apostate creature, and going to worship the omniscient God: a wretch who deserves to perish, yet looking to sovereign mercy a sinner called by the gospel, and trusting in the great atonement; confessedly insufficient for the work on which I am entering, but relying on the aids of grace." This will produce deep solemnity, tempered with devout delight: which mixture of holy awe and sacred pleasure should accompany the christian, and especially the christian minister, whenever he approaches the Supreme.

Remarkable and important is that saying: — "Let us have grace whereby we may serve God acceptably, with reverence and godly fear: for our God is a consuming fire." Very observable is the language of David: "I will go to the altar of God, to God my exceeding joy." May the import of these passages united, exert its force on your very soul, whenever you take the lead in public worship! Then your graces as a christian, and your gifts as a minister, will be exercised at the same time. Your graces being excited, you have communion with God: your gifts being exerted, the people are edified.

Whereas, were you to enter the pulpit merely to exercise your ministerial talents, though others might be fed by the truths delivered, your own soul would starve. This, I fear, is the case of many who preach the gospel.

But, what a figure, in the eye of Omniscience, must that preacher make, who is not habitually desirous of exercising devout affections in the performance of his public work! Like an index on the high-road, he directs others in the way to heaven; but he walks not in it himself. He may prophesy with Balaam, or preach with Judas; his learning and knowledge, his natural parts and spiritual gifts, may excite admiration and be useful to others; but, being destitute of internal devotion, his heart is not right with God, and he is a wretched creature. "Sounding brass, or a tinkling cymbal," is the character by which he is known in sacred Scripture.

When, however, commencing public service, it is needful to remember, that you appear, not only as a worshipper of God, but as a minister of Christ. Being such, it is your indispensable duty to preach Christ, and not yourself: that is, with sincerity and ardour, to aim at displaying the glories of his person, and the riches of his grace; the spirituality of his kingdom, and the excellence of his government: not your own ingenuity—or eloquence—your parts, or learning. Guard, then, my brother, as against the most pernicious evil; guard, as for your very life, against converting the gospel ministry into a vehicle to exhibit your own excellence; or prostituting the doctrine of Christ crucified to the gratification of your pride, or that it may be a pander to your praise. For who can estimate the magnitude of that guilt which is included in such conduct? Yet, with this enormous and horrible evil, I cannot forbear suspecting, many ministers are more or less chargeable. Nay, to the commission of this outrage on the honour of Christ and of grace, every minister should consider himself as liable. For so polluted are our hands, that, without grace preventing, we defile every thing we touch. So depraved are our hearts, that we are in danger of committing a robbery on the glory of our divine Lord, even when it is our professed business to exalt it.

Pastoral Cautions

As, when entering on public devotion, you should endeavour to act becoming your character, tinder the notion of a guilty creature, in audience with the King Eternal; and as a minister of Christ, whose business it is to display his glory; so you are further to consider yourself as the servant of this church. When standing up to address your people, it should ever be with an earnest desire of promoting their happiness. They having chosen you to the pastoral office; you having accepted their invitation; and being now solemnly ordained to the important service; that mutual agreement, and the interesting transactions of this day should operate as a threefold motive to the faithful performance of your public work. Yes, you are bound affectionately to aim at doing them good, by laying divine truth before them in such a manner as is adapted to enlighten their minds, to affect their hearts, and to promote their edification.

Though the occasional exercise of your ministerial talents in other places, may be both lawful and commendable; yet, as it is here only that you stand in the pastoral relation, you ought, except in extraordinary cases, to fill this pulpit yourself; and not leave the deacons to procure supplies, in a precarious manner, while you are serving some other community. It is here, as a public teacher, that your proper business lies; and here, at the usual times of assembling, your voice must be heard. When a pastor of a church discovers an inclination to avail himself of almost any pretext from being absent from his people, in order to serve others; he gives reason of suspicion, whatever his pretences may be, that, either filthy lucre, or a lust of popularity, has too much place in his heart; and that he accepted the pastoral office, rather as an article of convenience, than as matter of duty. It is, indeed, much to be lamented, that though dissenting ministers in general justly exclaim against the non-residence and the holding of pluralities, which are so common among the clergy; yet the conduct of some pastors among the nonconformists, makes near approaches to that of pluralities in our national establishment, and is a violation of pastoral duty.

Abraham Booth

You should seek, with peculiar care, to obtain the approbation of conscience in each of your hearers; as appears by the following words: — "By manifestation of the truth, commending ourselves to every man's conscience in the sight of God." This illustrious passage presents us with a view of Paul in the pulpit; and a very solemn appearance he makes. He has just been adoring in secret, at the feet of the Most High; and, recent from converse with the Most Holy, he is now going to address his fellow sinners. Penetrated with the importance of his office, and the solemnity of his present situation, he manifestly feels—he seems to tremble. Nor need we wonder: for the subject on which he is to speak, the object he has in view, and the witness of his conduct, are all interesting and so solemn to the last degree. Truth, conscience, and God—the most important and impressive thoughts that can enter the human mind—pervade his very soul. Evangelical truth is the subject of his discussion; the approbation of conscience is the object of his desire; and the omniscient Holy One is the witness of his conduct. An example this, which you, and I, and every minister of the word are bound to imitate. Make it your diligent endeavour, then, to obtain the approbation of conscience, from all that hear you; for without *deserving* that, none of your public labours can be to your honour, or turn to your own account, in the great day of the Lord.

A minister may say things that are profoundly learned, and very ingenious; that are uncommonly pretty and extremely pleasing to the generality of his hearers; without aiming to reach their consciences, and to impress their hearts, either by asserting divine authority, or by displaying divine grace. When this is the case, he obtains, it may be, from superficial hearers, the reward which he sought; for he is greatly admired and applauded. But, alas! the unawakened sinner is not alarmed; the hungry soul is not fed; and *the Father of mercies is* defrauded of that reverence and confidence, of that love and obedience, which a faithful declaration of the gracious and sanctifying truth might have produced. Yes, my brother, it is much to be suspected, that many ministers have

Pastoral Cautions

recommended themselves to the fancies, the tastes, the affections of their hearers; who never deserved, and who never had, in a serious hour, the approbation of their consciences.

Be ambitious, therefore, of obtaining and preserving the suffrage of conscience in your favour, whether admired, and honoured with verbal applause, or not. For it is evident from observation, that a preacher who is endued with a competent share of learning and fine parts, a retentive memory and good elocution, may recommend himself to the admiration of great numbers; while their consciences, in the hour of solemn reflection, bear testimony against him. Because, as a minister may have all those engaging qualifications, while habitually proud and covetous, deceitful and vain: so the *conscience* never feels itself interested in the fine imagination, the genius, or the learning, which a minister discovers in his public services. It is worthy of remark, my brother, that though none of us can command success to our labours, were we ever so pious, diligent, and faithful; and though it may not be in our power to obtain the applause of literature, of genius, or of address; yet, in the common course of things, if we be assiduous, benevolent, and upright in our labours, we may secure the approbation of conscience, in the generality of our stated hearers; which is an article of great importance to the tranquillity of a minister's own breast.

Now, my young friend, if you keep conscience in view; if you remember that God himself is a witness of your latent motives, and of your public labours, you will not choose an obscure text, principally that you may have the honour of explaining it: nor will you select one which has no relation to the subject you mean to discuss, in order that your acumen may shine, by making it speak what it never thought. The more you keep the approbation of conscience and the presence of God in your eye, the more dependent will you be on divine assistance, in all your ministerial addresses. Yes, bearing in mind, on every occasion of this kind, that your business here is to plead for the interests of evangelical truth, under the immediate inspection of Him who is the truth; you cannot but feel your incapacity, and look for assistance to God, whose cause you mean to promote. The more you keep the consciences of men and the presence of God in your view, the more will you be impressed with the importance of your subject, and the more earnest will you be in addressing your hearers: for that minister must have a strange set of passions, who does not feel himself roused by such considerations. The more you keep the approbation of conscience and the inspection of God in remembrance, the less will you be disposed to indulge a light and trifling spirit, and the more devotional will you be, in the course of your administrations: for the ordinances of God are too sacred to become the vehicles of entertainment, and his presence is too solemn to permit the smile of levity.

Again: keeping the consciences of men, and the searcher of hearts in view, it will afford you much more pleasure to find, that persons who have been hearing you, left the place bemoaning their apostate state, and very deeply abased before the Most Holy; than to he informed, that they greatly admired you as a preacher, and loudly applauded your ministerial talents. Because, for a person to depart from public worship, in raptures with the minister's abilities, is no proof that he has received any spiritual benefit. But if, smitten with a sense of guilt, he cry out,— "How shall I escape the wrath to come? God be merciful to me a sinner!" Or if he exclaim, "Who is a god like unto our God? How great is his goodness, and how great is his beauty! What shall I render to the Lord for all his benefits?" then it looks as if the preacher had commended himself to his conscience, and as if the truth had reached his heart. For language of this kind, from a reflecting hearer, has a devotional aspect, and gives glory to God.

It indicates a soul, either as being apprehensive of deserved ruin, or as rejoicing in revealed mercy; as having a good hope through grace, or as revering divine authority. Whereas, barely to admire and praise the preacher, is quite consistent with reigning depravity, and with rooted enmity to God. As it

Pastoral Cautions

is written, "They sit before thee as my people, and they hear thy words—With their mouth they show much love, but their heart goeth after their covetousness. And lo, thou art unto them as a very lovely song of one that bath a pleasant voice, and can play well on an instrument: for they hear thy words, but they do them not."

Once more: in proportion as the approbation of conscience, and the inspection of God are properly kept in view, the pleasure you have, arising from verbal commendations of professed friends, and the pain of strong opposition from the avowed enemies of evangelical truth, will be diminished. For conscience does not often express itself in the language of noisy applause; which, when free from hypocrisy, is commonly the fruit of a weak understanding, under the influence of strong passions. Hence it is not unfrequent for those who have been the most liberal in praising a minister, to be found among the first who entirely desert his ministry. As to unfounded censures, and violent opposition; the testimony of a good conscience, and the countenance of scripture, are adapted to afford the needful support.

Take heed to yourself, with regard to that success, and those discouragements, which may attend your ministry. —Should a large degree of apparent success, through the favour of heaven, accompany your labours, there will be the highest necessity to guard against pride and self-esteem. A young man, of good ministerial abilities, and honoured with great usefulness, is in a delicate situation respecting the prosperity of his own soul: for, through the want of experience and observation, such concurrence of pleating particulars has proved to some very promising characters, the innocent occasion of disgrace and ruin. Shining abilities, and a blessing upon their labours, have rendered them popular. Popularity has intoxicated them with pride. Pride has exposed them to various temptations. Temptations have prevailed; and, either precipitated them into some enormous offence or laid the foundation of a gradual departure from the truth, and from the practice of real piety. If the former, their character has been killed, as by the stroke of an apoplexy. If the latter, their comfort and usefulness have been destroyed, as by a consuming hectic.[18] Agreeable to that saying, "Pride goeth before destruction, and a haughty spirit before a fall."

Remember, therefore, my brother, that though it is your indispensable duty to labour and pray for prosperity in your work; yet, that a season of remarkable success will generally prove an hour of peculiar temptation to your own soul. Take heed to yourself, at such a time, and watch the secret motions of your own heart. The number of your hearers may increase, and your church may flourish; while, in your own breast, devotional affections and virtuous dispositions are greatly on the decline: nor need I inform you, that every degree of such declension has a tendency to final ruin.

Besides, if there should be an appearance of extensive utility attending your labours, for which I sincerely pray; you may do well to remember the old proverb, "All is not gold that glitters," numbers there are that seem to "receive the word with joy," who, "in time of temptation, fall away." Many evangelical and popular preachers, I am very suspicious, have greatly over-rated the usefulness of their own labours. For, the longer I live, the more apprehensive I am, that the number of *real* converts, among those who profess the genuine gospel, is comparatively very small: according to the import of that alarming declaration, "Many are called, but few are chosen."

On the other hand, should you meet *with many and great discouragements,* take heed that you do not indulge a desponding temper, as if you had been of no use in the ministerial work. With discouragements you certainly will meet, unless providence were to make your case an exception to the general course of things; which you have no ground to expect. Very painful discouragements, for instance, may sometimes arise, from the want of liberty and savour in your

---

[18] Si minister verbi laudatur, versatur in periculo, says the famous Augustine.

Pastoral Cautions

own mind, when performing public service. This, there is reason to suppose, is not uncommon. I, at least, have had frequent experience of it; and, once, to such a degree, that I began to think very seriously of giving up the ministry: supposing that the great Shepherd had nothing further for me to do, either in the pastoral office, or in preaching the word at large. This exercise of mind, though exceedingly painful for some weeks, was both instructive and useful. Before that well-recollected season, I had frequently *talked* about the necessity of divine influence, to render a minister savoury in his own mind, as well as profitable to others; but then I felt it.

Be not discouraged, then, "as though some strange thing happened unto you," that never befell a real minister of Christ; if a similiar trial should occur in the course of your ministry. For it may be to you, as I trust it was to me, of no inconsiderable benefit: because I reckon, that whatever curbs our pride, makes us feel our insufficiency, and sends us to the throne of grace. Seldom, alas! have I found any remarkable degree of savour, and of enlargement in public service, without experiencing more or less, of self-elatement and self-gratulation on that account. Instead of complaining, therefore, that I have not more liberty in my work, or more success attending the performance of it; I have reason to wonder at the condescending kindness of God, in that he gives to my extremely imperfect labours the least saving effect, and that he does not frequently leave me to be confounded before all my hearers. Such, brother, have been the feelings and reasonings of my own mind, and such my confessions before God many a time.

It is not unlikely that, in a course of years, some of your people, who had expressed a warm regard to your ministry, and perhaps considered you as their spiritual father; may become without any just reason, your violent opposers, asperse your ministerial character, and wish to be rid of you. This, though very trying, is far from an unexampled case: no, not with regard to much greater men, and far better ministers, than either of us. Witness the language of Paul, in various parts of his two epistles to the church at Corinth, and in his letter to the Galatian churches. Witness also the life of that excellent man, Mr. President Edwards, of New England.

Among the dissatisfied, it is probable, some will complain of your ministry being dry, legal, and of an Arminian cast: while others, it may be, will quarrel with it under a supposition, that you dwell too much on the doctrines of divine grace, and verge toward Antinomianism. My own ministry, however, has been the subject of loud complaint, in these opposite ways, and that at the very same time. Nor have we much reason to wonder at it. For if a minister, to the best of his ability, display the glory of sovereign grace, in the election, redemption, and justification of sinners; he will be sure to offend the pride of multitudes, who are seeking acceptance with God by their own obedience. Persons of this character will probably draw the same inferences from his doctrine, and form the same objections against it, as those by which the ministry of Paul was opposed, If it be so, they will cry, "Why does God yet find fault? for who hath resisted his will? Let us do evil that good may come; and continue in sin, that grace may abound. The law is made void, and personal holiness is quite superfluous."

Does the same preacher insist upon the necessity of that "holiness, without which no man shall see the Lord" —upon that conformity to the example of Christ, and that spiritual-mindedness, without which all pretensions to faith in the Son of God are vain? the covetousness and carnality of others will be disgusted. They will pronounce him legal, and consider his doctrine as inimical to the prerogatives of sovereign grace and this, because he maintains, that evangelical truths have a holy influence on all who believe them; or, in the language of James, "that faith without works is dead."

Again: you may, it is highly probable, have painful opportunities of observing, that while some of your people embrace pernicious doctrines, verge to wide extremes and are exceedingly desirous of making proselytes to their novel peculiarities; others of them are giddy and flighty, rambling about from one place of worship to another, admiring almost every fresh preacher they hear; but quite dissatisfied with your ministry, though they hardly know for what. Nor is there any reason to doubt, that others, among the objects of your pastoral care, will administer occasions of grief, by formality and lukewarmness in their profession; by their pride, extravagance, or sensuality; by their envy, avarice, or injustice; or, finally, by malevolent attacks, in unfounded charges upon your own character, as in the case of Paul, among the Corinthians. You must guard, however, against desponding discouragement, when any of these painful particulars occur to your notice. Nay, should a variety of them appear at the same time, you must not conclude that God has deserted your ministry, and entirely forsaken your church. But, while firmly determined to promote the exercise of strict and impartial discipline; and while careful, except the case be quite peculiar, never to bring the bad conduct of any individual into your public discourses; examine your own ways—humble yourself before God[19] —increase your pastoral exertions—cry mightily to the Father of mercies for assistance—endeavour, as it were, to levy a tax upon these trials; that they may, at least, afford private advantage to your own soul[20]—and, then, leaving your cause with God, "be of good courage."

I said, Endeavour to levy a tax upon your trials. For even malevolent attacks, and unfounded charges, upon a Christian's character, if his own temper be under proper government, may prove an occasion of promoting his best interests. In such cases, and for this end, it behoves him to examine his heart and ways, to see whether he have not contracted the guilt of some greater evil, than that which is falsely laid to his charge. If, on impartial inquiry, his conscience attest the affirmative; it will soon appear, that he has much less reason to redden with indignation at his

---

[19] 2 Cor. xii. 20, 21.
[20] Rom. viii. 28.

accuser's unfounded charge, than he has to admire the goodness of God in permitting an arrow to be aimed at his character, which he can easily repel by the impenetrable shield of a good conscience; while greater evils of his heart, or conduct, for which he cannot but severely condemn himself, are entirely hidden from his accuser. Besides, the Christian, in such a predicament, may justly say, "Though free from the charge alleged, it is not owing to the superior holiness of my heart; but must be ascribed to divine, preserving care.'

A Christian, therefore, who, in such a conjuncture of circumstances, is wisely seeking his own emolument; will be disposed to consider the unrighteous allegation, as a gracious, providential warning, lest at any time he be really overtaken of that very evil, with which, at present, he is falsely accused. Little do we know of the spiritual danger to which we are continually exposed; the temptations by which we may be, unawares, powerfully assaulted; or how near we may be to the perpetration of some awful evil, from which we have commonly imagined ourselves to be most remote. Neither, on the other hand, is it possible for us thoroughly to understand all the ways and means, by which our heavenly Father communicates those hidden provisions of preventing grace, which are continually administered for our preservation.[21] But, alas! how seldom it is that any of us have humility and wisdom sufficient, thus to improve such an event!

Once more: Take heed that you pay an habitual regard to divine influence: as that without which you cannot either enjoy a holy liberty in your work, or have any reason to erect success. We have heard with pleasure, that the necessity of such an influence, to enlighten, to comfort, and to sanctify the human mind, makes one article in your theological creed. An article, doubtless, of great importance. For as well might the material system have sprung out of nonentity, without the almighty *fiat;* as an assemblage of holy qualities arise in a depraved heart, without supernatural agency. As well

---

[21] Dr. Owen's *Sermons and Tracts*, p. 49.

might the order, harmony, and beauty of the visible world be continued, without the perpetual exertion of that wisdom, power, and goodness which gave them birth, as the holy qualities of a regenerate soul be maintained and flourish, independent of the Divine Spirit.

Now, my brother, as the knowledge of any truth is no further useful to us, than we are influenced by it, and act upon it; as doctrinal sentiments are not beneficial, except in proportion as they become practical principles, or produce correspondent feelings and affections in our own hearts; so you should endeavour to live continually under the operation of that sacred maxim, "Without *me* ye can do nothing." With humility, with prayer, and with expectation, the assistance of the Holy Spirit should be daily regarded. In all your private studies, and in all your public administrations, the aids of that sacred agent should be sought. Consistency of conduct, peace in your own breast, and success in your own labours, all require it; for, surely, you do not mean, merely to compliment the Holy Spirit, by giving his work a conspicuous place in your creed. Were you habitually to study and preach your discourses, without secret, previous prayer for divine assistance; the criminality of your neglect would equal the inconsistency of your character. If christianity be the religion of sinners, and adapted to their apostate state, it must provide, as well for our depravity, by enlightening and sanctifying influence, as for our guilt, by atoning blood.

Our Lord, when addressing his disciples, relative to the gracious work of the Holy Spirit, says, "He shall glorify me: for he shall receive of mine, and shall show it unto you." By which we are led to infer, that when a minister sincerely seeks and mercifully obtains divine assistance in preaching the word, his discourses will have a sweet savour of Christ and his offices will display his mediatorial glories—will exhibit his excellent characters, and condescending relations, that are suited to the necessities of miserable sinners. Thus he will feast the mental eye, and excite admiration of the Saviour's person and undertaking, in the believing heart;

even though the elocution and manner of the preacher be of an inferior kind. Hence you may learn, my brother, how to appreciate those discourses, which, whether heard from the pulpit, or perused from the press, frequently excite admiration of the minister's talents; but are far from raising the same passion to an equal degree; by exhibiting the personal and official excellencies of the adorable Jesus.

Nor or can you pray over your bible in a proper manner, when meditating on the sacred text, without feeling a solemnity in your ministerial employment. That solemnity should always attend you in the pulpit: for, a preacher who trifles there, not only affronts the understanding of every sensible and serious hearer, but insults the majesty of that divine presence in which he stands. Guard, therefore, against every appearance of levity in your public work. In all your studies, and in all your labours, watch against a spirit of self-sufficiency, from which that profane levity often proceeds. Remember, that your ability for every spiritual duty, and all your success, must be from God. To him your eye must be directed, and on his promised aid your expectations of usefulness must be formed. In thus acting the part of a christian, while you perform the work of a minister for the benefit of others, your own soul will feel itself interested in the doctrines you preach, and in the duties you inculcate; in the promises you exhibit, and in the reproofs you administer.

I will now, my brother, for a few minutes, direct your attention to another divine precept, and then conclude. Paul, when addressing Titus in the language of apostolic authority, says, "Let no one despise thee."[22] A singular and remarkable saying! *No one;* whether a professed christian, an unbelieving Jew, or an idolatrous gentile. Observe, however, it is not said, Let no one *envy,* or *hate,* or *persecute* thee; but, let no one *despise* thee. How, then, was Titus to preserve his character from contempt? By the penal exercise of miraculous powers, on those who dared to treat him with indignity? No such expedient is here intimated. By assuming

---

[22] Titus ii. 15.

PASTORAL CAUTIONS

lordly titles, appearing in splendid robes, taking to himself state, and causing the vulgar to keep their distance? Nothing less. For that would have been directly contrary to an established law of Christ, and inconsistent with the nature of his kingdom. But it was, as the apostle in another place plainly intimates, by becoming a bright "example of the believers, in word, in conversation, in charity or love, in spirit, in faith or fidelity, in purity."[23] Or, by being preeminent among those who "adorned the doctrine of God our Saviour."

Yes, a minister of the gospel, who "takes heed to himself" to his christian character, to his official duties, and to his various relations in life, whether domestic, religious, or civil; is not very likely to be sincerely *despised* by those that know him. His supposed religious *oddities* may be treated with contempt, and he may be hated for his conscientious regard to evangelical truth, and to the legislative authority of Jesus Christ: but the manifest respectability of his moral character will find an advocate in the breast of each that knows him, and especially in the hour of serious reflection. For, a series of conduct, bearing testimony to the reality of religious principle, to the fear of God, and to the social virtues reigning in his heart, *will* generally secure him from deliberate contempt. Hence it has been observed, by an author of eminence in his literary station: "It was a pertinent advice that Paul gave to Titus, however oddly it may appear at first: — "Let no one despise thee." For we may justly say, that in ninety-nine cases out of a hundred, if a pastor is despised, he has himself to blame."[24]

Yes, and how respectable soever for literature and science, if he entered upon his office, chiefly under the influence of secular motives; or if he be habitually trifling and vain, proud or covetous; if, in his general conduct, there be more of the modern fine gentleman, than of the primitive pastor; and much more of the man of this world, that of the *man of God;*

---

[23] 1 Tim. iv. 12.
[24] Dr. G. Campbell's *Lectures on Ecclesiastical History*, vol, i. p. 174.

he deserves, under the *pastoral* character, to be despised. For the feelings, and sympathies, and turn of his heart, are neither congenial to those of the great shepherd, under whom he should serve, and with whom, in order to feed the flock, he must have frequent spiritual intercourse; nor adapted to meet the necessities of any people that know the chief Pastor's voice.[25] He is a man of the world; and, as such, a cure in the national establishment seems more congenial to him, than a pastoral charge among the dissenters. For, a protestant dissenting minister, who is not *above* the world, is very likely to be *despised by* the world.

Take heed, then, my brother, that no one may have any reason to despise you; and that this church may never, like the church at Colosse, come under the obligation of that precept, Say to Archippus, "Take heed to the ministry which thou hast received in the Lord that thou fulfil it."[26] An apostolic injunction this, which, it is to be feared, attaches to many churches, respecting their lukewarm and negligent pastors. Nay, who, that is daily lamenting over the plague of his own heart; that reflects on the state of religion in what is called the Christian world; that considers the ministerial work and the pastoral office; as being both sacred and important; and, finally, that demand of the supreme Judge, "Give an account of thy stewardship;" can forbear to acknowledge the propriety of Dr. Owen's pathetic language, when he says, "The Lord help men, and open their eyes before it be too late! For, either the gospel is not true, or there are few who, in a due manner, discharge that ministry which they take upon them."[27]

"Take heed, I once more charge you, take heed to yourself. This duty performed, you can scarcely forbear taking heed, either to the doctrine you preach, or "to the flock over which the Holy Ghost hath made you an overseer, to feed the

---

[25] John x. 4.
[26] Col. iv. 17.
[27] On Epist, to the Hebrews, chap. vi. 11. vol, iii. p. 118. Folio.

Pastoral Cautions

church of God, which he hath purchased with his own blood."
AMEN.

A
BIOGRAPHICAL SKETCH
OF
ABRAHAM BOOTH
(1734-1806)

BY
JOHN FRANKLIN JONES

A Biographical Sketch of Abraham Booth (1734-1806)

Abraham Booth — General-turned-Particular Baptist, teacher, pastor, author — was born May 20, 1734 at Blackwell, in Derbyshire, England. In the first year of his life, his parents removed from Blackwell to Annesley Woodhouse, Nottinghamshire. The oldest of a family of numerous children, Abraham assisted his father in his agricultural concerns well into his teenage years. Though his circumstances prevented a formal education, his father taught the boy to read, and a robust mind early appeared in him. He was almost entirely self-taught in writing and arithmetic and pursued his studies avidly during his leisure hours ("Memoir"). Brought up with a reverence for the national establishment of the Church of England, at about ten years of age he became acquainted with the dissenters via the preaching of some plain and illiterate General (or Arminian) Baptists teachers who occasionally visited his neighborhood. Their influence first awakened Booth to a concern about salvation, and he applied for admission to the General Baptists. He was baptized by Francis Smith at Barton in 1755 at about age twenty-one ("Memoir").

He pursued stocking-making from age sixteen to twenty-four. At twenty-four, he married Miss Elizabeth Bowmar, the daughter of a neighboring farmer; they were married more than forty years. Assisted by Mrs. Booth, he opened a school at Sutton Ashfield to instruct youth. Mrs. Booth taught needle-work to the female pupils ("Memoir").

The General Baptists recognized his abilities and occasionally invited him to preach. He soon became a leader among them and in their neighboring districts. Upon their organizing their churches and appointing pastors over them in 1760, Booth became superintendent of the church at Kirby-Woodhouse. He labored among them successfully for several years but declined to accept the office of pastor ("Memoir").

Booth strenuously advocated the General Baptist-Armenian doctrine of the universality of divine grace and published same in a poem, "Absolute Predestination," in his twentieth year. In the poem, he reviled election and particular redemption ("Memoir"). Later, he wrote of the poem:

I thought it my duty in a particular manner to bear a public testimony to that important part of revealed truth, having in my younger years greatly opposed it, in a poem on "Absolute predestination" which poem if considered in a critical light is despicable, if in a theological view, detestable, as it is an impotent attack on the honor of divine grace in regard to its glorious freeness, and a bold opposition to the sovereignty of God. So I now consider it and as such I here renounce it (Matrunola, 2).

His convictions underwent such a change, though, that he could no longer maintain his relationship with the General Baptists. Regarding the deep convictions he came to hold, he later wrote:

The doctrine of sovereign, distinguishing grace, as commonly and justly stated by Calvinists, it must be acknowledged, is too generally exploded. This the writer knows by experience, to his grief and shame. Through the ignorance of his mind, the pride of his heart, and the prejudice of his education, he, in his younger years, often opposed it with much warmth, though with no small weakness; but after an impartial inquiry, and many prayers, he found reason to alter his judgment; he found it to be the doctrine of the Bible, and a dictate of the unerring Spirit. Thus patronized, he received the once obnoxious sentiment, under a full conviction of its being a divine truth ("Memoir").

After many cordial and lengthy discussions with them upon his now-firm convictions, he withdrew from the General Baptist ranks ("Memoir") in 1765 (Armitage). His departing remarks upon the occasion were from the parable of the unjust steward. He said: "Fraud and concealment of various kinds may obtain the favor of men, but, when favor is gained by these means, he who gains it and those who grant it, are chargeable with injustice peculiarly censurable" (Matrunola).

Booth would not obtain favor by such fraud and concealment.

Shortly after his withdrawal from the Arminians, Booth procured Bore's Hall, at Sutton Ashfield, and gathered a small group of Calvinistic or Particular Baptists. At Sutton Ashfield, and afterwards, at Nottingham and Chesterfield, where he preached alternate Sundays, he delivered a series of discourses from which came his excellent work, *The Reign of Grace* (1768). That work indicated both the bent of his thoughts at the time and the subjects of his preaching--the reign of divine grace in its nature and properties in election, effectual calling, pardon of sin, justification, adoption, sanctification, perseverance, and eternal glory ("Memoir").

He showed the manuscript to some friends. One of them showed it to Henry Venn, an evangelical clergyman well known for his popular work, *The Complete Duty of Man*. Venn recommended that Booth publish the work and Venn himself wrote a recommendatory preface to it. Booth published the work in April 1768 ("Memoir").

The Particular Baptist Church in Little Prescot Street, Goodman's Fields, London, needed a pastor and contacted Booth. He accepted their call October 1, 1768 and was ordained to that position February 16, 1769. Thereupon he publicly delivered a detailed confession of his faith, which confession was afterwards printed ("Memoir").

Booth moved to London to begin a new era in one of the most respectable among the churches of the English dissenters, and he well-discharged his pastoral duties. Taking full advantage of the opportunities to satisfy his insatiable thirst after learning, he acquired the assistance of a former Roman Catholic priest, an eminent classical scholar, and studied Latin and Greek ("Memoir").

His study of Latin provided the ability to examine the erudite professors of the foreign universities--Witsius, Turretine, Stapferus, Vitringa, and Venema. He examined the ecclesiastical historians--Dupin, Cave, Bingham, Venema, Spanheim. He studied the Magdeburg Centuriators, Lewis, Jennings, Reland, Spencer, Ikenius, Carpzovius, Fabricius of Hamburgh, and others on Jewish Antiquities. He studied English writers, especially John Owen. To Owen he acknowledged great obligation. Excepting Scripture, he quoted Owen more often than any ("Memoir").

In 1770, only a year after his ordination, Booth published *The Death of Legal Hope, the Life of Evangelical Obedience, in an Essay on Gal. 2:19*. The essay demonstrated that grace relaxes no obligations to holiness but produces godliness. That grace denies the moral law as a rule of life to believers--a pernicious sentiment--was rampant in England at the period, and Booth continually opposed the idea both in his writings and his pastoral ministry ("Memoir").

A challenge to the deity of Christ delivering many respectable, established church clergy to the Socinians and their anti-Trinitarian theology occurred about the time Booth came to London. In 1777, Booth presented an improved, revised, corrected, and fortified new edition of *The Deity of Jesus Christ, essential to the Christian Religion*, originally penned in French by James Abaddie, dean of Killaloe in Ireland ("Memoir").

In 1778, he published *An Apology for the Baptists, in Which They Are Vindicated from the Imputation of Laying an Unwarrantable Stress on the Ordinance of Baptism*. This work opposed the more or less prevalent principle of mixed communion introduced to the English churches about the middle of the seventeenth century. Into this book Booth incorporated a series of letters he had written at the request from a fellow minister whose own convictions also opposed the practice ("Memoir").

In 1784, he defended the practice of baptism in his *Pædobaptism Examined, on the Principles, Concessions, and Reasonings of the Most Learned Pædobaptists*. Booth took up the Pædobaptists' principles, facts, interpretations of Scripture, and concessions, met them upon their own grounds, and thoroughly refuted them. In 1787, he published a second edition, which he enlarged with additional material ("Memoir"). His *Pædobaptism Examined* was "never fairly answered" (Armitage, 570).

The *Essay on the Kingdom of Christ*, published in 1788, showed how the kingdom of Christ in its nature so differed from the kingdom of David as to disallow using events occurring under the Mosaic economy being applied to the Christian church. The Christian church differs in its nature, origin, subjects, means of establishment and support, laws by which it is governed, immunities, riches, and honors from the kingdom. Those differences explain and necessitate its dissent from the national establishment and all political efforts to impeach Christ's dominion in His own kingdom ("Memoir").

First appearing in 1796 and followed by a second edition in 1800, *Glad Tidings to Perishing Sinners; or, The Genuine Gospel, a Complete Warrant for the Ungodly to Believe in Jesus Christ* addressed the issue of the persons to whom the Gospel is to be preached and their obligation thereto ("Memoir").

The Amen to Social Prayer, Illustrated and Improved (1800) was a sermon previously delivered at a monthly meeting of Particular Baptist ministers belonging to the Particular Baptist denomination. A series by different ministers addressed the Lord's prayer, and Booth treated the concluding word of the prayer, "Amen." The sermon demanded some extrication from Booth. In *Essay on the Kingdom of Christ*, Booth had solemnly protested the practice of taking a single word or phrase of a text for preaching. Despite his condemnation that the practice disgraced the pulpit and profaned the sacred ministry, on this occasion he admirably met his challenge ("Memoir").

Approaching seventy years of age but with undiminished mental powers, Booth discoursed at one of the monthly meetings of his Baptist brethren on the subject of divine justice. Soon afterwards in 1803, he published the sermon as *Divine Justice Essential to the Divine Character* ("Memoir").

In the last year of his life--1805--he published *Pastoral Cautions*. This work summarized the substance of twenty years of pulpit ministry. He delivered it as a charge at the ordination of Thomas Hopkins as pastor of the Baptist Church in Eagle Street, Red Lion Square, London. Booth had now completed fifty years of ministry, more than thirty-five as pastor of the church in Prescot Street. He cautioned the ministers' behavior in the house of God, in their families, and in the world. He exhorted them to exemplify the character of the Christian pastor and adorn the high, honorable office in which they are placed. Booth's sermon expressed the profitable experience of his maturing years ("Memoir").

Several "Funeral Sermons" and "Addresses" reflect Booth's occupation with the great truths of the Bible--the uncertainty of life, the certainty of death, the necessity of being prepared for death, the folly of taking lightly the interests of the immortal soul and neglecting everlasting peace, and the Gospel as alone giving effectual relief to a sinner under the dread of death and the judgment. The messages contain little regarding the decedents' character. Nor do they contain compliments to surviving relatives ("Memoir").

Though generally blessed with good health, Booth became increasingly afflicted with asthma, especially during the winter months. Some months before his death and en route home from a meeting of his ministering brethren in the city, he suddenly took ill. Henceforth he largely retired from public labors and demonstrated to his oft-calling friends that his mind retained all its clarity, calmness, and serenity. His uniform answer to their inquiries was "I have no fears about my state. The gospel bears my spirit up. A faithful and unchanging God lays the foundation of my hope in oaths, and promises, and blood" ("Memoir").

The several months preceding his death were occupied with revising and completing *An Essay on the Love of God to His Chosen People and A Conduct Formed under the Influence of Evangelical Truth*. He committed them to a friend for publication ("Memoir").

A few days prior to his death, he gave the same friend the manuscript for *Thoughts on Dr. Edward Williams's Hypothesis Relative to the Origin of Moral Evil*. Notwithstanding the difficulty of the metaphysical topic, Booth's treatment of it demonstrated his mental competence to grapple with the subject at such a late stage in his life. He carefully examined William's theory and exposed its fallaciousness. Regarding his position upon the subject, Booth wrote:

> I have no opinion upon the subject; nor dare I form conjectures about it. . . Of this, however, I have no doubt, that the existence and prevalence of moral evil in the rational creation, are completely consistent with all the perfections of God, and with all his eternal decrees; and that under the management of Supreme Wisdom, when the great system of Providence respecting both angels and men is finished, the conduct of God in reference to evil, both moral and natural, will be to the praise of his glory, in the eyes of all holy creatures ("Memoir").

JOHN FRANKLIN JONES

This declining period left many testimonies to the steadfastness of his faith and hope and the importance he attached to the doctrines he had published throughout his life. Among those testimonies: "I now live," said he, "upon what I have been teaching others" ("Memoir").

To an esteemed friend on the Saturday preceding his death, he communicated his last instructions with a testimony, "I am peaceful but not elevated." To the son of the same gentleman the following day, he replied to the inquiry regarding his health and added:

> Young man, think of your soul; if you lose that, you lose all. Be not half a Christian. Some people have just religion enough to make them miserable; not enough to make them happy. The ways of religion are good ways. I have found them such these sixty years ("Memoir").

On the Lord's day prior to his death, he affectionately spoke to one and then to another of his friends who visited him. To one he said, "But a little while and I shall be with your dear father and mother." To another, "I have often borne you on my heart before the Lord; now you need to pray for me, and you must pray for yourself." To a third, referring to a well-known Socinian minister, he solemnly remarked, "Beware of _____'s sentiments" ("Memoir").

He spent the evening with his endeared family. Two of his daughters and their husbands continued with him. One of the latter led a time of family worship prior to their departure, and the dying Booth joined the time. Without struggle or sigh, he died the next day at age seventy-one ("Memoir").

The Little Prescot Street church records contain many references to its loving regard for the pastor of thirty-seven years. A marble tablet displays its public appreciation for Booth ("Memoir").

A Biographical Sketch of Abraham Booth

Booth and William Newman of Bow attempted to revive a Baptist education society organized earlier. Posthumously, the actions were bolstered by wealthy members of his church to become Stepney Academy in 1810 and later, Regent's Park College. From the outset, he was a supporter, though lesser known than others, of the Particular Baptist Society for Propagating the Gospel among the Heathen, formed at Kettering in 1792. In the 1790s, Booth and his church joined the protest of the African slave trade (Matrunola, 10).

Bibliography

ARMITAGE, THOMAS. —*A History of the Baptists; Traced by their Vital Principles and Practices, from the Time of Our Lord and Saviour Jesus Christ to the Year 1886*. With an introduction by J. L. M. Curry. New York: Bryan, Taylor, & Co., 1887, 569-70.

MATRUNOLA, K.F.T. —*A Brief Account of the Life and Labours of Abraham Booth 1734-1806*. Rushden Northamptonshire, England: Fauconberg, 1981.

"Memoir." In *The Reign of Grace, from the Rise to its Consummation*, by ABRAHAM BOOTH. With an introductory essay by Thomas Chalmers. Corrected ed. Grand Rapids: Eerdmans, 1949.

By JOHN FRANKLIN JONES
CORDOVA, TENNESSEE
JULY 2004

THE BAPTIST STANDARD BEARER, INC.

a non-profit, tax-exempt corporation
committed to the Publication & Preservation
of the Baptist Heritage.

CURRENT TITLES AVAILABLE IN
THE BAPTIST *DISTINCTIVES* SERIES

KIFFIN, WILLIAM	A Sober Discourse of Right to Church-Communion. Wherein is proved by Scripture, the Example of the Primitive Times, and the Practice of All that have Professed the Christian Religion: That no Unbaptized person may be Regularly admitted to the Lord's Supper. (London: George Larkin, 1681).
KINGHORN, JOSEPH	Baptism, A Term of Communion. (Norwich: Bacon, Kinnebrook, and Co., 1816)
KINGHORN, JOSEPH	A Defense of "Baptism, A Term of Communion". In Answer To Robert Hall's Reply. (Norwich: Wilkin and Youngman, 1820).
GILL, JOHN	Gospel Baptism. A Collection of Sermons, Tracts, etc., on Scriptural Authority, the Nature of the New Testament Church and the Ordinance of Baptism by John Gill. (Paris, AR: The Baptist Standard Bearer, Inc., 2006).

CARSON, ALEXANDER	Ecclesiastical Polity of the New Testament. (Dublin: William Carson, 1856).
BOOTH, ABRAHAM	A Defense of the Baptists. A Declaration and Vindication of Three Historically Distinctive Baptist Principles. Compiled and Set Forth in the Republication of Three Books. Revised edition. (Paris, AR: The Baptist Standard Bearer, Inc., 2006).
BOOTH, ABRAHAM	Paedobaptism Examined on the Principles, Concessions, and Reasonings of the Most Learned Paedobaptists. With Replies to the Arguments and Objections of Dr. Williams and Mr. Peter Edwards. 3 volumes. (London: Ebenezer Palmer, 1829).
CARROLL, B. H.	*Ecclesia* - The Church. With an Appendix. (Louisville: Baptist Book Concern, 1903).
CHRISTIAN, JOHN T.	Immersion, The Act of Christian Baptism. (Louisville: Baptist Book Concern, 1891).
FROST, J. M.	Pedobaptism: Is It From Heaven Or Of Men? (Philadelphia: American Baptist Publication Society, 1875).
FULLER, RICHARD	Baptism, and the Terms of Communion; An Argument. (Charleston, SC: Southern Baptist Publication Society, 1854).
GRAVES, J. R.	Tri-Lemma: or, Death By Three Horns. The Presbyterian General Assembly Not Able To Decide This Question: "Is Baptism In The Romish Church Valid?" 1st Edition.

	(Nashville: Southwestern Publishing House, 1861).
MELL, P.H.	Baptism In Its Mode and Subjects. (Charleston, SC: Southern Baptist Publications Society, 1853).
JETER, JEREMIAH B.	Baptist Principles Reset. Consisting of Articles on Distinctive Baptist Principles by Various Authors. With an Appendix. (Richmond: The Religious Herald Co., 1902).
PENDLETON, J.M.	Distinctive Principles of Baptists. (Philadelphia: American Baptist Publication Society, 1882).
THOMAS, JESSE B.	The Church and the Kingdom. A New Testament Study. (Louisville: Baptist Book Concern, 1914).
WALLER, JOHN L.	Open Communion Shown to be Unscriptural & Deleterious. With an introductory essay by Dr. D. R. Campbell and an Appendix. (Louisville: Baptist Book Concern, 1859).

For a complete list of current authors/titles, visit our internet site at:
www.standardbearer.org
or write us at:

The Baptist Standard Bearer, Inc.
NUMBER ONE IRON OAKS DRIVE • PARIS, ARKANSAS 72855
TEL # 479-963-3831   FAX # 479-963-8083
EMAIL: Baptist@centurytel.net   http://www.standardbearer.org

Thou hast given a standard to them that fear thee; that it may be displayed because of the truth. — Psalm 60:4

www.ingramcontent.com/pod-product-compliance
Lightning Source LLC
Chambersburg PA
CBHW021135230426
43667CB00005B/121